The Stupidity Watch:
An Atheist Speaks Out on Religion and Politics

The Stupidity Watch
an atheist speaks out on religion and politics

S. T. Joshi

Expanded Edition

Sarnath Press • Seattle

Contents

Preface

This book is a collection of my essays, reviews, and columns in the *American Rationalist,* a freethought journal I have been editing since the summer of 2011. When I was offered the editorship of this periodical (the longest continuously running freethought magazine currently published in the United States), I stipulated that I be allowed to write a column of satirical commentary entitled "The Stupidity Watch," and the Center for Inquiry (now the publishers of the *American Rationalist*) readily agreed.

I imagine I was chosen for the editorship because of my previous work in atheism and secularism. I had long been interested in this subject, especially as it pertained to what is in fact my chief focus of scholarly interest, supernatural fiction. H. P. Lovecraft (1890–1937), aside from being a pioneering author of "weird fiction" (as he called it) in the twentieth century, also revealed himself (chiefly in letters published long after his death) as a trenchant and vigorous atheist, as well as a pungent critic of the intellectual, social, and political follies of orthodox religion. My interest in Lovecraft—which, among other things, led me to write a philosophical study, *H. P. Lovecraft: The Decline of the West* (1990), in which I analyzed the particulars of his atheism—compelled me to undertake an historical study of atheism in Western culture. This in turn led to the compilation of an anthology, *Atheism: A Reader* (Prometheus Books, 2000). I had noted that this publisher had issued Gordon Stein's *An Anthology of Atheism and Rationalism* (1980), as well as a follow-up volume in 1987. Large and substantial as these anthologies were, I felt that they had omitted certain significant texts that illuminated the history of atheism. My compilation was readily accepted and remains in print to this day.

I had long had an interest in political and religious satire, fueled by my scholarly work on Ambrose Bierce and H. L. Mencken, two of the leading satirists in American literature. Under their posthumous tutelage, I wrote a polemical treatise, *God's Defenders: What They Believe and Why They Are Wrong* (Prometheus Books, 2003), in which I held up the buffooneries of such pious folks as C. S. Lewis, William F. Buckley, and Jerry Falwell to the ridicule they deserved. Some reviewers deprecated my studied impoliteness, but I felt that the volume had succeeded well enough that I wrote a kind of sequel, *The Angry Right* (Prometheus Books, 2006), in which I lampooned such redoubtable figures as Rush Limbaugh, Ann Coulter, and Sean Hannity.

I was then asked to assemble a volume entitled *Icons of Unbelief* (Greenwood Press, 2008), in which leading scholars addressed the atheism and free-thought of such individuals as Bertrand Russell, Friedrich Nietzsche, and Richard Dawkins. I myself wrote four of the essays in the book, and these essays served as the basis for my own study, *The Unbelievers: The Evolution of Modern Atheism* (Prometheus Books, 2011). This book is in fact a kind of trial run for what I hope will be a comprehensive world history of atheism and secularism, although that work may take years of research to complete. In the meantime, I assembled other volumes—*The Agnostic Reader* (Prometheus Books, 2007); *The Original Atheists: First Thoughts on Nonbelief* (Prometheus Books, 2014), an anthology of writings by French, German, English, and American freethinkers of the eighteenth century—that pointed in the same direction.

I do not believe the contents of the present book require much commentary. I was pleased—and, indeed, enlightened—to write reviews for the *American Rationalist,* whether it be on books about (or promoting) atheism or on Christian apologetics. The latter, as can be imagined, allowed me to hone my satirical in additional to my analytical skills. I do not profess to be a scholar on religion, whether Christianity or any other; but I do believe that my understanding of the history of atheism—extending back to the ancient Greeks and proceeding up to the "New Atheists" of today—give me some intellectual perspective to assess the arguments of those who (futilely, to my mind) continue to argue in favor of religious belief in spite of the mountain of evidence against it.

In terms of my political broadsides, I do not apologize for my unremittingly hostility to conservative individuals and conservative policies, since I regard both as being dangerously inimical to the highest ideals of American and civilized society. And I do not retreat one millimeter from my contention regarding the imminent demise of the current incarnation of the Republican Party. The unexpected election of Donald J. Trump not only is no refutation of that contention but may actually validate it: he is no friend of orthodox Republican doctrine and may do more to bring it crashing down than any other individual ever has. It is difficult for many of us, in an age that bombards us incessantly with news (fake or otherwise) and factoids, to take a long view of politics, society, and general culture; but the long-term ascendancy of liberalism is assured, chiefly because younger people are substantially more liberal and less religious than other segments of the population, and they show little inclination to shed these stances as they age. They are our ultimate saviors from short-term threats of fascism and authoritarianism, but we others also have our parts to play in this struggle.

—S. T. JOSHI

Seattle, Washington

Introduction: Living in a Religious Society

The number of atheists, agnostics, secularists, and the religiously indifferent may have reached around 30% of the American population, if recent surveys are reliable—and the number may in fact be higher than that, given the opprobrium that in certain circles still attaches to the very idea that one might be irreligious. Since, therefore, we are still a minority (although a larger minority than fundamentalist Christians, whose numbers have probably declined to under 20% of the populace), the question remains: How do we live in a society where the visible tokens of religion (churches, the motto on our currency, whole television channels devoted to Christian proselytizing, and much else besides) confront us from all directions?

The solution may be simpler than we think. Unless one has the misfortune to be a closeted atheist in some fundamentalist compound, or unless one is so fervently antireligious that one cannot resist attacking or lampooning people of faith in person or on social media, one can navigate the atheist/religious divide with a suitable amount of tact that does not in any way constitute a fatal compromise of one's principles. My own experience, which may or may not be representative, may shed some light on the matter.

I came to this country with my family when I was five years old, in 1963. As immigrants from India, we had the good luck to live in a succession of university towns in the Midwest, where the overall political liberalism of our friends and acquaintances not only tolerated whatever Hindu customs my family wished to practice (as a matter of fact, only my mother was devout, and she observed her faith largely in private), but made little mention of the subject of religion. Even in that era, most educated Americans wore their religion lightly; it had already become bad form even to speak about the issue in public—it would be rather like talking about mending one's underwear. I do recall one well-meaning American family taking me (without my two sisters or my parents) to a Catholic service when I was about eight years old, but the ceremony baffled and bored me and left no impression aside from the fact that I was denied the wafer: I had become somewhat hungry and could have used a snack about that time.

I've gone on to live in liberal enclaves, either on the East Coast or the West Coast, for most of my adult life. Living in New York City during the 1990s, I had a succession of Jewish girlfriends: they were themselves largely non-religious, but were in varying degrees eager to adhere to Jewish cultural traditions. One of them took me to her family's Passover seder. Somehow it had become known that I was an atheist, and one earnest young female member of the family looked at me solemnly and asked, "Why don't you believe in God?" I replied calmly, "It doesn't seem to me that there is sufficient evidence to support belief in a deity." The woman had nothing further to say on the subject, and the seder proceeded uneventfully.

The one time I lived in an area of the country that could be considered politically or religiously conservative was when I spent a few years (2005–08) in upstate New York, in the Finger Lakes area. Here, in spite of the proximity of the very liberal Ithaca and its intellectual cornerstone, Cornell University, I lived in a small town that seemed to have been unchanged since the 1950s. My then wife had secured a job at the small public library in town; and on her first day on the job she was asked bluntly by an elderly staff worker, "How many children do you have and what church do you attend?" My wife answered "None" and "Catholic," respectively. But in all those three years she attended exactly one service at the local Catholic church. Why? Well, this church's congregation had dwindled to such an extent that it could no longer support a live-in priest; instead, a roving priest would conduct a single service at 8:30 A.M., then move on to at least two other churches in the area. That service was far too early for my wife, who liked to sleep in on a Sunday!

Aside from those three years, I have lived in Seattle since 2001. Washington is a state with one of the lowest rates of church attendance in the nation, and Seattle itself is famously secular. I cannot recall a single discussion of religion among my neighbors—Christian, Jewish, or unaffiliated. I quickly joined a community choir—one of dozens in the city—as I found choral singing a welcome form of diversion from my literary duties. The choir director was a very pious African American man who concluded each rehearsal with an explicit prayer to Jesus. Did that bother me? Not in the least. It was his choir; he was a private individual, not a government official; and I could endure sitting quietly and unobtrusively through thirty seconds of a prayer in exchange for the abundant musical training I was absorbing. I have had the great privilege of singing some of the great (sacred) choral works of Western culture—Handel's *Messiah*, Bach's *B Minor Mass*, Mendelssohn's *Elijah*, *Requiems* by Verdi, Fauré, Duruflé, Rutter, and others, and much else. To this day I shed tears (as Handel himself did) when I hear the gorgeous alto solo "He was despisèd."

There is no denying that religion has been the source of an enormous quantity of the great art, music, architecture, and (to a lesser degree) literature in the West, and it would be foolish and self-defeating not to appreciate it merely because one happens not to agree with its religious orientation. If a religious person counters that I cannot really "understand" the essence of St.

Peter's in Rome or Bach's *St. Matthew Passion* or Milton's *Paradise Lost* because I am an unbeliever, I can counter that the average religious person who is untrained in architecture, music theory, or literary analysis is similarly at a disadvantage. One could go further: on this same principle, no one today (indeed, no one for at least fifteen hundred years) can "understand" Homer's *Iliad* and *Odyssey* because no one since about 500 C.E. (except, apparently, some self-styled Wiccans) has believed in the Greek pantheon. There is no illegitimacy in a purely aesthetic appreciation of religious art; many of the creators of such art were themselves not especially pious, and such works are not intrinsically dissimilar to great works of art, ranging from Beethoven's Ninth Symphony to the plays of Shakespeare, which are resolutely secular.

In short, I believe that in most circumstances it is fairly easy for atheists to avoid the taint of religion in their daily lives. I am not, of course, recommending utter passivity in the face of religious encroachments upon our rights and freedoms—as in current claims that "religious freedom" is an excuse to discriminate against same-sex couples, the transgendered, and other groups whom some Christians abominate. Such encroachments must always be combated, politically and legally: not only are they in themselves obnoxious, but there is always the possibility that they could be turned against atheists in ways that would constrain our own freedom of thought, action, and association.

I am, however, not persuaded by the claims of certain atheist activists that the death of religious belief is imminent. We have heard confident assertions of this sort before, and they have always been proven false. However much religion—especially the Christian religion—may be on the wane in both Europe and the United States, I think we are obliged to acknowledge that it will be an all but permanent factor in the intellectual and social makeup of a large segment of the American public. The great majority of Americans—and perhaps human beings in general—lack both the education and the courage to lead a purely secular life; and even if religion becomes a purely private matter with little influence on our laws, our political institutions, or even on our behavior, it is unlikely to disappear altogether. As such, potential conflicts between the religious and the irreligious will be an ever-present reality. I see no reason to create needless discord among our religious acquaintances by speaking abusively about their faith, so long as we also make it clear that our own atheism is firmly and intelligently held. A détente may be the best we can hope for—but that is probably good enough.

I. Essays and Reviews

A Confession of Unfaith

I have been editing THE AMERICAN RATIONALIST for more than three years, but have never given an overview of the sources of my own religious or anti-religious beliefs or my current stance on certain controverted issues relating to this subject. I am writing this piece now in part to correct certain small errors embedded in an otherwise flattering *New York Times* article on me that appeared this spring;[1] but in general I feel that a clarification of my own views might allow readers to have a better sense of the course and direction of this journal.

The title of this article is borrowed from an essay that H. P. Lovecraft wrote in 1922 in which he outlined his own shedding of religious belief. Unlike Lovecraft, however (whose family attempted to indoctrinate him into the Baptist faith to which they adhered), I never received even the rudiments of any religious training—not even the Hinduism that was theoretically my heritage as a person born in India in 1958. My father, the economist T. M. Joshi, was not an atheist, but was definitely an agnostic. He and I did not talk much about religion, but my mother (the mathematician P. T. Joshi) informed me that he told her not to inculcate any religious belief into me or my two sisters; we should be allowed to come to our own decisions on the subject when we were intellectually and emotionally mature enough to do so. He apparently said to my mother (who for many years was a devout Hindu and a believer in reincarnation, although she now has doubts about this and other tenets): "If you wish to pray, pray in secret." This may seem high-handed (another example of the patriarchal bias still rampant in India and among Indians everywhere), but it did have the advantage of relieving me from any painful "deconversion" in later years. I am acquainted with any number of atheists and agnostics who have testified to the severe trauma they suffered when the religious beliefs they absorbed through childhood brainwashing encountered the uncompromising wall of scientific truth. Whether this absence of indoctrination prejudiced me *toward* atheism is debatable. I doubt that it did so, because my sisters and I were encouraged to examine the tenets of the major religions of the world, and nothing would have prevented our becoming Hindus or Buddhists or Muslims or Christians or Jews if we so wished. In-

---

1. Mark Oppenheimer, "Spreading the Word on the Power of Atheism," *New York Times* (March 15, 2014).

deed, some of our well-meaning American friends, ever since my family came to this country in 1963, attempted to do just that, taking me to various church services that I found a trifle baffling at that early age.

It was, indeed, H. P. Lovecraft who was the central figure in guiding me toward atheism. I had become a devotee of what he called "weird fiction" at an early age and began devouring the work of Edgar Allan Poe, Ambrose Bierce, and other masters of the genre. It was natural that I would come to Lovecraft, even though he was still quite an obscure figure at this time (early 1970s). But as I began to explore Lovecraft and read his writings beyond his exemplary fiction, I found that he had written thousands of letters to all manner of individuals; and it is in these letters that he embodies a fearless, forthright atheism that is surprisingly comprehensive in scope, addressing social, political, and cultural concerns relating to the issue as well as doctrinal and scientific ones. From here it was a simple leap to the writings of Nietzsche, Bertrand Russell, and others who influenced Lovecraft's thought.

My academic studies at Brown and Princeton, initially undertaken for the purpose of securing an advanced degree in classics (the study of Latin and Greek), led me to the study of ancient philosophy, particularly Democritus, Epicurus, and Lucretius. From these writers I gained a perspective on the history and development of atheistic or agnostic thought, and I still hope someday to find the time and leisure to write a full-scale and probably multi-volume history of atheism. No such comprehensive study appears to exist in English, although one appeared in German some time ago.[2] But even this work necessarily fails to cover the "New Atheists" of the past decade or more.

My work in ancient philosophy inevitably led me to study certain trends in early-modern and contemporary philosophy, from the sixteenth century to the present. Naturally I was fascinated by the *philosophes* (Voltaire, Diderot, Holbach, d'Alembert, Montesquieu, La Mettrie), such scientifically inclined thinkers as Thomas Henry Huxley, and many others. This work eventually led to my assembly of *Atheism: A Reader* (2000), my first book for Prometheus Books. Prometheus had previously published two impressive anthologies of atheism compiled by Gordon Stein, but I felt that Stein had omitted certain important works that had a material influence on the development of atheist thought. The acceptance of my anthology has led to several other works written or compiled for Prometheus Books.

My current stance is that, in the West, religion is now merely an irritating nuisance. Over the course of the past two to three centuries it has been "defanged" in such a way that it no longer exercises the political and judicial

---

2. Hermann Ley, *Geschichte der Aufklärung und Atheismus* (1966–89; 5 vols. in 9).

power over citizens that it once did, and its moral sway is also now in tatters. The fact that, in this religion-soaked country, atheists still face prejudice (more so, it appears, than gays or Muslims) is simply an amusing confirmation of the general anti-intellectualism of the average American citizen. Since I am prevented by law from running for president, it matters not a whit to me that 53% of Americans (by one recent survey) would refuse to vote for an atheist candidate!

I call myself an atheist, and am happy with that designation. There are those in the freethought community who eschew the term, thinking it either too negative or too confrontational. I deny both assertions—or rather, I deny the first and welcome the second. If atheism is negative ("there is [probably] no god"), it is so because it is addressing a very specific query: *Is there a god or gods?* One either affirms it or denies it or sits on the fence. The chances of any theistic conception of the world being true are, to my mind, so infinitesimally small that I would feel like a pedant or a hypocrite if I did not declare myself a full-fledged atheist rather than an agnostic. And if that word *atheist* alarms or frightens people—well, good! They deserve to be alarmed and frightened. I have not the slightest inclination to convert anyone to atheism; in any case, reasoned argument rarely accomplishes the deed. Satire, ridicule, and repartée are actually a bit more effective, which is why I enjoy spoofing and lampooning religion and its adherents. But even if these methods convert no one, I am not concerned—they have provided me with some transient amusement, and that is enough.

If anything gets my blood boiling these days, it is the antics of the current Republican party. As the son of professors, I dwelt in university towns (in Illinois and Indiana) during my adolescence, and have tended to stick to the coasts (east or west) in adult life. I am not at all convinced that mere environmental influence has led to my liberalism; indeed, my parents talked as little about politics to me as they did about religion. But, just as I have trouble comprehending the religious point of view (at least from an emotional or psychological perspective—why, for example, so many people appear to *need* to believe, or have such difficulty shedding obviously erroneous beliefs), I similarly have difficulty understanding the seemingly inveterate and increasing imbecility of so many Republican politicians. (I am not referring necessarily to rank-and-file Republicans—at least two of whom are contributing editors to this venerated journal!) These politicians appear to live in a world of their own imagining, increasingly cut off from anything that can be called reality—a world that denies environmental and other dangers merely for the sake of preserving business profits that overwhelmingly end up in the pockets of executives and shareholders instead of workers; a world that professes distaste for governmental interference in a citizen's life (usually interpreted as an excess of tedious regulations in economic matters) but looks on with insouciance at governmental interference in the most intimate personal matters facing human beings (abortion, contraception, same-sex marriage); a world that blandly denies the obviously corrupting influence of immense sums of money given to political candidates and their surrogates; a world that mechanically rejects even the faintest hint of increased taxation for necessary governmental tasks even though the United States has one of the lowest taxation levels of any country in the industrialized world; a world that seeks to curry favor with religious fanatics for purely political reasons by denying plain facts such as evolution and global warming; and so on and so forth.

On every major political, social, and cultural issue, the Republicans seem to me transparently and overwhelmingly in error—and yet, *mirabile dictu,* they still command votes! But that may be coming to an end. There is every reason to believe that this party, unwilling or unable to face up to the demographic and other changes facing this country, will become a permanent minority party—and that is where they belong, unless they make radical changes in their program.

There is much more I could say, but I trust this is enough for now. I hope that my views are not fixed in stone—that would be unhealthy for anyone. But I doubt that the pious will be able to present the mountainous evidence they would need to accumulate to counteract the incalculable evidence supporting the atheistic worldview.

What Apostates Have to Say

Faith No More: Why People Reject Religion. By Phil Zuckerman. New York: Oxford University Press, 2012. 224 pp. Hardcover, $24.95.

Faith No More is a fascinating and eye-opening book that should be in the library of every atheist, agnostic, and freethinker. It is a sociological study of eighty-seven Americans whom Phil Zuckerman—a professor of sociology at Pitzer College and the author of a previous work, *Society without God: What the Least Religious Nations Can Tell Us about Contentment, Atheism and Secularity* (2008)—interviewed in detail about their "apostasy." These individuals were raised in a religious environment but later shed their faith; Zuckerman uses the terms *apostasy* and *apostate* not pejoratively but as a precise way of indicating that these people did not merely switch from one religion to another but actually gave up religion to become either full-fledged atheists or, at the very least, agnostics.

I will confess that I have led a sheltered life. By this I mean that I was not indoctrinated with any religious belief, even though my mother remains to this day a devout Hindu; my father, a secularist, insisted that his children not be inculcated into religious belief but rather that they be allowed to study religions on their own, when they were intellectually and emotionally ready to do so. If at that time we wished to become Hindus or Christians or Muslims or anything else, we would do so through our own conscious choice.

As a result, the tales that Zuckerman recounts of the pain, guilt, and outright anguish that many of his interviewees experienced in renouncing the religion of their birth were, to me, a revelation. The very first chapter tells the striking story of Robert, a boy who was raised in a fundamentalist household in which his mother hired herself out as a practicing exorcist. (How can you not love a book whose first chapter is titled "Mother Was an Exorcist"?) As a result, Robert grew up believing implicitly that demons, as well as Satan himself, were constantly hovering nearby, waiting to seize upon the least little "sin" or indiscretion that the Bible forbade. And yet today both Robert and his brother Ed are secular humanists.

Zuckerman has done a good job in hunting out all manner of religious adherents—fundamentalists, Mormons, Muslims, Catholics, Jews, and many others—and letting them tell the story of their de-conversion. Understandably, these various individuals shed their faith for many reasons: for some, the tenets of their religion simply "stopped making sense"; for others, it was the sexual repression that their religions enforced that proved too much to bear; for still others, it was the reprehensible behavior of their religious guardians—priests, Sunday School leaders, and the like—that created the first crack in their faith.

My own understanding of the Mormon faith is poor, and Zuckerman's chapter on the subject was especially revelatory. Here he recounts the narratives of two ex-Mormons, a woman named Cecilia and a gay man named Andrew. For Cecilia, the first element that caused her break from the church was underwear. You see, Mormons are obliged to wear a cumbersome two-piece pair of underwear that is a "symbolic reminder of the holy covenants made in Mormon temple ceremonies, as well as a reminder of an individual's relationship with Jesus Christ." But this underwear—which is "believed to be endowed with certain magic or spiritual powers that protect the wearer from physical harm"—is a trifle uncomfortable, and Cecilia, who lives in California. was mighty keen on wearing tank-tops but could not do so because of the underwear. From this point, her departure from the church was inevitable.

Andrew is a very different case. It is well known that Mormons have a strong antipathy to homosexuals, even stronger than Catholics or Protestant fundamentalists; this element—particularly the Mormon church's extensive funding of Proposition 8, which overturned the brief legalization of gay marriage in California—was the straw that broke the camel's back for Andrew. It hardly need be stated that this kind of sexual repression proves to be a widespread cause for many individuals to depart from the church in which they were raised. In one plangent case, a boy named Frank, raised in a "conservative Christian home," took to masturbating to a J. C. Penney catalogue! Later, his father—a well-respected church deacon—afraid of Frank's burgeoning homosexual tendencies, actually hired a high-class prostitute to spend two weeks with Frank in Hawaii! What happened? Frank tells the story: "Oh, she was great. A really nice woman. Very kind. We didn't have sex together, but we partied a lot together—we went out to the bars at night and picked up men. It was a lot of fun." I bet it was.

One doesn't wish to be flippant, but the stories that Zuckerman tells are full of such charming and amusing details—at the same time, they are also full of the anguish that many former adherents felt at the shedding of their faith, which frequently involved estrangement from friends and family, mental and emotional struggles in relinquishing "truths" they had been fed since infancy, and other painful scenarios. For the most part, Zuckerman lets his interviewees tell their own tales, and his own conclusions—that increasing intellect strongly tends one toward secularism; that personal loss (say, the death of a parent) or, more generally, the witnessing of the immense amount of suffering and tragedy in the world, leads many to doubt their faith—are fairly self-evident. In one telling account, a young woman attending a community college found her faith being shaken when she took a sociology class; predictably, her friends—who were attending a Bible college—warned her, "You need to stop going to that class. Don't go to class anymore, Elizabeth. It's ruining your faith." A clearer case of the anti-intellectualism on which religions rely to maintain their adherents would be difficult to find.

Zuckerman is strong in emphasizing that atheists and agnostics, far from being immoral, selfish, or self-indulgent, actually have, on the whole, a superior moral bearing than their religious counterparts; the former actually *think* about what it means to be moral, as they cannot rely on the teachings of a scripture to tell them what to think or how to behave. Zuckerman goes on to say that "morality actually *improves* after individuals undergo a transition from being religious to secular. As many apostates emphatically explained to me, their own personal morality was sharpened, enhanced, and ultimately became mature once they left religion behind."

One of the most important messages to draw from this book, for atheists, agnostics, and freethinkers, is that the tide is running in our favour. The fact that from 2003 to 2008 the number of self-confessed "nonreligionists" in the United States doubled (from 10 percent to 20 percent), and the fact that, among Americans born after 1981, only 53 percent believe in God, means that we should only redouble our efforts to spread the word to the benighted. Zuckerman pungently refutes the implausible notion that religious belief is somehow hardwired in us (he quotes Paul Froese as stating that religion is an "essential part of the human condition," that God beliefs "lie at the core of human understanding"), stating bluntly: "We need to simply accept that some men and women find that life is better, freer, richer, or more honest without faith in God and/or religious involvement." It is a message of which few readers of this magazine need to be reminded.

Circling the Wagons

Mere Apologetics: How to Help Seekers and Skeptics Find Faith. By Alister E. McGrath. Grand Rapids, MI: Baker Books, 2012. 197 pp. Hardcover, $16.99.

For several years Alister E. McGrath has been providing us much merriment at his own expense. Like a mosquito attempting to irritate a heavyweight boxer, he has been nipping at the heels of his intellectual better, Richard Dawkins. He first wrote *Dawkins' God* (2005), then, upon the immense success of Dawkins's *The God Delusion* (2006), he produced a feeble little treatise called *The Dawkins Delusion?* (2007). In that work he maintained that he was once an atheist but later renounced it, since "Christianity was a much more interesting and intellectually exciting worldview than atheism." Well, I suppose that theosophy, occultism, and similar complicated systems of gibberish can be "interesting" to certain mentalities. What McGrath neglects to mention is that he was raised as an Irish Protestant and attended the Methodist College Belfast. It would appear that the childhood crippling of his brain has produced an unsurprising boomerang effect. He now attempts a defense of Christian doctrine aimed at both believers and "skeptics," but the results are, to put it mildly, curious.

McGrath begins with the platitude that, in the light of modern science, "truth" is now a matter of statistical probabilities. Well and good; but what McGrath ignores is that, the more incredible the event, the higher the threshold of evidence required to confirm it, or even make it remotely plausible. In another context he compares the resurrection of Jesus from the dead to Julius Caesar's crossing the Rubicon, thereby initiating the Roman civil war. But the two events are, from an evidentiary standpoint, very different. For the latter, there are any number of contemporary accounts testifying to its occurrence, including the testimony of Caesar's own writings; even without this evidence, it does not strain credulity that it could have occurred. For the former, however, the only "evidence" is the Bible—and that is no evidence at all, for the writers of the Bible had a vested interest in affirming that the event occurred. But how likely is it? I have never seen a person revived from the dead, and all the knowledge we have accumulated about biology and chemistry suggests that it could not have occurred. So why should one believe it? More pertinently, how is it that an entire religion gets founded on such an unlikely event?

McGrath devotes a chapter to the "reasonableness" of Christianity, but offers no arguments to support this contention. Instead, he merely quotes *other people* who affirm it, also without evidence. For example, he asserts that "There is a growing consensus that belief in God is perfectly rational." What is his source for this surprising "fact"? None other than Alvin Plantinga! Theists like McGrath, Plantinga, and Richard Swinburne need to stick together—a kind of circle-the-wagons tactic so that bad old atheists don't strip them and others of their precious faith.

It was to be expected that McGrath would carp at the New Atheists. He maintains that these thinkers have presented a "metanarrative . . . of the former enslavement of humanity to primitive superstitions. Through the intelligent application of reason and science in the last few centuries, humanity was able to break free from this age-old oppression and enter a bright new world of liberty and enlightenment." He claims that this simplistic historical interpretation is transparently false. I don't know where he got this view from; I cannot find it in anything written by Dawkins or Hitchens or Sam Harris.

The real atheist "metanarrative" has to with the progress of human thought—as I have put it elsewhere, the systematic replacement of supernatural causation by natural causation. This process, to McGrath's discomfiture, continues up to the present day. Consider the scientific account of lightning. This account is now so satisfying that the earlier religious account—that lightning-bolts were hurled by God to punish sinners—has fallen by the wayside. No scientist has bothered to refute the religious account; it is simply a casualty of the advance of knowledge. McGrath tries to save religion by declaring: "Events within the created order can exist in complex causal relationships, without in any way refuting their ultimate dependency upon God as final cause." But this formulation falls victim to Occam's razor. The idea that there is an extra layer of causation above and beyond natural causation is, at a minimum, cumbersome and inelegant. That extra layer must be cut away, especially given that there is not the slightest evidence (and McGrath offers none aside from mere assertion) that that extra layer of divine causation exists at all.

I don't have space to examine every one of McGrath's actual apologetic arguments, but I do wish to address his notion that the existence of widely diverse life on Earth renders plausible the idea that God created a "universe designed for life." The reasoning here is a trifle opaque. Whatever one's views on the possibility of extraterrestrial life, one surely cannot dispute that life—at least, carbon-based life such as is found on this planet—is fabulously rare throughout the universe. The idea that God would create a universe of almost incalculable extent for the single or dominant purpose of populating a tiny little world with "life" while leaving nearly the whole of the rest of the cosmos "dead" is passing strange. It lacks a certain economy of means.

McGrath fails entirely when dealing with the intersection of Christianity and morality. He yearns for an objective (i.e., God-given) set of ethical rules, because he doesn't see how one can combat ethical-political evils like Nazism with merely the relativist or subjectivist ethics of the standard atheist; but replacing one totalitarian system with another doesn't seem much of a solution. I'm happy to acknowledge that my own ethical beliefs are nothing more than subjective preferences, generally induced by my upbringing, education, and place in history; but if McGrath thinks this is an insufficient impetus to action, he'll find me a pretty tough opponent if he and his fellow Christians try to enforce a theocracy here or anywhere else.

The wish for an objective basis for ethics is a fool's errand. Dawkins has treated this matter magisterially in *The God Delusion*. There he speaks of a theist who maintains: "If you don't believe in God, you don't believe there are any absolute standards of morality. . . . Only religion can ultimately provide your standards of good and evil. Without religion you have to make it up as you go along." Dawkins shrewdly points out that this dilemma is shared not only by atheists but by nearly everyone—including most Christians. Why? Because a number of the actual ethical doctrines propounded by the Bible are ones that cannot possibly be accepted by any sane person today—things like the condoning of slavery, the ownership of wives by their husbands, the death penalty for adulterers, sabbath-violators, and homosexuals, and so on and so forth. I will charitably assume that McGrath does not ascribe to any of these dogmas; but the moment he abandons any one of them, he has implicitly rejected the Bible (and therefore Christianity) as an *authoritative* (i.e., objective) source for moral behavior. Therefore, he, like everyone else, makes up his ethics as he goes along.

McGrath also brings forth the idea that belief in God is rendered more plausible by the "argument from desire"—the desire that some people have for the comforts of religion, especially those of a loving god and of immortality. But this desire (what McGrath explains by the statement "We have a hunch we were made for more than just this life") is so obviously accounted for by psychological need and cultural conditioning that it actually forms a clinching argument in support of atheism. All the (spurious) comfort that Christianity has provided to some is counteracted by the misery it has inflicted on others who spend their lives quaking in fear of an imaginary hell for the "sins" they have committed.

The most curious thing about *Mere Apologetics* is that it does not actually deal with the specifically *Christian* facets of Christian doctrine. Even if one were to accept the idea of God as a first cause, as McGrath does, this need not be the Christian god; any creator-god would do. Indeed, this argument usually entails the god of the Deists, who started the whole show at the outset and then sat back to watch his handiwork; and this is certainly not the god McGrath wants, because he believes God is a "person" with whom one can have an intimate relationship. What about such thorny doctrines as biblical inerrancy, the Trinity, the divinity of Jesus, or heaven and hell? What of the fact that Jesus unequivocally stated that his second coming would occur within the lifetime of those who heard him? How could such a "divine" figure be so embarrassingly wrong about so central a facet of his teaching? These are surely some of the dogmas that make it difficult for many to be Christian today; but McGrath is stonily silent about them.

What about other faiths? If Christianity is so "natural" and "reasonable," why do more than two-thirds of the world's people not ascribe to it? Why is it that large swaths of Western Europe are now resolutely secular? Why is it that only 5% of people in McGrath's own country (he teaches at Oxford) attend Anglican services? Why, even in the God-besotted United States, is the fastest-growing segment of the population that group that declares no religious affiliation? These are deeply uncomfortable issues for most Christians, but McGrath cannot trouble himself to address them.

I do not know why this book was written; it seems to have no reason for existence. I cannot imagine a single individual being persuaded by it. It is not merely that McGrath's arguments are poor, although they are; it is that, for large stretches, he provides no arguments at all. He seems to have come up with a new hermeneutical method for ascertaining the truth: "This is true because I say it is." Well, maybe this is not so new after all; for isn't it the principle on which all the sacred texts of the earth were written?

Yearning for Paradise Lost

Religion for Atheists: A Non-Believer's Guide to the Uses of Religion. By Alain de Botton. New York: Pantheon, 2012. 320 pp. Hardcover, $26.95.

The subtitle of this book says it all. Alain de Botton, who runs something called the School of Life in London, claims that religion has more "uses" than many atheists are willing to grant—that, in simple terms, we shouldn't throw out the baby with the bathwater. Many atheists and secularists think that there *is* no baby in the bathwater—that it is all bathwater, or perhaps ditchwater. But de Botton's support for his claims is so weak that one is more inclined to seek a psychological rather than an intellectual account for the very existence of this deeply silly little book. (I say "little" because the book's size is largely deceptive: nearly every other page is filled, not with text, but with fatuous pictures of one sort or another, usually of religious iconography or of pious persons engaging in prayer.)

De Botton ingenuously declares that he was raised as an atheist by secular Jews, but that "in my mid-twenties I underwent a crisis of faithlessness." It is pathetically obvious that de Botton yearns for many of the outward trappings of religion, although he is too intelligent to ascribe to its metaphysical underpinnings. The result is that he not only maligns secular culture for faults that are not properly attributable to it, but presents an idealized—even fantasized—image of religion that entirely ignores that religion actually is and has been.

Consider his discussion of the purported loss of "community" in contemporary life, a matter lamented by many stewards of our culture. We have become isolated units, cliquishly adhering to a small band of like-minded individuals but paying no heed to the society at large. But, at least in the United States, religious belief and church attendance remain high; why, then, should this lack of community be such a plague here? In contrast to the simple-minded sociology in which de Botton engages, it is a brutal truth that much of the decline in community is a result of the "rugged individualism" brand of capitalism that now dominates this country—a brand that our outwardly pious Republican friends are doing everything in their power to foster. And maybe religions really don't deserve as much credit for preserving "community" as they customarily get. Many churches and sects are now so clannish and suspicious of "outsiders" that they are augmenting rather than counteracting the decline of social cohesion.

Then there is de Botton's treatment of (secular) higher education. Evidently on the basis of a single afternoon spent sitting in on some classes at an unnamed London university, de Botton concludes that secular humanities departments have become nothing more than the haven of pettifogging pedantry are betraying the ideal of the secular university as propounded by Matthew Arnold and others—the ideal of an institution that preparing a person to lead an engaged and moral life. I don't know what college (if any) de Botton attended, but I can attest that my enrollment at two Ivy League institutions for eight years did in fact have a transformative effect—vastly broadening my intellectual horizons, making me more self-aware, and clarifying my moral, social, and political outlook. Is my experience typical? I believe it is, if my acquaintance with hundreds of other college graduates is any guide. (One gets the feeling that de Botton's tawdry caricature of higher education, as of secular society as a whole, for its supposed inability to instruct people in how to lead an emotionally fulfilling life is a not-so-subtle plug for his own School of Life, which purports to address this very point. This from someone who—plausibly enough, as it happens—decries the ubiquity of advertising in contemporary culture.)

De Botton's remedies for the dreary state of affairs he purports to find in modern culture are even more fatuous than his analyses. In regard to community, he soberly proposes what he calls an Agape Restaurant, where complete strangers will sit down with one another and pour out the darkest secrets of their hearts while passing the salt. Compounding his folly, he later recommends the reinstitution of the mediaeval Feast of Fools, in which all members of society behave buffoonishly, and licentiously, without penalty. De Botton comes up with the brilliant conclusion that these Agape Restaurants would be the perfect venue for a recrudescence of such a feast, in which we would be allowed "to party and copulate randomly and joyfully with strangers [not a wise move in the age of AIDS, but let that pass], and then return next morning to our partners, who will themselves have been off doing something similar." Yes, my friends—that is a direct quote; I couldn't have made it up. As for education, de Botton places another dunce-cap on his head by maintaining that all university professors should be "trained by African-American Pentecostal preachers." For you see, these latter are able to *persuade* their congregants with rolling of eyes and foaming of mouth. But it never dawns upon de Botton that such preachers really aren't trying to *convey truths* so much as to *indoctrinate their followers*. But the distinction is of no consequence to him.

The lengths to which de Botton is prepared to go in letting religion off the hook for its past and present derelictions is evident in his passing comment about "the ongoing charm and utility of the idea of Original Sin." This whopping claim ends up being nothing more than the provocative formulation of the banal truism that we are all imperfect; but it is difficult to credit that de Botton is unaware of the catastrophic moral harm that Original Sin has caused. It was, let us recall, what led Augustine to declare that infants were "limbs of Satan"—that they would go straight to hell if they were not baptized before death. And it is what led C. S. Lewis blandly to ignore the immense amount of suffering and misery in the world; for after all, such misery is a natural and *deserved* concomitant to our "fallen" nature. Isn't it?

This must surely be one of the most foolish and useless books ever published. The pious are going to take umbrage at de Botton's cherrypicking certain phases of religious life and practice while jettisoning their metaphysical foundations; and secularists are going to conclude, correctly, that every supposed "benefit" that religion claims to offer can be achieved in a better and less intellectually degrading fashion without religion or the trappings of religion. De Botton may see the baby in the bathwater, but that is only because of the bitter tears he has shed at the inevitable loss of his own faith.

The Caspar Milquetoast Humanist

The God Argument: The Case against *Religion and* for *Humanism.* By A. C. Grayling. New York: Bloomsbury, 2013. x, 269 pp. Hardcover, $26.00.

I recently referred to Bertrand Russell as a "philosophical schizophrenic."[1] By this I meant that, while writing prodigiously technical treatises on the philosophy of mathematics, philosophical logic, language analysis, and other abstruse subjects, Russell also wrote rather elementary and even simple-minded treatises—*Marriage and Morals* (1932), *Religion and Science* (1935), etc.—intended for the great unwashed, in the (probably vain) hope that they would crawl out of their cavern of inspissated ignorance and actually learn something about the world and universe they occupy.

It seems that A. C. Grayling, in *The God Argument,* has adopted much the same strategy. Grayling has written books on Berkeley, Wittgenstein, and other such weighty thinkers. I have not read these books, but I imagine their contents are correspondingly weighty. But *The God Argument* is clearly intended to appeal to a much broader public, especially those who might be in doubt about the "truths" of religion or any specific religion and might therefore come into the atheist/freethinker/secularist class, which is in any event growing by leaps and bounds. The very title of Grayling's book appears to be a deliberate alternative to Richard Dawkins's *The God Delusion* (2006), suggesting that Grayling won't be quite as open about kicking religion's butt as Dawkins was. But, sadly enough, the end result is that Grayling's book is written in a curiously flaccid, Caspar Milquetoast fashion that makes one wonder (a) whether he himself is sufficiently engaged in the issues in question, and (b) whether he has any hope of convincing fence-sitters by his very mild rebukes of religion and even milder advocacy of humanism.

And yet, on one subject he goes beyond Dawkins and other "new atheists." Startlingly, Grayling declares that "agnosticism, as the position that entertains the possibility that there *might be* or *could be* one or more supernatural agencies of some sort, is an irrational position." What Grayling is arguing is that it is in fact possible to eliminate the "nanometre" (as he calls it) of doubt as to whether anything resembling a god could exist. I think this position goes

---

1. See my "Bertrand Russell: The Sage of Cambridge," in *The Unbelievers: The Evolution of Modern Atheism* (Amherst, NY: Prometheus Books, 2011), 155.

too far, much as I would like to ascribe to it myself. Grayling appears to have forgotten that the inventor of the term agnosticism, Thomas Henry Huxley, maintained that both atheists (in the proper sense of the term—those who "know" that a god does not exist) and theists "had attained a certain 'gnosis,'—had, more or less successfully, solved the problem of existence; while I was quite sure I had not, and had a pretty strong conviction that the problem was insoluble."[2] (Huxley was, I believe, concerned about the emergence of a dogmatic atheism that would be, epistemologically and psychologically, indistinguishable from dogmatic theism; and I think this was and is a genuine concern.) Grayling claims that Bertrand Russell, in denying that it can ever be definitively proven that a god *does not* or *cannot* exist, is claiming that he (Russell) is somehow looking for a "demonstrative proof" (i.e., a "proof in a formal deductive system"). But Grayling himself knows that any statements about the existence or non-existence of a god are *empirical propositions,* which modern physics has established are only a matter of statistical probabilities. It may well be "irrational" to be a theist (for the probability of theism being true are vanishingly small), but that is precisely why it is *not* irrational to be an agnostic. As H. P. Lovecraft declared, "In theory I am an *agnostic,* but pending the appearance of radical evidence I must be classed, practically and provisionally, as an *atheist.*"[3] In other words, that "nanometre" of doubt about the existence of a god can never, by the nature of things, be eliminated. Possibly Grayling is addressing those agnostics who think there is a 50/50 chance of theism being true; but whether there really are any agnostics of this sort is seriously in question.

The rest of the first half of Grayling's book, devoted to arguments against religion, are pretty routine and say little that has not already been said before. Grayling has a somewhat ampler discussion of the Intelligent Design charlatanry than what Dawkins provided, but because Grayling appears not entirely well-versed in science, he merely cites others' work on the subject. And yet, it is extraordinary that, in discussing the argument from design, he never mentions the theory of evolution, which definitively destroyed this last remaining crutch of theism. This is precisely why Dawkins said that "Darwin made it possible to be an intellectually fulfilled atheist."[4] Grayling only brings up

2. Thomas Henry Huxley, "Agnosticism," in *Science and Christian Tradition* (New York: D. Appleton & Co., 1896), 238.

3. H. P. Lovecraft, Letter to Robert E. Howard (August 16, 1932), *Selected Letters: 1932–1934,* ed. August Derleth and James Turner (Sauk City, WI: Arkham House, 1976), 57.

4. Richard Dawkins, *The Blind Watchmaker* (New York: W. W. Norton, 1986), 6.

Darwinism in the chapter on Intelligent Design, never making clear how central it is to the establishment of a fully secular worldview.

One would have supposed that the second part of the book, outlining Grayling's understanding of humanism, would be a bit more lively and engaged; but it is nothing of the sort. To be sure, he propounds a fairly orthodox farrago of liberal social and political stances—support for abortion rights, women's rights, gay rights (but no mention at all of same-sex marriage), animal rights, euthanasia, legalization of drugs, and so forth, but some of these subjects (especially on animal rights) are treated so briefly and sketchily that one would be right to question Grayling's devotion to them. He appears to come out in favor of legalizing prostitution, but cannot quite bring himself to say so explicitly. Once again, I suspect he is fearful of offending his middle-class audience by taking so seemingly "radical" a stand (but one that strikes me as eminently sensible and, indeed, inevitable).

It is perhaps this fear of offending that leads Grayling into another serious philosophical error. He states (correctly) that moral (or ethical)[5] views are very various—among different eras, among various cultures, even in a single individual over time—but seems frightened at being branded a "moral relativist," so he opts for the untenable position of moral objectivism. (Sam Harris, in a recent book, has done so as well, from a different but equally erroneous perspective.[6]) Morality, in Grayling's view, is "an objective matter" because "there are objective facts about human needs and interests that constrain any possible morality." What Grayling doesn't understand is that moral positions and systems are not themselves *facts*, but *emotional responses to facts*. The logical positivist position on this issue, articulated by Russell, A. J. Ayer, and others, has never been answered. In saying "Killing is wrong [or bad or evil]," one is saying two things: (a) there is such a thing as killing; and (b) I happen not to approve of it. The first is a fact; the second is an emotional response to the fact. In effect, all ethical utterances are statements of preference—no different in kind from a preference for chocolate ice cream over vanilla ice cream, and no more subject to truth or falsity. It is not (factually) *wrong* to like chocolate ice cream over vanilla ice cream.

Grayling goes on to say that moral objectivism is based on a "good general understanding of the minimum conditions for human flourishing"—and

---

5. Grayling, like others, undertakes an artificial and unworkable distinction between "ethics" and "morals," apparently unaware that these terms are, respectively, merely the Greek (*ethos*) and Latin (*mos/mores*) terms for approximately the same conception. But this is an argument for another day.

6. See *The Moral Landscape* (2011).

this gets to the heart of the error. To say "the human race should flourish" is to say (a) there is such a thing as the human race, and (b) it should flourish. The first is a fact, the second a preference. It is perfectly possible to construct a systematic and coherent ethical system based on the preference that the human race should *not* flourish—that, in fact, it should be extirpated. It doesn't matter whether anyone actually espouses such a view (although I seem to be gravitating toward it more and more with each passing day); the fact that it can be espoused without committing any factual error or self-contradiction shows why moral subjectivism is the only viable stance. And much of Grayling's discussion is predicated on such a stance in any event.

I really wanted to like this book. I in fact agree with about 95% of it. But Grayling has expressed himself with such a lack of fire and passion, and with such a dearth of distinctiveness and innovation, that one wonders why the book was written at all. Well-informed atheists and humanists will learn exactly nothing from it. Whether some of those fence-sitters out there may fare better remains to be seen.

A "Christian Intellectual" Speaks

Conscience and Its Enemies: Confronting the Dogmas of Liberal Secularism. By Robert P. George. Wilmington, DE: ISI Books, 2013. xii, 290 pp. Hardcover, $29.95.

Robert P. George is the McCormick Professor of Jurisprudence at Princeton and is evidently regarded as a leading Christian conservative "intellectual." In this new book, he seeks to shatter a number of "dogmas" espoused by "liberal secularism," but he claims not to do so from religious presuppositions, since of course his opponents would not accept criticism on this basis. He asserts magnanimously that "I do not base my arguments on theological claims or religious authority"; instead, he maintains that he is only using science (in some cases "new" scientific evidence) to support his views. But in reality, George has cherrypicked those scientific "facts" that he believes support his own dogmas and prejudices while ignoring or downplaying others that would qualify or altogether undermine them. The result is a sadly tendentious and disingenuous screed that is not likely to convince anyone not already on George's side.

Most of George's book is devoted to attacking same-sex marriage and legalized abortion. He bases many of his arguments, especially on abortion, on "natural law" philosophy derived chiefly from the Christian tradition. I will state bluntly that I flatly reject this conception. I am happy to be one of those "moral skeptics who deny that there are moral truths," since to me it is plain as can be that all ethical systems are culturally conditioned preferences (whether "rationally" arrived at or not) to which standards of truth and falsity do not and cannot apply—any more than they can apply to my preference for chocolate ice cream over vanilla ice cream. I have made my arguments on this point elsewhere and do not have the space to elaborate them here.[1] In any event, George's stance leads him to assert (and to do no more than assert) that human beings accordingly have "intrinsic value"—that, indeed, "man is made in the image of God"! (Somehow I thought he was going to present his arguments without relying on theological claims or religious authority, but let

---

1. See my *God's Defenders: What They Believe and Why They Are Wrong* (Amherst, NY: Prometheus Books, 2003), 269–79; *The Unbelievers: The Evolution of Modern Atheism* (Amherst, NY: Prometheus Books, 2011), 226–31.

that pass.) In my view nothing in the universe has any "intrinsic" value; indeed, the very formulation is oxymoronic. To say that something has "value" is not to utter a fact; it is to utter a subjective preference. A gemstone only has (monetary) value because we, as a society, collectively agree to grant it such. George is free to base a philosophical theory on this principle, but he should be prepared to have his views rejected *tout court* by those who don't accept his premise.

In any case, let us consider what objections George has to same-sex marriage. I have read and re-read the several chapters of his book on the subject and still find myself befuddled as to what his precise argument is. He apparently wishes to maintain that only a man and a woman, because of the "complementarity" of their sexual organs, can achieve full "bodily union" and therefore become, in the biblical phrase, "one flesh." Silly me! I just thought this was a poetic metaphor. Does any couple ever become "one flesh" during coitus (or any other time) except moony teenagers and characters in Harlequin romances? George seems to think so, and presents the grotesque spectacle of making this metaphor the basis for a restrictive and prejudicial social policy. For after all, gays don't have the right (i.e., complementary) sexual organs! If he thinks he can win any adherents with this line of reasoning, he must be more delusional than I thought he was. His reasoning (if it can be called that) on marriage is so arid, abstract, and theoretical that it fails utterly to consider how marriage (including heterosexual marriage) is actually conducted in present-day society. Let me quote a representative sentence: "The central and justifying point of sex is not pleasure, however much sexual pleasure is rightly sought as an aspect of the perfection of marital union; the point of sex, rather, is marriage itself, considered as an essentially and irreducibly bodily union of persons—a union effectuated and renewed by acts of sexual congress." If you can attach a coherent meaning to any of this, you are doing better than I. And I still fail to see why either gays or unmarried straight couples cannot achieve this "bodily union," and why only heterosexual married couples can.

George denies that marriage is "a mere legal convention or cultural artifact," but of course it is exactly that. And more, it has historically been used as a license for sex, as even his own scripture declares (see Paul's celebrated comment "It is better to marry than to burn"). But now that the irrational stigma over pre-marital sex has dissipated (the very word "fornication" can now only be used parodically), marriage itself has lost a bit of its overriding rationale. I suspect that much of George's ire against same-sex marriage, as against other forms of "non-traditional" unions, is their implicit (and sometimes explicit) rejection of religion's stranglehold on marriage practices and on human relations altogether.

George attempts to frighten his conservative readership with the specter of "polyamory" if same-sex marriage gains wide acceptance. Let it pass that this also has biblical precedent, if the many wives of David, Solomon, and other worthies are considered. In reality, there is no legitimate (i.e., non-religious) objection to any such arrangements that people willingly enter into. As Ambrose Bierce repeatedly said, I have no objections to polygamy so long as it is not compulsory. ("Polygamy" needs to be understood not only as one man with multiple wives but one woman with multiple husbands, or any other combination thereof.)

The plain fact that George refuses to countenance is that marriage (whether heterosexual or homosexual) is now only one of several viable means of forming the family unit—including unmarried but committed gay or straight couples, single parents, and so on. George whines that "ideologies hostile to marriage" are causing or augmenting all manner of social ills; but the problem is not with marriage (or the lack of it), but with poverty. George must know that unmarried couples and even single-parent households of the more affluent sort are doing just fine in regard to childrearing, largely because they have the resources to secure day care and other services—something the poor cannot manage. So the solution is not simply to encourage poor people to get married, but to put measures in place to get them out of poverty.

In the matter of abortion, it is not what George says that is of interest, but what he doesn't say. In all his laborious and repetitious discussions of the matter (which include a tedious and largely irrelevant disquisition on embryology), one reasonably significant figure in the whole debate is noticeably absent. George devotes not one sentence to the moral, legal, or even biological role of the pregnant mother. It is as if the fetus magically develops on its own with no input from the mother carrying it. One typical sentence states that the embryo, "if left to itself in a *suitable environment*" (my emphasis), will develop normally. So now the pregnant mother is reduced to a mere "environment"! This fanatical focus on the "personhood" or "humanity" of the fetus, and the implicit denial of the humanity of the mother, is typical of the misogyny at the heart of the anti-abortion movement. It is no accident that abortion was legalized during the height of the feminist movement of the 1970s, and that it is opposed by those who continue to find female independence disturbing and even vaguely sacrilegious. George's stance leads to the bizarre conclusion that "we were never parts of our mothers; we were, from the beginning, complete, self-integrating organisms that developed to maturity by a gradual, gapless, and self-directed process." Is that so? Then I suggest that George take a three-day-old (or even a three-month-old) fetus, abstract it from its mother's womb, place it on a table, and see how well it "develops" on its own.

What all this means is that the fetus cannot possibly be regarded—legally, morally, and biologically—as an *independent* entity until it is capable of living outside the mother's womb. George, who thinks he has science on his side, does everything he can to obfuscate the only scientific fact of any relevance to the *public policy debate* about abortion—the fact of fetal viability. He does so because he would otherwise be forced to admit that, according to well-established science, the fetus is not viable until the third trimester—and that is exactly why the Supreme Court correctly decided on this boundary line as the threshold for legalized abortion. Before viability, the fetus can only be regarded as a part of the mother, to be dealt with as she sees fit. Anything else would lead to intolerable tyranny over pregnant women.

Consider the scenario in a world run by Robert P. George. Here is a living, breathing woman who for years or decades has been making independent moral decisions for herself and, perhaps, for other members of her family; but the moment she becomes pregnant, she suddenly loses her moral autonomy—in effect, her "personhood"—and becomes nothing more than an incubator, and a ward of the state. So much for the "limited government" that George trumpets in other contexts! Conversely, if the fetus is a "person" from the moment of conception, what follows? Should we give it a Social Security number? Should the parents receive a child tax credit from the moment of conception? Shall a pregnant mother, in filling out a census form, say that there is already one extra person in the household?

The underlying fact that those in the anti-abortionist camp (and perhaps some in the abortion rights camp also) fail to grasp is that pregnancy is an anomalous condition that requires careful deliberation and compromise. The idea of any kind of equivalency between a living, mature woman and an entity that is not even born is absurd on its face; and even if we grant some kind of "personhood" to the fetus, we must also acknowledge that the woman also has *some* rights, as opposed to *no* rights as under George's scheme.

George's other concern in this book is to raise the specter of repeated and intolerable infringements on the "conscience" of religious people as a result of liberal "dogmas" on abortion and other issues. It is, however, odd that George never specifies what conscience exactly is, nor does he specify exactly where it comes from. I imagine his answer to the latter question is that it comes from God. Of course it does; how could I forget? But doubts linger. . . . Once again, is it not evident that the *content* of our consciences is entirely time-bound and culture-bound? My conscience tells me that religion is the greatest evil the world has ever known and that I should devote my life to working toward its eradication. So where does *my* conscience come from? The Devil? Maybe so . . . but I suspect it comes more plausibly from my genes, upbringing, education, and my place in history—just as George's own does.

But let that pass. Exactly how are the consciences of religious people being infringed upon? He cites the notorious instance of the "pharmacist who declines to dispense abortifacient drugs," going on to say that this denial "coerces no one." But of course it does, and the one being coerced is *not* the pharmacist (no one, after all, is forcing *her* to take the drug). Remember that we are dealing with a legally available medical product that any woman has a right to secure. Why should she be forced to go to some other pharmacy to secure it? What if she lives in a remote part of the country where the next-closest pharmacy is 30 or 50 or 100 miles away? Are we now to call up our pharmacists ahead of time and ask them, "Oh, by the way, are you morally or religiously opposed to filling my prescription?" What if the pharmacist objects to dispensing drugs to treat schizophrenia and other mental illnesses? After all, it was long the teaching of the Christian church that such ailments were indicative of demonic possession (and the church for centuries stood in the way of the rational and humane treatment of mental illness), so maybe this pharmacist thinks that the luckless patient would be better off going to a priest and getting an exorcism. We can, I think, all agree that the pharmacist could do everyone (including herself) a favor by finding a different line of work.

George similarly complains that, with the advent of same-sex marriage in some states, private individuals and companies are now being forced to serve such people when their "conscience" objects to it. This line of reasoning also gets George into trouble. He knows that the courts have declared that discrimination on the grounds of race, religion, and sex is in most contexts no longer permissible, even if a religious rationale is brought forward; and he himself states that religious "freedom" has its necessary limitations. Let us take the example of a devout Christian who operates a flower shop. A menstruating woman, an atheist (or some other "heretic"), and a person who regularly violates the Sabbath by working for a living on that day wish to purchase some flowers. Now from the point of view of scripture, all these individuals are just as much *personae non gratae* as a gay married couple (or, in fact, a homosexual of any sort); indeed, the Bible specifically decrees the death penalty for heretics, Sabbath-violators, and gays. Why does George not complain about the menstruating woman, heretic, or Sabbath-violator being served, but only about the gay couple? The only answer is that prejudice against homosexuals is one of the last vestiges of bigotry deemed permissible in some quarters, and so George leads a rearguard defense of it. But scripturally speaking, it has no more or less validity than prejudice against those other undesirables.

And, of course, George repeats the tired canard that the Affordable Care

Act will force private companies to provide contraception for their female employees in defiance of the "conscience" of the bosses. But whose conscience is being violated? No one is forcing bosses to use contraception if they don't wish to do so; and no one is preventing bosses from speaking out against the "evils" of contraception. On the other hand, are we to countenance a situation where a female employee is at the mercy of her boss as to whether she secures contraception or not? Is this something a woman will need to raise at a job interview? It is all too absurd. I suppose it is to be expected that George nowhere mentions the plain fact that increased use of contraceptives (most of which are not in fact "abortifacients") materially reduces the very abortions he abominates. But this whole kerfuffle about contraceptives is, in the twenty-first century, simply a piece of lunacy. One might as well object to the proposition that the earth revolves around the sun (an objection that in fact has scriptural support: the Catholic Church did not acknowledge the truth of the heliocentric theory until 1822).

George also appears to believe that the very existence of legalized abortion constitutes some sort of infringement on his "liberty of conscience." He himself is not a woman; even if he were, no one (certainly not the government) is forcing him to get an abortion if he doesn't want one. And no one (certainly not the government) is forcing him to approve of abortion or is suppressing his ability to speak out against it if he so chooses. So where is the infringement? Conversely, there *would* be an intolerable infringement if a woman who wished to terminate her pregnancy in the first two trimesters was legally prohibited from doing so. Support for abortion is (*pace* George) not self-evidently vicious, and it is held by hundreds of millions of people around the world. What right has the government to intervene in the matter except under certain specified conditions (i.e., the third trimester)?

In other words, George is in the position of sensing an infringement on his conscience by the mere existence of other people being legally allowed to believe and act in ways he does not approve of. The classic definition of fascism is that you are not satisfied in acting or thinking in a certain way yourself; you require that *everyone* act and think in that way, especially on controverted subjects where uniformity is difficult or impossible to obtain. By this definition, I am sorry to report, Robert P. George is a fascist.

George, as I say, thinks the facts are on his side; but these moral issues are not themselves facts, only value judgments. It is not a "fact" that gay people can never establish "bodily union," or that "bodily union" (whatever it may be) is the only legitimate basis for marriage; it is not a "fact" that abortion constitutes the "death of a child" (this loaded and prejudicial language is typical of the anti-abortionists' attempts to argue rhetorically rather than logically). All these things are merely George's tortured interpretation of the facts, and that does not give him the right to impose those views, by statute or legislation, on others who disagree with him.

The uncomfortable position in which George finds himself in this entire treatise is that he is attempting to use reason and logic to defend the irrational. He has brainwashed himself into toeing the Christian party line on all manner of subjects and now seeks to find pseudo-intellectual arguments to justify them. But he fails at every turn. He proclaims his support for "governmental respect for individual freedom," but this principle falls to the ground on issue after issue (abortion, same-sex marriage, euthanasia) at exactly the point where it needs to be sustained. And it does so because sustaining it would lead to conclusions precisely opposite to those he holds.

There are many other silly and objectionable stances in George's book, but they are largely incidental. He has a brief and cranky chapter on a few conservative professors who have presumably been dismissed or censured merely for their opinions (although in one instance—that of Crystal Dixon, who publicly denied that sexual orientation should be included along with race, religion, and sex in anti-discrimination statutes—we appear to be dealing with both an idiot and a bigot). But George must know that cases of this sort are, historically speaking, far more likely to involve the left than the right, as the instances of social activist Scott Nearing, the many intellectuals destroyed during the McCarthy era, and the recent case of Ward Churchill attest.

And George is either staggeringly naïve or plainly disingenuous when he asserts that conservative Catholic priests' threats to deny communion to (mostly Democratic) politicians who support abortion rights are not being political, writing blandly: "No one is compelled by law to accept ecclesiastical authority." Surely George is aware that these threats always surface conveniently around an election and are manifestly meant to sway the election. And George remains stonily silent on the fact that such pious clerics never make such threats to the many (mostly Republican) politicians who support the death penalty—a violation of the Catholic "pro-life" stance quite as severe, it would seem to me, as support for abortion.

George provides a predictably superficial and misleading account of the constitutionality of the Affordable Care Act, claiming that for the first time in history people will be penalized for "inactivity" (i.e., the failure to purchase health insurance). But he fails to grasp the obvious fact that, in the matter of health care, this "inactivity" is only on the surface, and that it has serious economic consequences that Congress can legitimately legislate. Everyone will use health care at some point or other; and the great majority of the uninsured are not able to pay for it, especially if a serious illness or injury occurs.

Who then *does* pay for it (when, e.g., the uninsured go to the emergency room)? We all do. Gee, that sounds an awful lot like socialism to me! Does George really want tens of millions of the uninsured freeloading on the health care system, creating immense waste and inefficiency? What is his solution to the crisis? It is exactly what other conservatives have offered—i.e., nothing at all.

And George is living in a dangerous fantasy world if he thinks that the "much maligned" Tea Party (which, as I write, is hurtling this nation recklessly into the abyss of a government shutdown and default) has any concerns about the constitutionality of the individual mandate (which, as he fails to point out, was a conservative invention—cooked up by the Heritage Foundation in the early 1990s) and is not in reality guided by purely ignorant, selfish, and hypocritical motives (who can forget the exquisitely oxymoronic demand: "Hands off my Medicare!")—to say nothing of the fact that the Tea Party is largely funded by equally self-serving right-wing individuals and organizations.

George writes repeatedly, as if it were a mantra by which he is attempting to convince himself, that heterosexual marriage and the free enterprise system are "the two greatest institutions ever devised for lifting people out of poverty and enabling them to live in dignity." Really? Has George paid attention to the fact that, for the first several centuries of industrial capitalism, both here and in Europe, the working classes suffered grinding poverty of the sort that we cannot even imagine—saved in part only by the slow emergence of the labor union movement and sane laws enacted by governments (minimum wage, limitation of working hours, old age pensions) that properly curtailed "free enterprise"? Or has he considered that, during the past forty years, the top 1% of the population has seen its income increase by more than 400% whereas the incomes of everyone else have largely stagnated, resulting in increasing inequality that is destabilizing the entire society? It is now the view of a fair number of economists that the one time when capitalism delivered prosperity proportionately to the entire populace (the twenty-five years following World War II) was an historical aberration, and that capitalism cannot deliver these boons unless it is strongly reined in by government and other forces. I daresay George and his party will be slow in absorbing these plain truths.

I am a liberal, so my heart bleeds—and it bleeds for Robert P. George. He must be a very unhappy man. On multiple fronts, his side is not winning, and he is angry and resentful. Secularism is growing by leaps and bounds; "limited" government (if it means a government before the necessary reforms instituted by FDR and his successors) has been permanently consigned to the dustbin of history; same-sex marriage is set to become universal throughout the West; and even abortion in some form is still supported by a majority of the American population and is likely to remain legal, especially as the crassly political attempts by some states to curb abortion rights are systematically being shot down by the courts.

George is one of those many conservatives who live in the past—and, moreover, a past that never existed. For all his avowed advocacy of a "dynamic" society, he looks back to a time when safely married heterosexual couples raised happy and well-adjusted children; when government weighed lightly on people's (and especially corporations') backs (aside from minor incursions upon individual liberty such as African American slavery, prohibition of women to vote or own property, and attempts to ban the consumption of alcoholic beverages); and when religious institutions were looked upon with respect (in spite of trivial derelictions such as support for slavery, hostility to freethinkers, women, immigrants, and other dubious characters, brainwashing of children into religious dogma, and embarrassing revelations of clerical malfeasance).

If Robert P. George is the best "intellectual" that Christian conservatives can produce, then their movement is in deep trouble.

Religious Freedom or Religious Coercion?

Taking Liberties: Why Religious Freedom Doesn't Give You the Right to Tell People What to Do. By Robert Boston. Amherst, NY: Prometheus Books, 2014. 190 pp. Paperback, $19.95.

This is a compact, hard-hitting book that confronts one of the most urgent and vital issues facing us as a nation today: where is the precise line separating "religious freedom" (for both believers and nonbelievers) from religious coercion? Robert Boston, director of communications for Americans United for Separation of Church and State, makes a compelling case that religious fundamentalists, both Protestant and Catholic, are disingenuously misusing the notion of "religious freedom" to advance an agenda whereby *their own* freedom to practice their religion insidiously metamorphoses into forcing others to adhere to it as well. And that, as Boston implies, is not freedom—it is tyranny.

Boston's main point, presented especially at the conclusion of his slim book but really implicit throughout, is that the Religious Right is really seeking to regain lost ground. He is well aware, as we all should be, that the representatives of religion, for centuries or millennia, enjoyed near-total domination of many of the critical functions of human life and society—government, society, culture, and much else besides, especially as embodied in such central elements as sex, marriage, law, scientific inquiry, political involvement, and even death. It is not his purpose to engage in a lengthy historical disquisition on how this dominance came into existence and how it gradually fell by the wayside, but Boston pungently outlines how the freeing of humanity, especially in the United States, from the stranglehold of religion has caused the more fanatical religionists to fume over their increasing impotence. They no longer have the power to burn people at the stake; they no longer can force people to attend church or profess belief in God; they can no longer tell people whom to marry or the correct way to have sex. And so they are now undertaking a systematic effort to regain as much of that lost power as they can.

And they are doing so under the cloak of "religious freedom." That a pharmacist can refuse to supply a certain type of birth control; that a secular, for-profit business owner can refuse to allow his employees access to contraceptives; that similar for-profit businesses such as flower shops or wedding planners can deny services to same-sex couples—each of these things does not constitute "religious freedom," but rather a perversion of that concept whereby the religious seek to enforce their own biases and prejudices on others. Boston makes the particularly cogent point that religiously affiliated organizations such as Catholic-owned hospitals, by virtue of accepting taxpayer funds, necessarily subject themselves to at least some minimal degree of government oversight. There is, as Boston states, no obligation for such entities to accept taxpayer money; if they truly wish to be independent of the government and do whatever they wish, then they should declare themselves full-fledged private religious entities and eschew any such funding. But once they accept that money, they are obliged to adhere to regulations that all other such entities adhere to, such as non-discrimination, equal treatment of all citizens, and so on.

There are, however, times when Boston pulls his punches a bit. Early on he states that "Religion is not the problem. Fundamentalist religion that seeks to merge with political power and impose its dogma on the unwilling is the problem." There is some truth to this, but I suspect the comment—and, indeed, the overall tone of his book, which singles out the "Religious Right" but spares most other faith groups—is something of a sop to his boss, Barry W. Lynn, the executive director of Americans United for Separation of Church and State, whom Boston describes as a person whose "faith is genuine" and who is "comfortable enough with it to believe that it needs no support other than what he and his co-religionists are willing to give it." But I have to confess to a grudging admiration for certain religious fundamentalists who, unlike their more liberal or moderate counterparts, *actually believe* in what the Bible says and have sufficient courage in their convictions to act on it. Moderate religionists, it seems to me, often pay lip service to church doctrine and then blithely ignore it when it comes to certain stances (such as abortion or birth control or same-sex marriage) that they have come to find inconvenient with society's values and with their own evolving moral values. Catholic women who take contraceptives *really are* violating the doctrines of their own church, and to that degree they are no longer Catholics; but you won't find many of them making such an admission. The problem with religious fundamentalists in the United States is not so much that they adhere to a set of outworn dogmas but rather that they live in a country where the enforcement of those dogmas is specifically outlawed.

Boston is also in error in stating or implying that fundamentalists are seeking to impose their own interpretation of the Bible on others, and that one can always find some other passage in the Bible that contradicts their stance. This is a tad too simple; in any number of cases there is no dispute about what the Bible is saying. There is, for example, not the slightest doubt that the Bible is hostile to same-sex relations of any kind; indeed, even fundamentalists may, on this issue, lack the full courage of their convictions, since in at least one place the Bible recommends *the death penalty* for practicing homosexuals, something I personally have not heard many fundamentalists advocating. (Perhaps they have; I simply don't hang around in their circles enough to know one way or the other.)

Boston also tends to shy away from confrontation with more moderate faiths. He strongly protests the attempts by fundamentalists to prevent the teaching of evolution in public schools, even in its patently disingenuous disguise of "intelligent design"; but he feels it is "short-sighted" for tough-minded atheists to heap scorn on the notion that there can be any kind of reconciliation between religious faith and evolution, as when Catholic bishops say that evolution can be somehow guided or allowed by God. Boston writes: "Non-believers and those who insist that science has made faith obsolete should be careful. The United States remains a highly religious country. If people are told that they can't have both religion and science and that they must choose one, most will go with religion and shut out science." This strikes me as a somewhat hysterical reaction and a justification for pusillanimity. The practice of science will continue no matter how opposed the pious are to its overall implications—especially at the college level, where state legislators' meddling with the teaching of evolution or any other scientific doctrine is virtually nil.

Toward the end of his treatise, Boston's tone changes from outrage and indignation to a kind of mild contempt, especially when he treats the issue of the sad plight of fundamentalists in matters of art, literature, film, and general culture. Their power to control these venues is now so reduced as to be utterly insignificant. Indeed, every time they speak against some book or film or work of art that offends them, it only drives more people to sample that very item. Boston remarks tartly that William Donohue, the humorless buffoon who runs the Catholic League, is just about the "last guy on the planet you would choose to safeguard your entertainment options."

The only problem with this book is that it isn't long enough. Boston could have gone into greater detail on all the subjects at hand, and could have produced an even livelier treatise if he had recounted more exhaustively some of the specific legal and political battles that have been waged over these issues. His book is also written in a somewhat simple, even simple-minded, manner, with a bit more slang and colloquialism than I personally care for. But perhaps that is necessary to reach a broad audience today. Whether his work has any hope of penetrating the thick skulls of his opponents is, however, another matter entirely.

Satan, Monsters, and Bad People

Heaven Is for Real. By Todd Burpo, with Lynn Vincent. Nashville, TN: Thomas Nelson, 2010. 163 pp. Hardcover, $21.99. Paperback, $16.99.

I am reviewing this exquisite bit of buffoonery now because a major motion picture based on it will, by the time you read these words, have been released. I very much doubt that the film will be quite the blockbuster that the recent *Noah* will be; indeed, I suspect it will be a spectacular flop. But all that is beside the point. The book itself has generated a nice little cottage industry for its author and publisher: it has sold in the millions of copies, and there are such offshoots as a children's version and a "DVD-based study" and, presumably, sundry other lucrative paraphernalia. But what is remarkable about this fluffy bit of charlatanry is that virtually all the tools needed for an emphatic refutation of its main points lie in the unwitting words of the author himself.

Let us establish the background. Todd Burpo was (and, I assume, still us) a pastor at a Wesleyan church (a splinter group that split off from the Methodist church nearly two centuries ago) in Nebraska. A few months prior to his fourth birthday, Todd's son Colton suffered a serious illness. It was finally determined that his appendix had ruptured, and it required two operations to cure him. It is not clear from Burpo's account whether Colton really was close to death in this whole situation, so it cannot be determined whether Colton had a "near-death experience"; but whatever the case, Colton began spouting off about various visions experienced during his illness that led his father to believe he had been to heaven and back.

There are any number of anomalies in all this, but what is most peculiar is the readiness with which Todd Burpo swallows astounding, incredible, and supernatural accounts by his son without the slightest bit of skepticism. I have stated many times that incredible events have a very high threshold of evidence to be believed, chiefly because belief in them would upset longstanding scientific truths that have been verified over and over again. This applies not merely to religious hallucinations (for that is clearly what they are) of the sort experienced by Colton (and by many others, of many religions, over the millennia), but also things such as ghosts, vampires, haunted houses, and all kinds of other phenomena that are not directly religious in nature. If someone tells me that a person pole-vaulted eighteen feet at the Olympics, I would be inclined to believe it without having any first-hand knowledge of the matter; but if someone said that he saw a cow jump over the moon, I'd require a bit more evidence than merely his unsupported testimony. Why? Because this latter assertion overturns millennia of painstakingly acquired human knowledge that would require equally painstaking and overwhelming counter-evidence to refute.

We are told almost at the outset that one of the things Colton saw was Jesus (naturally); indeed, Colton claims that "I was sitting in Jesus' lap." Very nice; but Colton goes on to remark curiously about "markers" on Jesus' body, which Burpo finally figures out refers to Jesus' stigmata. This doesn't seem terribly remarkable, but Burpo reacts to the revelation with amazement. And he makes the incredible assertion: "I didn't know if my son had ever seen a crucifix." The son of a Wesleyan pastor, a boy who had already been attending Sunday school, had *never seen a crucifix?* What kind of suckers does Burpo think we are? If you believe this, there's a bridge nearby that I'd like to sell you.

This is only the most egregious of the whoppers that Burpo tries to put over on us. There are many others. Colton, for example, says that the children in heaven have wings—small ones, it is true, but wings nonetheless. (Evidently one's wings get bigger as one spends more time in heaven.) But the burning question I have is: *Where are the harps?* I want the harps, goddamn it! But alas, Colton apparently did not see or hear any harps, for there is no mention of them in Burpo's account. Colton also says that God himself sat on a big throne. Is this particularly remarkable? It doesn't seem so, especially since Burpo himself recounts this tidbit after telling of a children's book about Solomon (which has pictures of a golden throne) that he admitted reading to Colton from an early age. Jesus, predictably, is sitting to the right of God. Once again Colton thinks this is a remarkable revelation that must indicate some actual vision of heaven on his son's part. One wonders how many times Burpo had muttered the words "He sitteth at the right hand of God" in his son's presence without knowing it.

Colton also claims to have seen Burpo's maternal grandfather, but we get nothing even remotely precise about this person; all Colton can come up with is the fatuously trite "He's really nice." Then there is the matter of Colton's *two* sisters. Burpo makes a great deal of this, because in fact he has only one living sister, Cassie, two years his elder. Burpo and his wife, Sonja (who, incidentally, became acquainted with him at some institution of higher [sic] learning called Bartlesville Wesleyan College), suffered great emotional trauma when Sonja, two months pregnant, suffered a miscarriage. But now, Colton reveals awareness of this lost child. Let us quote Burpo directly: "Losing that baby was the most painful event of her [Sonja's] life. We had explained it to

Cassie; she was older. But we hadn't told Colton, judging the topic a bit beyond a four-year-old's capacity to understand." But does this mean Colton could never have known about this matter? Do you not think the likelihood is fairly strong that Cassie told Colton about it at some point? Siblings of that age are very close and are not likely to have secrets from each other. But Burpo makes not the slightest suggestion of this sort, because his dogmatic faith yearns to believe everything Colton is telling him.

Colton proves adept not only at seeing visions of heaven but also of predicting the future. He turns out to have a vision of Armageddon, saying: "There's going to be a war, and it's going to destroy this world. Jesus and the angels and the good people are going to fight against Satan and the monsters and the bad people. I saw it." Neither Colton nor his father specify who these "bad people are," but there are presumably quite a few of them, since there are any number of biblical passages suggesting that Jesus believed that the great majority of human beings would be consigned to hell. But Colton goes on to tell us that the "good guys win." Whew! What a relief! I was getting worried there for a minute. . . .

What is the moral of this fatuous little book for a rational person (as opposed to a Christian)? Surely it can be nothing less than the evils of brainwashing children into religion, a crime against humanity infinitely worse than anything that Vladimir Putin or Bashar al-Assad is currently engaging in. Indeed, one of the most revealing passages in the book is when, shortly after his recovery, Colton is attending a funeral and says with rage about the corpse: "He can't get into heaven if he didn't have Jesus in his heart!" Well, a nice little bigot in the making! Burpo, instead of chastising his son for his intolerance, actually praises him—or, rather, his religious training ("*Man, those Sunday school teachers sure are doing a good job!*"). Burpo blandly states that "most people who profess faith in Christ do so at a young age." You don't say! Most people who profess *any* faith do so at an early age. I am reminded of a wry comment by H. P. Lovecraft:

> Religionists openly give away the fakery of their position when they insist on crippling children's emotions with specialised suggestion anterior to the development of a genuine critical faculty. We all know that *any* emotional bias—irrespective of truth or falsity—can be implanted by suggestion in the emotions of the young. . . . If religion were true, its followers would not try to bludgeon their young into an artificial conformity; but would merely insist on their unbending quest for *truth*, irrespective of artificial backgrounds or practical consequences. With such an honest and inflexible *openness to evidence*, they could not fail to receive any *real truth* which might be manifesting itself around them. The fact that religionists do *not* follow this honorable course, but cheat

at their game by invoking juvenile quasi-hypnosis, is enough to destroy their pretensions in my eyes even if their absurdity were not manifest in every other direction.[1]

That passage could have been written as a review of *Heaven Is for Real.* In the meantime, all we can do is chortle at the credulity of Todd Burpo and his ilk who think the maunderings of a religiously brainwashed little boy can confirm a fairy tale that, for intelligent people, has been consigned to the dustbin of history for centuries.

---

1. H. P. Lovecraft, Letter to Maurice W. Moe (August 3, 1931), in *Selected Letters 1929–1931*, ed. August Derleth and Donald Wandrei (Sauk City, WI: Arkham House, 1971), 390–91.

Guns, Guns, and More Guns

The Second Amendment: A Biography. By Michael Waldman. New York: Simon & Schuster, 2014. xiv, 255 pp. Hardcover, $25.00.

"A well regulated militia, being necessary to the security of a free state, the right of the people to keep and bear arms, shall not be infringed." No part of the U.S. Constitution is more vexing and, in our current hyper-polarized political environment, more controverted than this single sentence. We are today faced with what Michael Waldman, in this compact, incisive, and pungently written treatise, calls "Second Amendment fundamentalists"—precisely analogous to Christian and Muslim fundamentalists, in more ways than they themselves realize—who foam at the mouth at the slightest suggestion of even the most commonsensical proposals for gun control and regulation, and the wholly mistaken belief that this one sentence grants them free and total access to weaponry without government interference. Waldman shows how this view—now enshrined in a titanically misguided Supreme Court ruling—is utterly and tragically mistaken.

Waldman provides us with a detailed history of the amendment and the political, military, and other issues that led to it. He notes that, prior to the American Revolution, citizen militias were widespread, and members (exclusively white and male) were *required* to own their own weapons (i.e., muskets). Militias also required universal (male) conscription: in theory, every white male of a given community or state was a militiaman. Both before and during the Revolution, as Waldman points out, the "right to bear arms" was *always* in the context of a "common defense." The basic motivation was the perceived need to counteract what was then called a "standing army"—i.e., a professional army, usually under the command of a king or Parliament. The idea was that a militia would be needed to balance the potential for mischief of an army not under the direct command of "the people"; for a standing army was then considered to be, in Waldman's words, "tyranny in the making."

James Madison, a believer in the need for a strong central government, did not feel any love for the militias, which by that time had proven themselves to be inefficient and largely incompetent. Many members no longer had the means or the desire to own their own weapons, and in many instances the state governments had to expend its own resources to purchase them. But, after the U.S. Constitution was ratified by the states, he and others con-

49

tinued to face extensive opposition from the Anti-Federalists (opponents of a strong central government) and grudgingly acquiesced in the drafting of a series of amendments to limit the power of Congress.

At this time, as Waldman points out, no one was talking about an *individual* right to bear arms. Although the right to self-defense was tacitly recognized by English common law, this issue was nowhere to be seen in the (relatively scant) discussions of the Second Amendment that survive. Indeed, the first draft of the amendment makes this quite clear: "The right of the people to keep and bear arms shall not be infringed; a well armed and well regulated militia being the best security of a free country; but no person religiously scrupulous of bearing arms shall be compelled to render military service in person." That final clause would have been utterly redundant if the amendment had anything to do with individual rights. That part of the amendment, dealing with conscientious objectors to military service such as Quakers, was eliminated by the Senate, and the clause about a "well regulated militia" was moved to the head of the sentence. That move itself is of consequence, although Second Amendment fundamentalists paradoxically do everything they can to obscure the fact. Waldman frequently notes the generally odd (by current standards) grammar and syntax of the entire sentence and mentions in passing that that opening clause is an English version of what in Latin is called the "ablative absolute." This is a grammatical usage that denotes *the conditions under which the terms of the main clause apply.* In other words, the "well regulated militia" clause is not some kind of "preamble" that can be blithely ignored in considering the true "meaning" (whether in the eighteenth century or today) of the sentence, but a critical component of it—and a component that strictly *governs* the scope and reach of the rest of the sentence. The "right to bear and keep arms" cannot possibly have any significance outside the context of a "well regulated militia."

In the century or so following the Revolution, the state militias rapidly declined, and gun violence increased throughout the growing nation. Some states did pass laws in the mid-nineteenth century that appeared to grant individuals the right to self-defense; but, as Waldman keenly points out, the federal courts—including the Supreme Court—*almost never made such a ruling in favor of individual rights.* Meanwhile, gun control legislation increased widely at the municipal and state level. No action was taken at the federal level, in part because of a curious Supreme Court ruling in 1876 that interpreted the Second Amendment as applying only to Congress, not to states. In the 1930s stringent gun control laws were indeed passed by Congress in the wake of the depredations of organized crime during Prohibition, where criminals used sawed-off shotguns and other heavy weaponry. These laws were upheld by the

Supreme Court—precisely on the basis of the "well regulated militia" doctrine.

Waldman also provides an illuminating history of the NRA, which began life in 1871 when "militia and army veterans created a new organization to train American men to shoot safely and accurately." The organization kept a low profile for decades and only recently metamorphosed into the radical, uncompromising entity that it is today. The extent of the deep paranoia infusing its leadership can be gauged by a comment in 1994 by its chief lobbyist, Neal Knox, who conjectured that the hideous political assassinations of the 1960s were "part of a gun control conspiracy"! And it is typical of the historical blindness of the organization that, when it moved into new quarters soon thereafter, it emblazoned the words of the Second Amendment on the wall of the lobby—*but not all of it!* The politically inconvenient clause about the "well regulated militia" was quietly excised, as if it didn't exist.

Waldman also recounts a systematic and incredibly tendentious conspiracy—no other word is suitable here—on the part of right-wing legal "scholars" to misread the Second Amendment. As Waldman observes, "There was no more settled view in constitutional law than that the Second Amendment did not protect an individual right to own a gun." But a tsunami of NRA-funded articles, beginning in the 1970s, supported the opposite view; and by continually citing one another in footnotes, the articles seemed to suggest a growing unanimity on the issue. Liberal scholars were clearly caught flat-footed on the issue—perhaps they couldn't imagine how such a perversion of the historical record could be made by purportedly conscientious law professors.

The end result is known to us all. In 2008, in *District of Columbia v. Heller*, the Supreme Court, by a predictable 5-4 majority, found an individual right to bear arms for the first time in American history. Justice Antonin Scalia was invited by Chief Justice John Roberts to write the majority opinion, and Waldman subjects it to such withering and vibrantly satirical dissection that one actually begins feeling sorry for the old duffer. Scalia, of course, relied on his patented legal methodology of "originalism"—the notion that every judicial decision must be made on the basis of what the Founders believed to be the meaning of the words of the appropriate statute in the Constitution. Aside from the internal incoherence of such a methodology (any literary critic could have told Scalia that it is next to impossible to determine in any precise and comprehensive way the "intent" of any author, especially a dead one), Scalia did not in fact even use originalism in any systematic or coherent way in writing his opinion. And he also, in a breathtaking lapse of consistency, also managed to weasel in some allowances for reasonable gun control—probably to secure the crucial fifth vote from Anthony Kennedy, who might have been uncomfortable in giving individual gun owners such broad rights in radical defiance of two hundred years of settled law. Amusingly, Waldman notes that several conservative legal scholars condemned both the *Heller* decision and Scalia's tortured and at times plainly erroneous reasoning (he denied, for example, that the phrase "bear arms" refers only to military service—a point in which he is flatly in error).

Waldman ends his treatise on an unduly depressing note. Although he notes interestingly that, overall, gun violence has indeed decreased from its height in the 1970s and that, although there are many more guns in the country (he gives the figure of 270 million, although I believe it is closer to 300 million), fewer households actually own guns (no more than 20%), he also believes that we are stuck with the *Heller* decision for the immediate and even distant future. I have no idea why this should be. If *Heller* does constitute (and I cannot believe how it could not) a notorious instance of an "activist" judicial decision, exactly of the sort that *Roe v. Wade* is in conservatives' eyes, I see no reason why this relatively recent decision could not simply be overturned by a differently configured Supreme Court. *Roe v. Wade* itself has already come close to the level of "settled law" and is not in my view likely to be overturned; and a single change in the makeup of the court could make things very different. Both Scalia and Kennedy would be eighty-eight years old by the time Hilary Clinton's second term ends in 2024; they are not likely to live that long. Even replacing one of them will suddenly turn a conservative court into a liberal one. So I think it is very likely that *Heller*—as well as *Citizens United* and other court decisions that overturned longstanding laws on campaign finance, civil rights, and other issues—will simply be reversed in the future.

Meanwhile we are still menaced by a relatively small but increasingly well-armed minority of the population. Exactly what they plan to do with their stockpile of guns is not entirely clear, but eternal vigilance is always warranted.

The Pious Fight Back

The Atheist's Fatal Flaw: Exposing Conflicting Beliefs. By Norman L. Geisler and Daniel J. McCoy. Grand Rapids, MI: Baker Books, 2014. Trade paperback, $14.99.

I suppose there is some benefit in having Christian apologists fight back against the onslaughts of atheists. For decades, perhaps centuries, Christians have been forced to engage in a defense of doctrines that have become more and more indefensible with each passing day. There was a time when nearly the whole of Christendom believed that the sun revolved around the earth; that witches with supernatural powers were prevalent in every village and town; that wives were the property of their husbands; and so on and so forth. Every one of these doctrines has clear biblical support, and for centuries it was regarded as heretical not to believe in them implicitly.

But the tide gradually turned. With the advance of science and human knowledge generally, one by one the pillars underpinning Christian doctrine fell by the wayside. As Tom Stoppard wrote in the play *Jumpers* (1972), "There is presumably a calendar date—*a moment*—when the onus of proof passed from the atheist to the believer, when quite suddenly, the noes had it."

The valiant authors of this slim treatise—Norman L. Geisler, Distinguished [!] Professor of Apologetics and Theology at Veritas Evangelical Seminary, and Daniel J. McCoy, an associate minister and Christian schoolteacher—attempt to stem the tide by accusing atheists of a multitude of inconsistencies in their attacks on Christian dogma. But their arguments are themselves so weak and inconsistent that they read like a parody of logical debate. If this is the best that Christian apologists can do, their cause is in deep trouble.

The basic premise of this book can be dispensed with in short order. This book is entirely devoted to the "problem of evil" or theodicy (which I have always thought should really be rendered the-idiocy), which the authors (falsely) maintain is the atheists' central argument against the existence of God. Why, in short, is there so much suffering in a world that was putatively created by an all-powerful and all-loving God? The authors claim that atheists make two mutually inconsistent assertions on this point: "In the first case, though initially indicting God for not fixing the problem of moral evil, the atheist then indicts God for his attempts to fix it." The authors rely on the

"God-in-the-dock" argument as enunciated by the unfortunate C. S. Lewis—the argument, as the authors state, "that place[s] God on trial for having contradicted his own nature."

But the authors have entirely misunderstood the atheist agenda. What atheists are doing is engaging in purely hypothetical arguments that initially presuppose God's existence in order to see where such a doctrine leads. If the atheist points out the awkward non-intervention of God in some instances of moral evil (say, the Holocaust) and then, in an entirely separate argument, criticizes the intervention of God in other cases (say, in the supposed death, resurrection, and ascension to heaven of Jesus), it is only *per argumentum;* no atheist actually believes any such things happened. What the authors therefore believe to be inconsistencies in the atheist position prove to be inconsistencies in Christian doctrine itself.

The fact of the matter is that the "problem of evil" is not a problem except for Christians who simultaneously maintain the inconsistent propositions of (an imaginary) God's omnipotence and benevolence. There really is no way around this difficulty, and the authors make little effort to propose any remedies. At one point they glancingly and half-heartedly point to the doctrine of free will as some kind of intellectual escape valve, but Walter Kaufmann destroyed this line of reasoning in *The Faith of a Heretic* (1961)—a book obtrusively absent from the authors' bibliography.

If our pious authors could ever emerge from their clouds of sophistry and venture into the clean, pure air of the real world, they would see how much *simpler* it is to account for "moral evil" without recourse to God. One of the central tenets of the philosophy of science is that the simpler the theory, the more likely it is to be true. The existence of bad people—such as Vladimir Putin, Bashar al-Assad, Donald Rumsfeld, Dick Cheney, and their ilk—can, for a secularist, be simply and plausibly attributed to common human failings such as greed, corruption, hypocrisy, selfishness, arrogance, and so forth. The moment a purportedly omnipotent and benevolent God is thrust into the equation, all manner of embarrassing and paradoxical issues arise that can only be dispensed with by a heroically tortuous logic-chopping that in the end convinces no one not already predisposed to believe in a deity.

The authors are so God-besotted that they can never really believe that atheists actually deny the existence of God; throughout their treatise they attribute such a belief to atheists who would no doubt repudiate it. This comes through especially toward the end of their book, when they outline the purported "inconsistencies" in atheistic attacks. After laboriously surveying atheist objections to the doctrine of heaven and hell, the authors ingenuously write: "Clearly, the atheist does not want to go to hell." How can I want (or not want) to go to a place that doesn't exist? This remarkable statement is followed by one still more flabbergasting: "It is understandable why the atheist would reject hell, but why reject heaven?" And still later: "The atheist thinks God ought to fix the problem of moral evil." But how can a non-existent entity fix anything? A page later the authors state: "God's existence, which is part of the system being attacked, makes . . . a worshipful morality not a vice but a virtue simply because there is, in fact, a Being worth worshiping." At this point I threw up my hands: do the authors not realize the staggering question-begging they have just committed? There is simply no arguing with people who cannot present an opposing view except through the lens of their own dogma and who assume the very existence of the entity in dispute.

The authors also seem to think that all atheists think alike on any and every point of doctrine. Even though they loftily maintain at the outset that "When we speak of 'the atheist,' we are merely referring to the atheist who holds the atheistic arguments under discussion," this reasonable supposition quickly goes by the board as they marshal one statement after the other from atheists over a period of centuries (or even millennia, as Lucretius is cited at one point) without the slightest concern whether any single atheist would ever agree with all the statements being offered. They reach the height of tendentiousness when they claim that, in the atheist view, "even if God *were* to exist, it would be positively immoral of him to demand . . . submission" to him. This comment is made in answer to Nietzsche's passing comment: "If any one were to show us the Christian God, we'd be still less inclined to believe in him." It should have been plain to anyone—but apparently isn't to our dogmatic authors—that Nietzsche was engaging in harmless hyperbole; but his view (which even he did not espouse) is now suddenly attributed to all, or many, atheists. (On the flip side, the authors plead plaintively that "If you want to argue against Christianity, let it be the real thing." But what *is* the real thing? The Christianity adhered to by Catholics or Protestants or Seventh-Day Adventists or some other sect? The one advocated by fundamentalists or by learned theologians? They never bother to say—or even to wonder whether there even *is* any one "real thing" that they are defending.)

And yet, this book is engaging for reasons exactly opposite to what the authors intended. The great bulk of it is a thoroughly entertaining and on the whole accurate account of atheist attacks on such doctrines as faith, punishment, heaven and hell, and so forth; and since the authors make virtually no effort to rebut the attacks, the atheists have the field largely to themselves for large stretches of this treatise. I suspect that any number of wavering Christians will be persuaded to slough off the remnants of their faith as a result of reading this book.

Consider the opening of the chapter on heaven and hell: "'Afterlives are fantasies,' laugh the atheists." (But aren't they?) "They are fairly tales and horror novels." (Does any sane person think otherwise?) "Some are written by the most cloud-headed among us, others by the most dark-hearted." (Well, aren't they?) "They are daydreams that escape and compromise reality." (N'est-ce pas?) "The deeper it delves into such fictions, the further religion banishes itself from credibility, says the atheist." (But doesn't it?) I couldn't have presented the case better myself!

On those few occasions where the authors do attempt to rebut their foes, they do so in such a feeble and fallacious manner that their own cause suffers serious damage. Let us consider the matter of faith. After repeating numerous atheistic arguments that faith (belief without evidence) is unreasonable, the authors put up the following defense: "The reasonableness or unreasonableness of faith depends on the trustworthiness of its object. Christians believe that God exists and can be trusted." Well, of course they do—but that is exactly the point in question. Atheists maintain that God does *not* exist, and therefore Christian "faith" is faith in a delusion. The evidence largely seems to be on their side. And yet, the authors pervert atheist doctrine by stating: "Atheists believe the postulated God of Christianity to be intrinsically untrustworthy." Once again, atheists are made to acknowledge an entity whose existence they have explicitly denied. "God" cannot be trustworthy or untrustworthy— because he does not exist! The authors continue: "Faith becomes necessary anytime knowledge is withheld." On the contrary! What is called for in such cases is skepticism, a suspension of judgment, and a provisional belief in the most probable hypothesis. Such things may be difficult for the credulous, who seem to need the security of some "certain" belief to continue existing, but the disciplined mind can and must train itself to them.

The authors state, as if it were a truism: "Of course, no one is being accused of having belief *despite* evidence, neither Christian nor atheist." Pardon me, but that is *exactly* what many atheists (I included) assert: we have reached the stage (as the Stoppard quotation suggested) where Christian tenets have become so implausible in the light of present-day knowledge that "faith" really has become belief in spite of evidence.

The authors also err in believing that the atheist seeks autonomy above all else; in their view, "liberation from God means uninhibited autonomy." Here again the authors attribute to atheists some kind of vestigial belief in God—as if we are unruly children who happen not to like a (really existing) god who is watching over us and judging us at every moment. But autonomy is only one of the atheist's goals, and not necessarily the supreme one. The authors themselves quote the *Humanist Manifesto I*—"In place of the old attitudes involved in worship and prayer the humanist finds his religious emotions expressed in a heightened sense of personal life and in a cooperative effort to promote social well-being"—but don't seem to grasp its obvious implications for atheist morality.

I want to return to the authors' assertion that the "problem of evil" is the chief argument in the atheist arsenal. It is nothing of the sort. Our chief weapon is merely the relentless advance of human knowledge, which has rendered every central tenet of Christianity (and Judaism and Islam and every other religion) so untenable that adherence to it is tantamount to adherence to astrology or phrenology or phlogiston. Atheists also rely on the sciences of psychology and anthropology to propound highly convincing reasons why religious belief was espoused in the first place, and why it continues to be espoused (childhood brainwashing, hundreds of thousands of years of cultural conditioning, the effects of hope, fear, and wishful thinking). The "problem of evil" really is a sideshow—as I have said before, it is a "problem" only for theists.

This sorry little treatise is not likely to stem to tide of atheism. We have the wind at our backs, and the evils and deficiencies of all the major monotheistic religions—Christianity, Judaism, and Islam—are becoming more and more apparent. The present age is, indeed, a bad time to argue for the existence of God. We are faced today with a great many societies where large numbers of individuals are gleefully killing each other solely and largely on religious grounds—Christians, Jews, Muslims, Hindus, even Buddhists. The fact that this is not happening very much or very often in the civilized West is only because, over the past several centuries, the Christian religion has been defanged and thrust out of political power, so that it is now only a minor nuisance rather than an active force for evil. The likelihood is that atheism, agnosticism, and secularism will continue to increase by leaps and bounds in the West; and one can only hope that other regions of the world will experience an enlightenment that will allow them to shed the fanatical religion that only causes them physical, intellectual, and spiritual harm.

As for Christianity, the words that John Beevers uttered nearly eighty years ago are truer today than when they were first set down: "I do not believe that Christianity holds anything more of importance for the world. It is finished, played out. The only trouble lies in how to get rid of the body before it begins to smell too much."[1]

---

1. John Beevers, *World without Faith* (London: Hamish Hamilton, 1935), 64.

Republicans: An Endangered Species

The Right Path: From Ike to Reagan, How Republicans Once Mastered Politics—and Can Again. By Joe Scarborough. New York: Random House, 2013. xxviii, 194 pp. Hardcover, $26.00.

This book came out just about a year ago. I have deliberately delayed review-ing it until now to gauge its impact on its chosen audience—Republicans in general and Republican politicians in particular. The results are not pretty for the author, a one-time congressman from Florida (1995–2001) who now hosts a popular show (which I have never watched) on MSNBC. A now em-barrassing press release quotes a pre-publication comment by one Mike Allen: "The buzz among GOP insiders is that 'The Right Path' has the potential to galvanize conservatives in the way Barry Goldwater's 'Conscience of a Con-servative' did half a century ago." The comparison itself is inept, because Scarborough's plea for conservatives to embrace moderation and steer away from Cloudcuckooland insanity is exactly the opposite of Goldwater's fire-eating extremism; but the more relevant fact is that Scarborough's book has, to put it mildly, not made much of an impression. If it did not exactly "fall dead-born from the press" (as David Hume said of one of his philosophical treatises), it is not exactly seen as "required reading" by anyone. Its current ranking on Amazon is 470,057—considerably lower than one of my horror anthologies (*Searchers After Horror*) published by a small press with virtually no publicity, which ranks at 197,862.

I am sympathetic with the basic tenet of this book—that Republicans should seek to be more pragmatic and moderate—but Scarborough's treat-ment is sadly deficient in a number of ways. He is entirely focused on the de-tails of presidential elections from Eisenhower to the present day, his fundamental point apparently being that it is only moderate Republicans who have succeeded in attaining the presidency. Even this simple formulation is subject to numerous caveats of which Scarborough appears unaware. If it is plausible enough that Eisenhower was a moderate (he did, after all, initiate the interstate highway system), and even that Nixon was in some senses a moderate (he did found the EPA), the case bogs down when Reagan and George W. Bush are considered. It is true that Reagan, although elected with an immense number of votes from the religious right, did little to foster their agenda (he could hardly do so in any event, since many aspects of their agenda were flatly unconstitutional), but otherwise his program of cutting taxes and increasing defense spending created huge deficits that only that sex-crazed draft dodger Bill Clinton was able to eliminate—only to have the deficits reinstituted by further tax cuts and massive defense spending by Bush.

Scarborough's argument also has to contend with standard Republican assertions that "moderates" do not generally win presidential elections, and they can point to such losers as Nixon (assuming for the nonce that he was a moderate) against Kennedy, George H. W. Bush against Clinton, Bob Dole against Clinton, and Mitt Romney against Obama. The only counter-example Scarborough has to offer is Goldwater, whose presidential run he rightly states "was less a campaign than it was an ideological crusade."

I could also have done without Scarborough's boot-licking paean to Reagan, who was little more than an empty suit with a slick delivery. Scarborough repeats the Republican party line that Reagan was largely responsible for the fall of the Soviet Union, when more impartial historians have come to substantially different conclusions on the matter.[1] And Scarborough makes no mention of the numerous embarrassments in Reagan's two terms. Remember James Watt, his disastrous secretary of the interior? Remember his assertion that ketchup was a vegetable? Remember Iran-contra, a scandal that tainted the entirety of Reagan's second term and induced many to believe that he had Alzheimer's disease well before he left office? Scarborough is blissfully silent on all these matters; all he can do is offer tender love-notes to his idol: "One wonders a generation later why the Republican Party has so totally forgotten the importance of Reagan's humanity and moderate temperament."

But Scarborough's entire enterprise is fatally flawed from the outset. By focusing so relentlessly and exclusively on the ups and downs of presidential campaigns over the past half-century, he utterly fails to note the broader social, intellectual, cultural—and, indeed, political—currents that have led us to where we are, and led the Republican party (as Scarborough plangently admits) to its current low state, where it seems virtually impossible for it to win at the presidential level. Scarborough identifies the period from 1965 (Johnson's signing of legislation on civil rights [which he correctly recognized as dooming Democrats' chances in the South for a generation], Medicare, and other issues) to 2005 (Bush's disastrous response—or lack of it—to Hurricane Katrina) as an era of conservative dominance. But it was exactly during this period that many issues central to the liberal agenda gained force, ranging from abortion rights (legalized in 1973, upheld by the Supreme Court in

---

1. See Martin McCauley, *The Rise and Fall of the Soviet Union* (Harlow, UK: Longman, 2008).

1992, and now fairly safe, for all the restrictions that some states have put on the practice), women's rights (which have made substantial progress in spite of the defeat of the Equal Rights Amendment), gay rights (no discussion necessary here—the likelihood that the Supreme Court will make same-sex marriage legal throughout the nation by next June is overwhelming), and other issues. And of course we now have something approaching universal health care. True, there have been setbacks from a liberal perspective, especially on matters relating to defense spending, taxation, gun control, and other issues—but there are flickers of hope even here.

What Scarborough is unable or unwilling to acknowledge is that the Republican party faces far more profound troubles than merely being afflicted with uncharismatic presidential candidates (Dole, John McCain, Romney); and even the idea that Republicans need to be more "moderate" is a pitiably weak formulation that doesn't get at the heart of the issue. The time is long past when the party could win the allegiance of a majority of young people, as Reagan fleetingly did; and the party's major troubles with huge sectors of the electorate—women, African Americans, Hispanics, Asians, Jews—is well documented. The plain fact of the matter is that the Republican Party is currently a party of angry, aging white males—not a recipe for success!

Scarborough makes passing reference to some of the problems facing the party without fully realizing their true import. "The political value of an army of shrill Limbaugh clones is suspect at least," he states in an exquisitely unconscious understatement. What has happened is that these "shrill clones" are keeping the Republican base in a state of perpetual rage and resentment against perceived foes, while gerrymandering and voter suppression (the only way Republicans can win elections even at the local level) have rendered so many districts "safely" Republican that politicians have more to worry from challengers on their right than on their actual Democratic opponents, with the result that they become further radicalized. This may work at the congressional level; but once we get into senatorial and presidential elections, where gerrymandering has no effect, the results are disastrous. At this moment, no Republican can win the presidency as far as the eye can see—barring some incredible scandal or blunder by the Democratic candidate.

Scarborough does launch into Republican demagogues from time to time: "Many Republicans today . . . seem less interested in moving voters to their position than in planting an ideological flag in the ground and declaring all those not in lockstep insufficiently conservative, unpatriotic, or worse." But there needs to be much more of this to make this treatise in any sense effective, or to break through the self-enclosed echo chamber in which most Republican politicians smugly dwell. And Scarborough needs to put forth more of a meaningful agenda aside from merely winning elections ("There is no substitute for victory"—a statement by General MacArthur—was written on a sign plastered above the door of his own campaign office) if he is to persuade anyone why Republicans should even be granted the privilege of winning.

Meanwhile, have Republicans heeded his message? Maybe not, given that we now hear of some Republican candidates asserting that Hillary Clinton is the Antichrist, that most African Americans have "no concept of the pride and joy when we, as parents, invest in our children," and that wives should be happy to be "within the authority" of their husbands.[2] The incredible thing is that a good many of these candidates will probably be elected to the U.S. House of Representatives.

Joe Scarborough claims to be a "proudly defiant" Republican who has developed dyspepsia because Republicans have lost the popular vote in five out of the last six elections. He is blithely confident that Republicans can change their ways ("I do not believe that will happen. I *know* that will happen"). I am forced into delicate understatement myself when I say that nothing in his treatise, nor in the current activities of Republican politicians, gives anyone the slightest confidence on this point.

---

2. Jonathan Weisman, "House Hopefuls in G.O.P. Seek Rightward Shift," *New York Times* (28 September 2014).

Christianity and Complexity

True Paradox: How Christianity Makes Sense of Our Complex World. By David Skeel. Downers Grove, IL: IVP Books, 2014. 175 pp. Trade paperback, $15.00.

The nonsensical title of this book is a fitting encapsulation of its nonsensical contents. A strong whiff of self-parody runs through the entire work—as if it were written by an atheist deliberately advocating weak, fallacious, and preposterous arguments for the express purpose of undermining Christian doctrine.

David Skeel, a professor of corporate law at the University of Pennsylvania Law School, thinks he is presenting a new take on Christian apologetics. He flatly admits that he cannot "prove" that Christianity is true; instead, what he hopes to show is that it provides a more plausible account of the "complexity" of human life than other religions or than "materialist" (i.e., atheistic) accounts. But in doing so he commits nearly every fallacy it is possible to commit, and the end result is confusion and disaster for his cause.

One of Skeel's chief fallacies, made throughout the book, is misrepresentation of his opponents' beliefs. He relies almost exclusively on atheistic explanations of various phenomena based on evolutionary biology (chiefly those expounded by Richard Dawkins and Steven Pinker, who seem to be virtually the only atheists he has read). The myriad other methodologies that atheists employ—ranging from psychology to anthropology to history to textual analysis—are all brushed aside as nonexistent. As a result, Skeel presents a simplistic, and often simple-minded, account of atheistic theories—and then criticizes them for being too simplistic to account for the "complexity" of the phenomena in question! If this isn't chutzpah, I don't know what it is. Consider Skeel's portrayal of the atheistic account of the naturalistic origin, growth, and continuance of religious belief—an account that, to my mind, is the atheist's trump card because it so thoroughly explains why people were and are religious in the first place. But Skeel is unsatisfied by this explanation because, among other things, it omits "its most important dimension: we are drawn to a particular religion or philosophy because it seems to us to better explain the nature of the universe than the alternatives." I don't know what atheistic accounts of religious belief Skeel has read; all I can say is that the work of anthropologists going all the way back to E. B. Tylor (*Primitive Cul-*

ture, 1871) and Sir James George Frazer (*The Golden Bough*, 1890-1915), psychologists such as Chapman Cohen (*Religion and Sex*, 1919) and Sigmund Freud (*The Future of an Illusion*, 1927), and many other scholars has indeed accounted for this very phenomenon—and every other phenomenon associated with religious belief—with subtlety, sophistication, and, yes, complexity. Has Skeel not heard of such things as childhood indoctrination? Does it not trouble him that the great majority of believers adopt the religion of their own culture and society?

Another major fallacy that Skeel commits is presenting a sanitized—indeed, whitewashed—account of Christianity. His bland account brushes myriad instances of Christian folly, duplicity, corruption, and error under the rug. He asserts that Christianity fostered the idea of "human equality," pointing to a celebrated biblical passage: "There is neither Jew nor Greek, there is neither slave nor free, there is no male and female, for you are all one in Christ Jesus" (Galatians 3:28). Skeel says that this passage proves that Christianity was and is opposed to slavery; but he neglects to observe that this is virtually the only passage in the entire Bible that fails to endorse slavery as a common and, indeed, approved element of human society. Later on Skeel maintains defensively that "the Bible at best tolerates slavery as a ubiquitous feature of the ancient Roman economy." Has he forgotten Paul's comment in Ephesians 6:5 ("Servants, be obedient to them that are your masters according to the flesh, with fear and trembling, in singleness of your heart, as unto Christ")? That seems to me a pretty enthusiastic endorsement of slavery!

Skeel even has the gall to claim that "Christianity leaves no doubt that sexuality and the body are good." Needless to say, he does not quote Paul's infamous comment "It is better to marry than to burn" (1 Corinthians 7:9), which can only mean that sex is pretty horrible and that you'd better do it, if at all, under the aegis of a (religiously sanctioned) marriage rather than to masturbate or fornicate or commit adultery (all practices violently condemned by the Bible).

A later chapter gets Skeel into more trouble as far as Christian history is concerned. This is where Skeel discusses what he calls the "justice paradox," which he defines as the belief among devisers of legal systems that their systems will inevitably lead to an elimination of the crimes and other bad behaviors they are seeking to abolish. "The dream of a *perfectly just* [my emphasis] social order is, Christians believe, a dangerous lie that we tell ourselves." Here Skeel is indulging in a classic straw man argument. No matter what people like Marx and others may have said about the efficacy of their political and legal schemas, it is ludicrous to believe that any realistic person would think that the mere establishment of a law will suddenly eliminate every single in-

63

stance of the crime that law seeks to eradicate. Every legal system (including those found in the Bible) seeks to criminalize murder, and yet murder continues to exist.

Skeel is awkwardly forced to admit that Christians themselves have tried to enforce exactly such "perfectly just" systems, with catastrophic results; but he is highly deceitful in recounting such horrors. Instead, he states with a straight face that "Although Christians have been responsible for too many abuses, Christianity is uniquely self-correcting." Is Skeel really aware of the centuries-long struggle in the West to purge legal and political systems of religious influence—a struggle that was led by brave freethinkers ranging from Voltaire to Charles Bradlaugh, and that leading Christian figures opposed with all their might? It was only by the nineteenth century that most countries in Europe finally prohibited Christianity from having the power of life and death over its citizens. Skeel presents a further whopper when he says: "When Christians seek to usher in the Kingdom of God through law, they are denying Christianity's teachings, not promoting them." Oh, yeah? What about "Thou shalt not suffer a witch to live" (Exodus 22:18)? That single sentence led to the executions of millions of suspected "witches" over many centuries in Europe. And the statement "Compel them to come in, that my house may be filled" (Luke 14:23) in one of Jesus' parables was plausibly interpreted as a justification for the forcible conversion of Jews, Muslims, freethinkers, and many others. I hardly need add that the repeated condemnations of homosexual sex in the Bible (both the OT and the NT) continue to be used today by Christians to deny gays and lesbians their civil rights.

Yet another fallacy that Skeel commits is to frame a question such that it leads inexorably to a predetermined answer. This fallacy is most prominent in his chapter on "Beauty and the Arts." Here he maintains that the natural human desire for beauty cannot be properly accounted for an evolutionary grounds; but note how he defines the phenomenon in question. "This perception that beauty is real and that it reflects the universe as it is meant to be . . . is the paradox of beauty." I cannot even attach a meaning to this sentence. I like to think that I have a pretty fair sensitivity to beauty: I have been a practicing literary critic for nearly forty years, meaning that I derive great enjoyment from literature; I have been a practicing musician for an even longer time; and I profess keen enjoyment of painting, sculpture, and other arts. But I have never felt, when listening to Beethoven's Ninth Symphony, that I am suddenly in the presence of "the universe as it is meant to be." I am simply appreciating a great work of art created by a human genius. Skeel goes on to say that "the paradox that God is both unity and diversity is very similar to the qualities that we associate with a beautiful painting or concerto." But every single thing in the universe could be thought to combine "unity and diversity"—such as, say, the atom. So one could just as plausibly say that a great work of art reflects the unity-in-diversity of the atom as that it reflects the unity-in-diversity of the Christian god.

Skeel concludes with a richly amusing chapter about the reality of heaven and hell. What is his evidence for the former? It is "the evidence of our longings. . . . The desires we experience as human beings always seem to have a real object." My dear man, do you realize what you are saying? If I have a longing to see a unicorn, does that mean that unicorns exist? But Skeel goes from bad to worse: "The testimony of Christians about how embracing Christianity has changed their lives is thus evidence of the reality of heaven." How this *psychological belief* can provide evidence for an *ontological proposition* escapes my understanding. In any case, similar testimonials from every other major religion—and, indeed, from atheists around the world—could be secured; but what bearing does that have on the truth-value of any of these systems of thought? It is noteworthy that Skeel says almost nothing about hell, even though Jesus was perfectly happy consigning the great majority of human beings to that warm place.

I am beginning to wonder why Christian apologists even bother anymore. Their screeds are so riddled with obvious fallacies that it is child's play to refute them. Meanwhile, atheism, agnosticism, and secularism continue to make strides in the West, while in other parts of the world it is becoming all too evident what horrors are produced by continuing adherence to religion. If any defense of religion is to be made, it will have to be done in a more intellectually cogent manner than people like David Skeel appear capable of doing.

The Problem of Islamic Extremism

The increasingly horrific outbreaks of violence associated with Muslim fanatics—not merely the continual outrages (beheadings, death by immolation, etc.) of the Islamic State but also such individual attacks as those at the office of the satirical magazine *Charlie Hebdo* in Paris and at a coffee shop in Sydney, Australia—is making it more and more difficult to maintain that all this is merely a series of "extremist" attacks unrelated to the religion of Islam. The question does need to be raised as to whether there is something inherent in Islam that makes such attacks both likely and in congruence with its essential doctrines.

But I think we should resist the tendency to make hasty judgments that Islam is intrinsically violent or barbaric. We need to take seriously the arguments of moderate Muslims that only a tiny fraction of the 1.5 billion Muslims in the world are exhibiting these signs of violence; and—for all the atrocities committed by loosely organized entities such as the Islamic State, Boko Haram in Nigeria, the Taliban in Afghanistan and Pakistan, and other such groups throughout the Middle East, Africa, and Asia—it cannot possibly be said that Islam today has any monopoly on violence and barbarity. When we witness Buddhists (yes, Buddhists!) happily slaughtering Muslims in Burma, Christian militias doing the same to their Muslim counterparts in the Central African Republic, and other instances of religiously motivated violence, it becomes clear that Muslims are not alone in viciously attacking their perceived enemies.

The current status of Islam—and, in particular, of the nations (mostly in the Middle East) with largely Muslim populations—is immensely complicated and involves a bewildering array of political, social, economic, and cultural issues beyond (and, in my judgment, superseding) the core issue of religion. To simplify a matter that cannot be simplified, it must be said that many of the countries in the Middle East, Africa, and elsewhere are facing the consequences of (a) an over-reliance on oil wealth, which has inhibited their societies from developing other means of employing its citizens, (b) autocratic governments that seem more intent on maintaining their own power than in engaging the political aspirations of the people they govern, and (c) a deep sense of resentment against the West for exactly the features of our society that make us civilized (religious tolerance, political freedom, cultural dynamism, and so on). What is left to most people in these regions is to cling to

Islam as a bulwark for the manifest failures of their societies.

And Islam itself, as I have stated many times, is in desperate need of an Enlightenment such as occurred in the seventeenth and eighteenth centuries in the West. There really is a sense in which Islam is in precisely the situation that Christianity was in before the Enlightenment (and, in some phases, even after it). In particular, the notion that religion has the right to be shielded from any kind of scrutiny—whether intellectual or satirical—appears to be deeply ingrained in the sensibilities of even well-educated Muslims. Consider this remark by a Turkish lawyer, Ercan Ezgin, commenting on the issue of *Charlie Hebdo* that came out after the attack on its offices, depicting Mohammad shedding tears over the attack: "Insulting the prophet can never be regarded within the context of media freedom. This cartoon bears the danger of deeply provoking billions [sic] of Muslims. It should never be acceptable to depict our prophet in such a cartoon, poking fun at him, showing him as if he's shedding tears." Passing over the question of whether the carton was "insulting" in the first place, the remark merely underscores the prevalent belief (a belief that, in many Muslim countries, can be enforced by law) that it is a criminal offense to "blaspheme" religion.

I am willing to believe that those Muslims who adhere to this belief are mistaken—that is, that the Quran does not endorse such a view. Heaven knows I am not an expert in Islam, but I found it of interest that Mustafa Akyol, author of *Islam without Extremes: A Muslim Case for Liberty*, cited this passage from the Quran: "God has told you in the Book that when you hear God's revelations disbelieved in and mocked at, do not sit with them until they enter into some other discourse; surely then you will be like them."

Well and good: the idea that you simply walk away from those who mock your religion, rather than killing them, seems eminently civilized. I have no idea, however, whether this single quotation is representative of the Quran's doctrines as a whole. I imagine that, like the Bible, one can cherrypick Islam's sacred text to make it conform to whatever beliefs a given individual may wish to put forth.

But in all this discussion, one immensely important issue has been largely overlooked: the degree to which Christianity behaved *much worse* and *for a much longer period* than Islam, past or present.

The matter has at last been brought to the fore by President Obama's assertion, during the National Prayer Breakfast on February 5: "Lest we get on our high horse and think this [i.e., the violence of the Islamic State] is unique to some other place, remember that during the Crusades and the Inquisition, people committed terrible deeds in the name of Christ. In our home country, slavery and Jim Crow all too often was [sic] justified in the name of Christ."

The remark inspired the usual squawking from the usual suspects—fundamentalist Christians and their lickspittles. Jim Gilmore, the former (Republican, naturally) governor of Virginia, stated: "He has offended every believing Christian in the United States." Bill Donohue, president of the Catholic League, predictably chimed in with the remark that Obama's comments were "insulting" and "pernicious."

The question becomes: Can a *true* remark be an "insult"? If someone is a fool and I call him a fool, does he have the right to be insulted? It does not appear so; he can only be insulted if he can demonstrate that he is *not* a fool. In this case, Obama was actually vastly *understating* the political and legal crimes that Christianity has committed over a very large portion of its two millennia of existence. Numbers in these matters are always uncertain, but at a conservative estimate it is likely that several *million* individuals—"witches," heretics, infidels, freethinkers, Jews, Muslims, and other undesirables—were, over the course of at least fifteen hundred years of Christian dominance in the West, either summarily executed or made to convert.

And—more significantly in terms of any parallels between Christian malfeasance and the actions of Islamic terrorists today—the great majority of Christian violence occurred precisely because of an insidious conjoining of religion with the legal apparatus of the state. It took centuries of work—largely by secularists—to kick Christianity out of government, with the end result that religious authorities no longer had the power of life and death over the citizenry. It would certainly be a welcome development if something similar occurred in Islamic nations; but I repeat that the atrocities we are currently witnessing are not, for the most part, caused by those nations themselves but by non-state actors who may wish to become a state (or a state within a state) but are in the long run very unlikely to do so.

So Christians in the West have no compelling reason to crow at how "civilized" their religion is in comparison to the "barbarity" of some aspects of Islam. Christianity was dragged kicking and screaming out of political power and continues to do all it can to regain that power. Its attempts will almost certainly be fruitless, but that is no justification for thinking that it is somehow superior to its fellow religion. A pox on both of them!

The Beatification of St. Kim

The buffooneries of American politics and religion are no doubt a source of endless amusement to the rest of the civilized world, and they have been on prodigious display over the last few months. Their focus lately has been on the unlikely figure of one Kim Davis. She is, you will recall, the county clerk in a rural part of Kentucky who, after the Supreme Court declared in late June 2015 that same-sex marriage was legal throughout the nation, refused to issue marriage licenses to anyone—gay or straight—because such a thing would infringe on her "religious freedom."

It transpires that Ms. Davis is an Apostolic Christian. Being woefully ignorant about the hundreds of Christian (mostly Protestant) sects that litter the earth, I was compelled to do some hasty research on this cult—er, sect. It appears that the Apostolic Christian Church of America is derived from a German sect founded in the mid-nineteenth century by one Samuel Heinrich Froelich; an American colleague of Froelich founded the American branch in 1847. The sect acknowledges a belief in the Bible as the literal word of God. There is nothing particularly remarkable about this; more to the point is that, for Apostolic Christians, marriage is deeply tied to their faith. At some point in his life a man feels that God has called upon him to marry. He seeks God's help identifying a suitable (female) mate for him. God somehow reveals the blushing bride to him, and the man relays the good news to his Elder, who then informs the female in question. She herself appeals to God for an answer to this pressing matter. Somewhat to my surprise, it is apparently acceptable if Mr. God instructs her to turn down the luckless wight, after which nothing more is said. But if the Big Guy gives the thumbs-up, then wedding plans proceed—and, of course, take place as part of the Sunday afternoon service.

I am not making this stuff up, folks. I do not see any provision for a woman to initiate the conversation with God as to whether *she* wants to marry someone or other, and to that degree this whole folderol strikes me as pretty anti-feminist; but at least the hapless female is not compelled to accept the hand of anyone who has gotten the word from On High.

All this makes clear why Ms. Davis has such hostility to same-sex marriage—although one would suppose that heterosexual marriage in which a man and a woman just decide to get married without God's approval would be nearly as offensive. But let that pass. (What we are to make of the fact that Davis herself has been married four times, thereby presenting an extreme instance of the contemporary trend toward serial marriage, is a conundrum. She has certainly kept that pipeline to God pretty busy!)

We all know the upshot. When Ms. Davis refused to grant the marriage licenses, even though that was an essential part of her job description, two homosexual and two heterosexual couples sued. In August, Judge David L. Bunning of the United States District Court for Eastern Kentucky, ordered Ms. Davis to resume issuing the licenses. She refused and appealed all the way to the Supreme Court. But the court refused to hear her appeal, and she herself was jailed for five days for contempt of court. During this whole time she not only refused to budge on her position but also instructed her deputies (one of which is her son) not to issue marriage licenses. All the deputies except one (you can imagine who that is) refused to follow her and started issuing licenses to gay and straight couples alike.

It was at this point that the beatification of St. Kim began. Her release from jail produced a kind of circus atmosphere, aided by her offensively aggressive lawyer, Mat Staver of the Liberty Counsel, and presidential candidate Mike Huckabee, who was apparently looking for some volatile issue that might allow him to break the media's love affair with the bombastic loud-mouth Donald J. Trump. Huckabee's presence when Davis was released had all the fervor of a revival meeting—and just as much intellectual heft.

But Davis and, especially, Staver refused to yield to the inevitable. First, Staver insisted that marriage licenses issued in Davis's absence "weren't worth the paper they were printed on," even though Kentucky Governor Steve Bashear stated otherwise. Then he tried to maintain that the appeals court ruling that went against his client applied only to the four couples who had sued and no one else—a preposterous and unheard-of reading of the law that the appeals court quickly shot down.

But all this is nothing new to the Liberty Counsel, which has just been declared a hate group by the Southern Poverty Law Center. Staver protested mightily against the attribution, whining pitiably that it was "irresponsible and reckless to call someone a hate group because you disagree with them." Well, my dear chap, there's a bit more to it than that. After all, it was Staver himself who declared, "To force someone like that to give a license for something that will legalize, that will put a stamp of approval on something that is absolute rebellion against God, sinful, then that is a direct collision of unprecedented magnitude." Evidently Staver has failed to note the obvious fact that the U.S. Constitution is not based on the Bible, so that acts that he thinks constitute an "absolute rebellion against God" are not necessarily illegal. Staver compounded his folly (and his malice) by saying that forcing Ms. Davis to issue marriage licenses to same-sex couples was equivalent to forcing her to "grant a license to engage in pornography, to grant a license to sodo-mize children or something of that nature." Charming fellow!

More buffoonery resulted when it was eventually learned that Davis had had a private meeting with Pope Francis toward the end of his visit to this country. The religious and political right, which had been mightily discour-aged at the failure of the courts to uphold St. Kim's "religious freedom" in decision after decision, began crowing that the Pope—who himself had dis-mayed conservatives by emphasizing the need to combat climate change and the needs of the poor—was on their side. He himself issued an unwise state-ment declaring that "Conscientious objection must enter into every juridical structure because it is a right, a human right." This whole affair negated a large part of the good will that the Pope's visit had elicited, so the Vatican immediately began to backtrack, saying that the meeting was not intended as staking a position in the American culture wars; but the damage was done.

Amidst all the furor and bluster, certain basic truths have apparently been overlooked. The essence of the matter is that St. Kim was properly jailed be-cause she was not fulfilling her oath of office, which was to uphold the laws of her state and of the U.S. Constitution. Same-sax marriage is now legal, and therefore it is a violation of the law to disallow same-sex people from marry-ing. But would the granting of licenses on St. Kim's part be a violation of her "religious freedom"? How can it be? She has every right to speak out against same-sex marriage as much as she wants; no one is compelling *her* to engage in marriage for a fifth time to a woman; and, most important of all, "religious freedom" does not come into play in the matter *because her job is not intrinsical-ly religious in nature*. It is well known that members of the clergy cannot be forced to preside over same-sex marriages if they do not wish to do so; but no such allowance can possibly be allowed to a county clerk—just as it cannot be allowed to a pharmacist who objects to handing out contraception or a florist who does not wish to offer his or her products to a same-sex wedding. St. Kim's actions do not constitute "religious freedom," but rather religious fas-cism—a means of coercing others to follow her chosen religious predilections.

Consider a counter-example. Suppose I was a county clerk, and I decided that I have a "conscientious objection" to Republicans marrying. After all, I am deeply troubled by Republican stances on a variety of political, religious, and social issues, and I believe it would be immoral for me to facilitate the propagation of Republicans in this country. My act of denying marriage li-censes to these people would of course be illegal (even though political affilia-tion is not a protected category, as race, religion, and gender are), and it would be right and proper that I be hauled off to jail. And one can only imag-ine the howls on the right side of the political spectrum if I were to defend my actions in the name of "religious" (or, in my case, moral) "freedom."

And so it goes. The saga of Kim Davis will probably be no more than a minuscule footnote in American history, but the principle it embodies—the need to separate one's personal beliefs from the (non-religious) job one occupies, or else to find another line of work—is of eternal relevance.

Atheism, Christianity, and Insanity

God's Not Dead: Evidence for God in an Age of Uncertainty. By Rice Broocks. Nashville, TN: W Publishing Group/Thomas Nelson, 2013. xx, 279 pp. Trade paperback, $15.99.

I do not know why I continue to review books of this sort: the arguments found in them are so weak and unconvincing that there is no longer any sport in refuting them. And yet, perhaps some salutary function is indeed served by demolishing the claims of Rice Broocks and other contemporary Christian apologists. Christianity is the prototypical example of what has been called the "zombie idea": an idea that is essentially dead but somehow continues to walk. And so there is some benefit in showing how writers like Broocks actually weaken the claims of Christianity for intellectual respectability by their preposterous and self-refuting arguments.

This book is apparently derived from a movie of the same name, released in 2014. Strangely enough, I do not find Broocks's name in the film's credits. Also, since I live in a notoriously godless city, the film apparently came and went without my noticing it. The book actually postdates the film, making the former a kind of "novelization" of the latter. I use that term advisedly, for this sorry excuse for a treatise is a work of fiction from beginning to end.

What is most notable about it is not its arguments—which are stale to the point of tedium—but the angry, resentful, and even hate-filled tone the author adopts. He is clearly alarmed at the rise of atheism, agnosticism, secularism, and freethought in the United States and elsewhere and seeks to do everything he can to stem the tide. He is particularly infuriated when believers are worsted in arguments by clever atheists, and he has accordingly written this intellectually flimsy book so that his side can be armed with suitable counterarguments. He fancies that he is already seeing some kind of religious revival among the young, but a wide array of surveys and polls do not support this contention.

Broocks is also irked at the ridicule and derision he senses coming from his opponents. He high-mindedly states early on: "The tactic of insulting the opposition has never worked in this debate." And yet, Broocks himself refers to his antagonists as "radical atheists" (whoever they might be), and at a later point writes breathtakingly: "Tragically, when skeptics try to assert the nonexistence of God, they lose touch with reality and sound reason and unwittingly head down the long, dark road to insanity." Well, lordy me! I for one do not feel any overwhelming compulsion to check myself into a madhouse, however much Broocks might wish to hurl me into one and throw away the key. But remember—no insults, please!

But Broocks is not done. It would appear that mass murders in our society are becoming more common "because of the decreasing presence of the knowledge of God in society." Moreover, the West is succumbing to suicide, drug use, and other miseries because of "the backlash of the meaninglessness of atheism and unbelief." Broocks cannot be troubled to wrestle with the immensely complex social, political, economic, and cultural factors that have led to this state of affairs—it's all the fault of atheists! All this reminds us of Jerry Falwell's claim that 9/11 was caused by feminism and the absence of prayer in schools. It's only because Broocks is a nonentity that he has not been roasted over the coals for these outrageous claims as Falwell was.

The number of fallacies to which Broocks subscribes could be taken as a textbook for unsound reasoning in a Philosophy 101 class. His book is filled with unsupported assertions that his opponents could not possibly accept, any number of straw-man arguments, appeals to authority, and so forth. The appeal to authority is one of his favorites. Whenever he can find anyone, no matter how daft, who echoes a view he wishes to put across, that is sufficient to confirm the truth of that view. He cites the usual suspects—William Lane Craig, Alvin Plantinga, and so on—but his pride and joy is the ineffable C. S. Lewis, who at one point is declared a "great writer" and, later, a "legendary writer and philosopher." Poor fellow! He is no doubt ignorant of John Beversluis's devastating refutation of the entirety of Lewis's philosophy and theology—a refutation so complete and unanswerable that it leaves one feeling a kind of objective pity that Lewis so exposed his intellectual failings for all to see.[1]

The issue that gives Broocks the greatest difficulty is the age-old one—the problem of evil, or why bad things happen to good people (or, indeed, why bad things happen at all). Broocks cannot wrap his mind around the true crux of the dilemma: the problem of evil is insoluble if a god is postulated as both omnipotent and benevolent. One of these tenets has to go if the god-idea is to be saved (or else, if one really has to be a theist, one has to adopt a Manichaean or polytheistic view whereby the "bad" things in the world can be

---

1. See John Beversluis, *C. S. Lewis and the Search for Rational Religion* (Grand Rapids, MI: William B. Eerdmans Co., 1985). I was heavily reliant on his work in my chapter "Surprised by Folly: C. S. Lewis" in *God's Defenders: What They Believe and Why They Are Wrong* (Amherst, NY: Prometheus Books, 2003).

attributed to some devil-god). But of course, as a Christian, Broocks cannot bring himself to do so. He is therefore obliged to resort to the false solution of free will. "The mess that results [from bad human behavior] is not God's fault. It's ours." This itself is paradoxical, because, if God is omnipotent, then he must be responsible for "evil" in the ultimate sense. And Broocks does not even consider the strong possibility—now espoused by an increasing number of philosophers and scientists—that free will does not in fact exist. Even if it did, it cannot perform the task that Broocks wants it to perform. The problem is too involved to go into here, but I would direct readers to Walter Kaufmann's stimulating discussion of this point—of which Broocks is manifestly ignorant—in *The Faith of a Heretic*. Kaufmann's conclusion ("The problem of suffering is of crucial importance because it shows that the God of popular theism does not exist") is irrefutable.[2]

Broocks compounds his folly by asserting that there is an objective morality and that this must come from God. He simply cannot conceive that any other basis for a sound morality could exist: "If there is no heaven, then there is no reward for any good deed done." The idea that a "good deed" can be done for its own sake rather than for some imagined super-plum after one dies is beyond Broocks's imagining. He entirely misunderstands secular ethics when he declares: "Without God, the absurd notion that everyone's morals are true becomes a living nightmare." No one's morals are "true" because *moral principles are not subject to truth or falsity*. This is because they are not facts but preferences. When I say "Killing is bad (or wrong or evil)," I am uttering a sentence that is *grammatically* similar to a statement of fact (say, "The earth is round"), but epistemologically very different. What I am really saying is: "There is such a thing as killing, and I happen not to approve of it." It is my preference that indiscriminate killing not go unpunished. But for Broocks, this is not good enough: it is not enough that an atheist would want to behave in a moral manner for the purpose of maintaining a decent, civilized society; for him, the separation of morality from an imaginary God only results in Dostoevsky's crude caricature, "Without God, everything is permissible."

It is of interest to note that, although Broocks employs numerous (bad) arguments to establish (in his mind) some kind of deific presence in the universe, he is particularly intent on establishing that it is the Christian god—as opposed to the approximately 30,000 other gods that humans have invented over the millennia—who really rules the roost. He does so by seeking to prove the validity of the Christ myth. You see, "The evidence of [sic] the historical

---

2. See Walter Kaufmann, *The Faith of a Heretic* (1961); excerpts in *Atheism: A Reader*, ed. S. T. Joshi (Amherst, NY: Prometheus Books, 2000), 250–59.

Jesus is beyond dispute." How so? Well, don't you know that non-Christian sources such as Tacitus and Pliny the Younger refer to the fellow? Let it pass that these accounts were written a good eighty years after the putative death of Jesus and were no doubt obtained at second or third hand. Once Broocks has accomplished this sleight-of-hand, he can swallow the whole story—crucifixion, resurrection, sitting at the right hand of God—with insouciance, even though this account is found only in Christian sources that pretty clearly have a vested interest in the matter. One might as well say that William Peter Blatty's novel *The Exorcist*, by the mere fact that it survives as a written document, validates the existence of the Assyrian demon Pazuzu.

I was most interested to see that Broocks repeatedly seeks to undermine the theory of evolution, especially as it applies to the evolution of humanity, by the now stale dodge of Intelligent Design. This is of interest not because he presents any new findings that make Intelligent Design—already thoroughly refuted by Richard Dawkins, Daniel C. Dennett, and others—any more plausible than before, but because he explicitly uses it to underpin his faith in Christianity. The proponents of Intelligent Design are generally a bit more cagey on the subject, deliberately neglecting to specify the exact properties of the "designer" in question. This is of course a ploy meant to further their (so far fruitless) attempts to secure a place for Intelligent Design in public schools; so it is most refreshing to see someone like Broocks expose the ploy for the disingenuous charade that it is.

But Broocks employs Intelligent Design for another reason—as a means of supporting the following whopper of a claim, printed in self-important italics: "*Humans did not evolve from lower life forms.*" Yes, my friends, Broocks is now on record as siding with his creationist colleagues in advocating the "special creation" of humanity by Mr. God! Does it matter that we humans share 98% of our genetic makeup with chimpanzees? Apparently not to Mr. Broocks. But because he is not quite so regressive as to declare that human beings, in the form of Adam and Eve, were created by God's magic wand in 4004 B.C.E., one begins to wonder why the Big Guy waited so long to create these paragons of the universe—maybe only a few hundred thousand (or at best a few million) years ago, after conjuring up the universe some 13 billion years before that.

But wait, it gets better. A throwaway passage in Broocks's book reads: "There are not only evil humans but evil spirits. . . . The skeptical mind scoffs loudly at this, but there is evidence of this unseen evil entity that inspires and energizes evil in humans." I am a bit puzzled by the shift from plural to singular, but no matter. What I want to know is: *How does Broocks know this?* Maybe he read it somewhere (Dante's *Inferno*? Milton's *Paradise Lost*? Blatty's *The Ex-*

orcist?). Maybe he had a dream about devils (or the Devil?) rampaging through the universe. In spite of that ominous "there is evidence" clause, Broocks provides no evidence for this all-important utterance. C'mon, guy, don't be a tease! Inquiring minds want to know.

I would have more respect for Rice Broocks if he had merely stated, "I'm a believer because I was brainwashed in infancy," or "I'm a believer because I'm terrified of the prospect of utter extinction after death," or "I'm a believer because I can't imagine a godless universe." Instead, he destroys whatever shreds of intellectual self-respect he may have had by making comical claims that his faith is "reasonable," and by lashing out furiously at his opponents and conjuring up demons out of his imagination. Broocks may want to consign atheists to Bedlam, but it is he who seems in desperate need of psychiatric assistance.

The Rise and Fall of Christianity

The Unexpected Christian Century: The Reversal and Transformation of Global Christianity, 1900–2000. By Scott W. Sunquist. Grand Rapids, MI: Baker Academic, 2015. xxiii, 213 pp. Paperback, $22.99.

I reviewed this book largely as a kind of experiment. I wished to examine whether a respected Christian academic (Sunquist is "dean of the School of Intercultural Studies and professor of world Christianity at Fuller Theological Seminary"), treating a not particularly controversial topic (the decline of Christianity in the West and its advance in Latin America, Asia, and Africa), could handle the subject in a fair-minded and non-tendentious manner. The results are not pretty.

It was, for example, not encouraging to hear Sunquist announce, at the very beginning of his treatise: "Jesus was a real person who lived in West Asia . . . He was not a generic or theoretical human being, but a specific, culturally embedded peasant and a wandering Jewish teacher who lived, taught, acted, was killed, and was buried. . . . He would not be the subject of this book if he had merely been a wonder-worker and then stayed in the ground." Surely Sunquist knows that every one of these statements is in fact hotly contested and that few outside the Christian penumbra would accept them wholeheartedly. It is not even clear why Sunquist felt the need to go on in this fashion, since nothing in his account hangs upon it.

But Sunquist's most notable failing is his failure to make even the barest mention of the critical role that secularists and freethinkers played in the decline of Christianity in the West over that last century or so. In an incredibly superficial opening chapter speaking of the spread of Christianity from the first century C.E. to the end of the nineteenth century, he never refers to countervailing tendencies that planted the seeds of Christianity's later collapse. The Renaissance goes all but unmentioned, but it is crucial to the story. The revival of learning in the fifteenth century served two key functions: (1) its rediscovery of a transcendently brilliant classical (i.e., pre-Christian) literature put into focus the millennium-long darkness of the Christian Middle Ages; and (2) its systematic scientific discoveries—embodied in the work of Copernicus, Kepler, Galileo, Newton, and so many others—led directly to the formation of a purely secular conception of a world and a universe that came to be without a creator god.

When Sunquist moves to the twentieth century, all he can do to account for the demise of Christian belief in the West is to point to the devastating effect of the world wars and the lamentable persecution of Christians by secular political movements such as Nazism and communism. He presents impressive statistics of the estimated number of Christians killed in Germany, the Soviet Union, China, and elsewhere in the last century; it would be churlish and false to suggest that this was some sort of payback for the millennium and a half of Christian persecution of Jews, Muslims, freethinkers, and other "heretics" (something Sunquist never mentions), but in any case he must know that persecution often strengthens a faith rather than crushing it. The continuing advance of the sciences, and the continuing role that Christianity and other religions played in blocking needed social reforms (chiefly the push to free women, gays, atheists, and other groups from prejudicial treatment), all had a far greater role in Christianity's demise in Europe and the United States than persecution.

Sunquist does reveal an amusing resentment against the higher criticism and other movements that demythologized Christianity and showed it to be a man-made religion just like any other. In reference to such thinkers as Rudolf Bultmann and Paul Tillich, he writes: "Christianity in the West, in an age of great comfort and affluence, slowly dissipated as it became its own worst enemy, dying by suicide, or at least by growing irrelevance." Just so!

But Sunquist is indeed pointing to a notable phenomenon—the dispersal of Christianity worldwide while it loses adherents in what used to be its home base. The numbers are striking: in 1900, 82% of Christians were in the West; by 2000, 62% were non-Western. The causes for this dispersal are multifarious, ranging from the continuing work of missionaries to vast migrations of populations and other factors. But it is telling that the greatest growth of Christian belief in Latin America, Asia, and Africa takes the form of what Sunquist identifies as a new and distinctive strain of Christianity—Pentecostal or other spiritual movements. It is plain that these movements constitute the most irrational and emotional branches of Christianity, and it is not surprising that they have taken root in areas where education is in short supply and poverty is widespread.

What we are to make of the tendencies outlined in Sunquist's book is not entirely clear. Christianity seems to be holding firm, with about one-third of the world population as adherents; but it appears that Islam has now overtaken it in absolute numbers, chiefly because Muslims breed at a greater rate than Christians. But the most spectacular rise by far in the course of the twentieth century is that of the unaffiliated—atheists, agnostics, secularists, and others who refuse to adhere to an established church. They now number about 16% of the world population, and their numbers are growing. It may be too soon to refer to the twenty-first century as the "unexpected atheist century," but I would not bet against it.

Christianity and Free Enterprise

One Nation under God: How Corporate America Invented Christian America. By Kevin M. Kruse. New York: Basic Books, 2015. xvi, 352 pp. Hardcover, $29.95.

For anyone who is a freethinker, a political liberal, or a believer in the separation of church and state, this book is one of the most dispiriting tracts one could read. I say that in praise; for what Kevin M. Kruse—a professor of history at Princeton—has portrayed in overwhelming detail is a carefully conducted campaign to infuse religion, religious imagery, and religious practice into the workings of the American government in defiance of the establishment clause of the First Amendment.

The important point that Kruse makes is that this campaign—symbolized by the insertion, in the 1950s, of the phrase "under God" into the previously secular Pledge of Allegiance and the motto "In God We Trust" on our currency—was in no way a benign or natural outgrowth of Americans' innate religiosity, but rather a conspiracy (no milder word will do) on the part of corporate executives, religious figures, and conservative politicians to use religion not only as a stick with which to beat their liberal foes but to effect a fusion of Christian morality with the free enterprise system that they felt was under siege.

The bugaboo that animated many of these figures was, of course, FDR's New Deal. We are all well aware that business leaders and Republican politicians habitually claimed that FDR's reforms were a harbinger of that most dreaded conception in the capitalist mind, socialism; what is new in Kruse's account is the extent to which FDR's opponents increasingly used Christianity as a weapon against him.

Kruse's account begins in 1940, when the National Association of Manufacturers sought to fight back against FDR by maintaining that the essence of Christianity was the salvation of the individual and—in a feat of rhetorical legerdemain—that this principle necessitated free enterprise shorn of tiresome governmental regulation or supervision. A central figure in this movement was James W. Fifield, Jr., a wealthy Congregationalist minister from Los Angeles who attacked the New Deal and—in an anticipation of the "prosperity gospel" of recent years—defended the accumulation of wealth and property as thoroughly Christian. A magazine, *Faith and Freedom*, embodied the principles of what Kruse calls "Christian libertarianism." The campaign gained strength throughout the 1940s (in spite of repeated electoral defeats at the presidential level), and Kruse meticulously details the extensive corporate funding for a series of "Freedom Under God" ceremonies that took place on July 4, 1951.

It was at this time that a young preacher named Billy Graham burst on to the scene, in a series of hugely popular rallies in Los Angeles in 1949. From the beginning, Graham linked Christianity with patriotism and free enterprise, embodied in his repeated use of the phrase "the American way of life." Kruse quotes a biographer of Graham who wrote: "When Graham speaks of 'the American way of life,' he has in mind the same combination of economic and political freedom that the National Association of Manufacturers, the United States Chamber of Commerce, and the *Wall Street Journal* do when they use the phrase."

A key development was the election of Dwight D. Eisenhower in 1952. Kruse well portrays the deep religiosity in Eisenhower's upbringing and temperament; and his landslide victory led him to believe that he had a mandate to effect a religious revival in the nation. "We *need* a spiritual renewal," he said soon after his election; and later: "Without God, there could be no American form of Government, nor an American way of life. Recognition of the Supreme Being is the first—the most basic—expression of Americanism."

There is, however, a question whether Eisenhower did more than just talk. Kruse admits that not only did he fail—to the immense disappointment of the corporate backers of the "back to religion" campaign—to undo New Deal reforms, but actually strengthened them; as Kruse notes, "In fundamental ways, he ensured the longevity of the New Deal." Where Eisenhower lent his support, and his bully pulpit, was on a more explicit acknowledgment of God by the government. In 1954 attempts were made to pass a constitutional amendment that would have read: "This Nation devoutly recognizes the authority and law of Jesus Christ, Saviour and Ruler of nations through whom are bestowed the blessings of Almighty God." Mercifully, this appalling proposal fizzled, but attention quickly shifted to amending the Pledge of Allegiance, which had been written in 1892 by Francis Bellamy. The Knights of Columbus had proposed inserting the words "under God" in 1951, and the measure was fostered by George M. Docherty, a Scottish-born Presbyterian minister who outrageously declared: "Philosophically speaking, an atheistic American is a contradiction in terms."

Kruse's account of the "under God" campaign is thoroughly researched and compelling; but his overriding point is that this modification of the Pledge of Allegiance had little to do with legislators' fears of the spread of international communism, but rather pointed to their determination to combat religious indifference at home and the spread of "socialistic" governmental programs. Naturally, the "under God" bill was quickly passed by the House and Senate and was signed into law by Eisenhower on Flag Day (June 14, 1954).

Kruse also studies the long campaign to affix the motto "In God We Trust" on our currency—a measure that had first taken effect on select currency during the Civil War. Kruse pungently quotes Theodore Roosevelt's belief that putting such a motto on money "comes close to sacrilege." Nevertheless, the campaign continued, and Eisenhower signed a bill mandating the placement of the motto on all our currency on July 11, 1955.

One of the several critical features lacking from Kruse's account is his failure to note how this particular measure, as well as the entire campaign by corporations to promote free enterprise as inherently Christian, is in fact contrary to the known teachings of Jesus. Bertrand Russell among others had plainly pointed out that Jesus and his immediate disciples were what in today's parlance would have been called socialists if not actual communists ("And all that believed were together, and had all things common" [Acts 2:44]). And we can also point to such well-known incidents as Jesus' expulsion of the moneychangers from the Temple and his celebrated remark that "It is easier for a camel go to through the eye of a needle, than for a rich man to enter the kingdom of God" (Mark 10:25). It would have helped if Kruse had emphasized some of these points; but his knowledge of the Bible and of biblical exegesis does not seem to be very strong, and so these matters are passed over in silence.

A more serious failing in Kruse's account is a rather one-sided approach that emphasizes the agenda he is seeking to advance—the dangerous fusion of explicitly Christian dogma, laissez-faire capitalism, and Republican politics—without noting a number of significant countervailing tendencies. A chapter titled "Pitchment for Piety" regales us with the surprising "conflation of piety and patriotism" that Walt Disney displayed when he opened Disneyland in 1955. This is all well and good—but what relevance does this now have? Anyone who goes to Disneyland or Disney World today is not likely to come upon anything remotely religious in any of the rides or displays. Kruse also goes on at great length about how the politically conservative filmmaker Cecil B. DeMille explicitly believed in the religious message of his film *The Ten Commandments* (1956)—to the extent of having hundreds of Ten Commandments monuments erected all over the country. But one wonders whether these monuments are still standing.

Surprisingly for a professional historian, Kruse fails even to attempt to provide sufficient historical context for the events he is chronicling. Even the

1950s was not so monolithically pious or conformist as his account suggests. What of film noir (and its literary antecedent, the hard-boiled detective novel, which enjoyed huge popularity in the work of Raymond Chandler, Ross Macdonald, John D. MacDonald, and Mickey Spillane), which portrayed a bleak, savage world where God was notable by his absence? What of Elvis, Little Richard, and other pioneers of rock music?

Kruse's single-minded approach is particularly unfortunate when it comes to events of the 1960s and later. He does provide detailed accounts of the Supreme Court's landmark decisions in 1962 and 1963 to prohibit prayer in public schools (although he curiously fails to refer to one of the prominent plaintiffs in these cases, Madalyn Murray, under her better-known name, Madalyn Murray O'Hair) and the subsequent outrage it provoked, leading to fruitless efforts to pass a constitutional amendment allowing or mandating such prayer. But Kruse neglects to indicate how a number of radical movements in the 1960s and 1970s—the youth movement, sexual liberation, women's liberation, gay rights—agitated religious and political conservatives to such an extent that they felt the need to respond by harnessing the latent political power of the religious right. Jerry Falwell's establishment of the Moral Majority in 1979 and Pat Robertson's founding of the Christian Coalition soon thereafter were manifestly *reactions* to what was perceived to be the rejection of Christian moral principles by the American people and popular culture—but we hear of none of this in Kruse's account.

Kruse examines in considerable detail how President Nixon turned Christian piety into a partisan weapon; but even here his emphasis seems a bit misplaced. Kruse goes on at tedious length about the overt religiosity of Nixon's inauguration—but who remembers this event? Nixon also instituted weekly prayer sessions in the East Room of the White House—events that frequently had sharply partisan overtones. And then there were the elaborate politico-religious ceremonies of Honor America Day (July 4, 1970)—but what effect did this have on the course of the Vietnam War or the protests that ultimately led to our withdrawal from the conflict? And as for Nixon's attitude toward governmental regulation, he clearly went in the opposite direction, as his establishment of the Environmental Protection Agency suggests.

A brief and sketchy epilogue traces the successful attempts by Ronald Reagan and his Republican successors to cultivate religious conservatives—but Kruse fails to note that Reagan did little but pay lip service to their cause, soliciting their votes but doing little virtually nothing to advance any of their programs. The same could be said of both Bush presidencies.

In effect, Kruse simply tries too hard to prove his point. He cannot bring himself to acknowledge that the events he chronicles are now largely historical curiosities. He makes a great point of showing how church attendance spiked during the 1950s, going from 49 percent in 1940 to 69 percent in 1959; but he fails to note that attendance has now fallen back to pre-1940 levels and is declining. He says nothing about the significant decline of the religious right in the past decade or so. As for the insertion of "under God" in the Pledge of Allegiance—well, I cannot be the only one who, throughout my years of grammar school, recited the Pledge without paying the slightest attention to its meaning or significance, nor did it have the slightest influence on my inexorable drift toward atheism. And who takes any note of "In God We Trust" on our currency? Has this motto ever augmented anyone's religiosity? And with online banking, credit cards, PayPal, and many other means of conducting financial transactions, who even uses cash anymore? All this makes Kruse's comment that, since 1955, "every act of buying and selling in America has occurred through a currency that proudly praises God" seem a trifle hyperbolic.

And yet, the story that Kruse tells in such exhaustive detail and such narrative panache is an important one. The cynical harnessing of piety by corporate executives, religious leaders, and conservative politicians was insidious and threatening to the very fabric of our nation. Even if this movement was a product of a specific historical period whose time has come and gone, there is no guarantee that it may not rise again.

The Bible and Gays

The Bible's Yes to Same-Sex Marriage: An Evangelical's Change of Heart. By Mark Achtemeier. Louisville, KY: Westminster John Knox Press, 2014. xv, 137 pp. Paperback, $17.00

God and the Gay Christian: The Biblical Case in Support of Same-Sex Marriage. By Matthew Vines. New York: Convergent Books, 2014. 213 pp. Paperback, $14.99.

These two books will provide much merriment to the freethinker, as its pious authors twist themselves into pretzels trying to reconcile the not very nice things the Bible says about homosexuals and homosexual sex with their fervent belief in both the moral soundness of same-sex marriage and its congruency with the "essence" (whatever that may be) of biblical teaching on love, marriage, and so forth. The funny thing is that they actually make a tolerably good case that several key biblical passages apparently condemning homosexual sex have been widely misinterpreted. Whether their arguments will have any effect on the Protestant fundamentalist or Catholic hierarchy in the near future is anyone's guess; and they leave themselves open to many other lines of attack in what can only be characterized as their tendentious readings of Scripture.

The two authors are a study in contrasts. Mark Achtemeier is a long-serving pastor in the Presbyterian Church (U.S.A.) and served for many years on the faculty of Dubuque Theological Seminary. Matthew Vines is much younger (he was born in 1990), but has lately received much wider press coverage for his pro-gay stance—chiefly because, as he bravely announces on the first page of his treatise, he is gay himself and has been wrestling with the apparent conflict of his inner nature with the Bible's seeming condemnation of same-sex relationships.

Both authors have difficulty establishing viable hermeneutical principles to interpret passages in both the Old and New Testaments regarding gays. Achtemeier deprecates the "fragment" approach to biblical interpretation, declaring plausibly enough that it is invalid simply to pluck random passages and hold them up for either praise or condemnation. Well and good; but there are strong suspicions that Achtemeier (and, even more so, Vines) uses exactly this method at times, deliberately brushing certain passages under the rug on the basis that they are somehow irrelevant or non-representative and vaunting others instead.

The method Achtemeier prefers is stated as follows: "Faithful interpreta tions of the Bible should make coherent, good sense." But he himself cannot possibly be unaware that the Bible itself may not be a "coherent" document as it stands, given the plain fact that in its totality (Old and New Testaments) it was written over a period of at least a millennium, and more likely a millen nium and a half, by writers of widely differing backgrounds and tempera ments. What kind of coherence can we expect in such a multifarious text? It is precisely this awkward fact that allows many individuals (Achtemeier engag ingly notes how a white supremacist in Idaho claimed to find justification for his views by citing various biblical passages, although this methodology has also been used by Jehovah's Witnesses and many others, including atheists) to pick and choose what parts of the Bible they think are of importance.

And as for "good sense"—well, that is also a highly subjective and time bound conception. What is good sense for one person, or one era, may not be so in another. In 1000 B.C.E. it made perfect "good sense" to regard wives as the property of their husbands, as emphatically noted in the tenth com mandment ("Do not covet your neighbour's household: you must not covet your neighbour's wife, his slave, his slave-girl, his ox, his donkey, or anything that belongs to him" [Exodus 20:17]).[1] It does not make such "good sense" today. (It always amuses me that proponents of public displays of the Ten Commandments are forced to present a kind of Reader's Digest Condensed Version of this commandment—"Thou shalt not covet"—that deliberately omits exactly those items that the Bible explicitly states should not be coveted.)

Vines's methodology is equally open to criticism. What he wants to do is to apply a passage in Matthew to biblical exegesis: "Beware of false prophets . . . You will recognize them by their fruit. . . . A good tree always yields sound fruit, and a poor tree bad fruit" (7:15–17). (Vines uses a different translation, which contrasts "good fruit" from "bad fruit.") This leads to a kind of instru mentalist ethic whereby the *effects* of a given biblical doctrine are the criterion as to whether it is sound or not. But once again, *how* is one to determine what is "good" or "sound" fruit and what is not? How is this not a totally subjective decision on the part of the commentator? For many centuries Christians be lieved that killing suspected "witches," based on a single passage in the Bible— "You must not allow a witch to live" (Exodus 22:18)—resulted in pretty good fruit: after all, the witches were dead! (And, not coincidentally, their property and assets were confiscated by the church.)

Both of our devout scholars are wary of what is found in the Old Testa-

---

1. I use the translation in *The Revised English Bible* (Oxford University Press/Cambridge University Press, 1989).

ment—and justifiably so, since it is here that the harshest condemnations of gay sex occur. Achtemeier flatly declares that "any correct understanding of the Bible's teaching should be grounded and centered in Christ." But of course! Why didn't I think of that? The author actually goes on to say that "the Law and the Prophets had been pointing to Jesus from the very beginning"—presumably referring to random passages in Isaiah that purport to predict the birth of Jesus. Aside from now succumbing to the "fragment" approach he has just condemned, Achtemeier glosses over the fact that our Jewish friends would presumably not agree about this Jesus-pointing tendency in the scriptures that their own distant ancestors wrote. Indeed, no fair-minded reader could possibly think that those passages in Isaiah had anything to do with Jesus. Achtemeier later concedes grudgingly that one cannot just dispense with the Old Testament altogether, much as he deeply desires to do so. But there are apparently ways to minimize its impact, as well as the impact of other embarrassing passages in both the Old and the New Testaments.

This sleight-of-hand comes out particularly in Achtemeier's discussion of slavery in the Bible. He ingenuously professes amazement that pro-slavery advocates both before and after the Civil War pointed to the Bible as the source of their stance. He then goes on to say that these passages were only meant for "an ancient Greco-Roman society that was wholly dependent on slavery for its economic survival." This gets Achtemeier into more trouble than he realizes. Firstly, the statement is plainly false, because the author has deliberately failed to cite any passages on slavery in the Old Testament, which could not possibly be intended for a Greco-Roman audience. Secondly, this idea that certain passages in the Bible can simply be dispensed with on the grounds that they only reflect the historical reality of the period in which they were written has long been used by secularists to point (correctly) to the wholly human—i.e., not divinely inspired—composition of the Bible. One would presumably expect an omnipotent and omniscient god to "inspire" his prophets to rise above the "temper of the times" to advocate doctrines of universal validity. Thirdly, other passages in the New Testament do in fact contradict Greco-Roman political and moral theory. Jesus' admonition to "love your enemies" stands in direct contrast to the principles of antiquity, most pungently embodied in a statement in Euripides' *Medea*: "[I am] hard on my enemies and well-disposed to friends."[2]

Vines gets himself into similar trouble by blandly passing off certain passages in the Bible (including some dealing with same-sex relationships) as reflective of the patriarchal tendencies of all ancient societies, which resulted in

---

2. See further Ruby Blondell, *Helping Friends and Harming Enemies: A Study in Sophocles and Greek Ethics* (Cambridge: Cambridge University Press, 1991).

women being considered of lesser moral, social, and political value than men. But there are significant differences in ancient societies: Roman law permitted women to inherit property, something that didn't happen in "Christendom" until the nineteenth century. Vines goes on to say that the coming of Christ makes it possible for us to abandon certain parts of the Old Testament as outdated or irrelevant. I am not at all sure how Vines accomplishes this interpretative prestidigitation, but he is plain on the matter: "Paul said in Romans 7 that the law existed to expose our sin, revealing our need for a Savior. But once our Savior has come, we no longer need the law. We could compare it to the way drivers no longer need road signs once they arrive at a destination." Well, if you believe that, there's a bridge nearby I'd like to sell you.

Achtemeier also thinks you can escape from the implications of certain biblical passages by regarding them as symbolic or metaphorical. He points to the notorious passages in Joshua that unmistakably suggest its author's belief that the sun revolves around the earth. But, Achtemeier says blithely, we refer constantly to "sunrise" and "sunset," knowing that these words are only meant figuratively. But again, this leads him into hot water. Exactly *which* passages in the Bible can or should be so interpreted? Why is it that only those passages that are today seen as contradictory to known fact are to be interpreted symbolically? Why not interpret the whole story of Jesus' death, resurrection, and ascension to heaven as one big metaphor? Common sense would surely lead one to such a view. But I suspect that this suggestion would horrify our devout commentators.

Turning to the actual passages (six or seven or eight, depending on how you count them) in the Bible that deal with homosexuality, the authors become a little more sure-footed. The famous passage in Genesis 19:1–19 (the story of Sodom and Gomorrah) is fairly easily dealt with: Achtemeier claims plausibly that this story doesn't condemn same-sex relations so much as it condemns "homosexual gang rape used as a weapon against foreigners." Vines claims that "the sin of Sodom had far more to do with a lack of hospitality and a bent toward violence than with any sexual designs the men had on Lot's visitors."

The passages in Leviticus (18:22 and 20:13) cause a bit more trouble. The second is so incendiary ("If a man has intercourse with a man as with a woman, both commit an abomination. They must be put to death; their blood be on their own heads!") that Achtemeier cannot bring himself to quote that second sentence, thereby concealing the fact that the passage advocates the death penalty for the practice. He maintains that this passage really just condemns certain customs of the Canaanite tribes, which God is declaring off-limits because it might lead to "gang rape and similarly violent forms of sexual aggression." But this is exactly the "slippery slope" argument that Achtemeier has scorned elsewhere. As for Vines, it is here that he brings forth Jesus' emergence as an excuse for avoiding the nastier parts of the Old Testament.

Other passages are dealt with likewise. Both Achtemeier and Vines make plausible arguments that what is being discussed in all these passages is violent or exploitative sex, not the committed, loving relationships that many gays practice today. But this very stance, valid enough as a hermeneutical tool in explaining away the Bible's apparent condemnation of gay sex, leads to further trouble. Achtemeier states: "Neither the Old nor New Testament writers have any concept of sexual orientation. This means that when the biblical writers consider same-sex behavior, they can understand it only as a deliberate rejection of fully available heterosexual options in service to out-of-control passions like anger, lust, or aggression." Well and good; but what this means is that the Bible can be used neither to *support* nor to *condemn* committed same-sex relations, much less gay marriage. But that is not enough for our brave commentators; they want the Bible to *sanction* such marriages. Achtemeier says: "God desires to bless and sanctify same-gender relationships no less than heterosexual unions." Vines goes even farther, heaping scorn on what he calls "non-affirming" scholars who think the Bible prohibits same-sex marriage: "It isn't gay Christians who are sinning against God by entering into monogamous, loving relationships. It is the church that is sinning against them by rejecting their intimate relationships." Take that, you bigots!

Both commentators are, I think, on solid ground when they say that the Bible has little concern with what has been termed "gender complementarity"—the apparent fact that male and female genitalia "fit" together pretty well (for the purposes of procreation, anyway), and therefore any other sexual practice must be "unnatural." But this argument—propounded recently by a leading conservative Christian scholar, Robert P. George—is highly tendentious and cannot be supported by scripture. Achtemeier refers to it scornfully as "the argument from plumbing." Both writers also find no benefit from some Christians' declarations that gays should just be celibate: Vines keenly points out that celibacy in the Bible must be regarded as something chosen willingly, not mandated upon an entire group of persons.

From our perspective, this whole internecine debate is rather amusing. It is to us pathetically obvious that the real solution to this whole dilemma is simply to leave the church and become happily secular. But of course that option isn't open to these pious gents. Vines makes no bones about his lifelong brainwashing: he flatly states that his indoctrination into Christianity began at the age of two. We atheists will be delighted to watch from the sidelines while these two sides duke it out. It may well be that Achtemeier and Vines are on the whole more right than their opponents; but I very much doubt that the latter will change their tune anytime soon.

Atheism in Classical Antiquity

Battling the Gods: Atheism in the Ancient World. By Tim Whitmarsh. New York: Alfred A. Knopf, 2015. x, 290 pp. Hardcover, $27.95.

This bracing account of the development of atheistic thought in classical antiquity should be read by anyone who doubts that, as the author states, "Atheism . . . is demonstrably at least as old as the monotheistic religions of Abraham." Tim Whitmarsh—A. G. Leventis Professor of Greek Culture at the University of Cambridge and the author of several books on Greek literature and philosophy—has written a history of Greco-Roman atheism that spans more than a millennium and is written in a non-technical manner accessible even to those without a firm grounding in classical literature, history, and thought. Indeed, at times the book becomes a bit simple-minded in explaining elementary facts of classical culture—but perhaps Whitmarsh is correct in pointing an accusing finger at "an educational system that fails to acknowledge the crucial role of Greco-Roman thought in the shaping of Western secular modernity." The time has long past when knowledge of Greek and Latin was expected of every civilized person—and, in my humble opinion, we are the poorer for it.

Whitmash begins his account with an overview of the nature and development of Greek religion. There are of course significant differences between Greco-Roman polytheism and the dogmatic monotheistic religions (Judaism, Christianity, and Islam). Whitmarsh notes that among the Greeks "those in charge of religious matters had no jurisdiction over secular matters," and that "the Greeks had nothing comparable to sacred scripture." The closest thing to the latter were the epic poems of Homer and also Hesiod's *Theogony*. In these works, the gods are not depicted as moral exemplars or even as having omnipotent powers even within the specific realms they putatively controlled (Poseidon as god of the sea, for example). Whitmarsh could have augmented his account by observing that polytheism is in a sense a refinement of primitive animism, where all natural objects are thought to be animated by some godlike entity (rivers flow downhill because a god is directing them to do so). Also, Whitmarsh neglects to say anything about Greek creation myths—perhaps because the Greeks themselves seemed to pay only lip service to them. Hesiod's *Theogony* opens with a depiction of "Chaos" somehow begetting "Erebus and black Night; but of Night were born Aether and Day, whom she conceived and bore from union in love with Erebus." It is difficult to imagine the Greek populace believing these begettings to be anything but symbolic.

Whitmarsh is correct in emphasizing the radical act of the pre-Socratic philosophers of the sixth century B.C.E. (Thales, Anaximines, Anaximander, and so on) seeking a *material* origin of the universe, whether it be water, air, fire, or whatever. Although these philosophers did not entirely reject the divine, the mere fact that they sought "natural" explanations for the origin of all entity is a significant gesture toward atheism. Some philosophers went farther, as when Xenophanes pungently ridiculed the very notion of anthropomorphic deities: "Now if cows, horses, or lions had hands, and were able to draw with those hands and create things as humans do, horses would draw gods in the form of horses, and cows in the form of cows, and create bodies just like what they had."

I had long thought that one Diagoras of Melos (c. 400 B.C.E.) was the first avowed atheist in classical antiquity, but Whitmarsh makes a case for that honor to go to Hippo of Samos nearly a century earlier. Little is known of Hippo aside from the fact that he identified the mind with the brain. A much more significant figure is Democritus (460?–370? B.C.E.), the co-founder (with Leucippus) of the atomic theory. Although the idea of god is not entirely absent in his thinking, his assertion that all entity consists of "atoms and the void"—as well as his rigid determinism—leaves very little room for gods to function. By this time secularism was spreading out well beyond the purely philosophical realm. The Hippocratic writers rejected divine explanations for disease—a pioneering act that would not be repeated in the West for close to two millennia. Historians such as Herodotus and Thucydides similarly denied the role of gods in human affairs. Whitmarsh asserts of the latter: "There is no room in his system for divine intervention or moral patterning in human fortunes."

The Sophists of the later fifth century B.C.E. became notorious for skepticism that verged closely on atheism. Protagoras wrote a treatise (now lost) called *On the Gods* in which he compactly articulated agnosticism: "Concerning the gods, I cannot know whether they exist or whether they do not, or what form they have, for there are many impediments to knowledge, including obscurity and the brevity of human life." Democritus pioneered the study of the natural origins of religious belief and could well be thought of as the first anthropologist in Western civilization. An obscure Sophist named Prodicus of Ceos may well have been an out-and-out atheist.

Greek tragedy might be thought of as hostile to atheist thought, since it was performed at a religious festival (the Greater Dionysia) and frequently involved the gods as characters. Sophocles' *Oedipus Rex* would seem to enforce the idea of divine prophecy, since Oedipus cannot escape the hideous prophecy that he will kill his father and marry his mother; but Whitmarsh makes a case that there is plenty of skepticism found even in this work. Euripides, indeed, gained a reputation in antiquity for atheism; one ancient critic noted that he "has persuaded all men that there aren't any gods." This is a bit of an exaggeration, but religious skepticism is found in abundance in his work.

Although the Greeks generally did not criminalize heresy or blasphemy, there were some notable cases of persecution in the later fifth century; but Whitmarsh notes that much of this was a result of political tensions, chiefly the Peloponnesian war between Athens and Sparta. It was at that time that a figure named Diopeithes emerged; he impeached the philosopher Anaxagoras for denying the gods. Later, Diagoras was prosecuted, nominally for profaning the Eleusinian Mysteries, but also for outright atheism.

Socrates, of course, was the most famous victim of persecution, and the charge against him—"not recognizing the gods the state recognizes"—was in fact probably true, since Socrates appealed to his own *daimonion* ("little god") as the source of his moral and other views. There is a certain irony in Socrates' relations with his most famous disciple, Plato. Although the Socrates depicted in Plato's earlier dialogues is probably more or less historical, in the later dialogues Socrates serves merely as a mouthpiece for Plato's own ideas—ideas that became more and more dualistic, theistic (the *Timaeus* frankly portrays an anthropomorphic creator-god), and fascistic. Plato, who early on deprecated the Greeks for persecuting a freethinker like Socrates, finds room in the late treatise *The Laws* for punishing atheists as a danger to the state. It is no wonder that the Christians found Plato an *anima naturaliter Christiana*.

With the advent of the Hellenistic period (fourth to second centuries BCE), a wide array of philosophical schools battled for supremacy, chief among them the Stoics, the Epicureans, the Skeptics, and the Cynics. The Stoics were deeply theistic, hence play little role in Whitmarsh's account. The Skeptics, whose chief assertion was the denial of all dogma and the impossibility of arriving at true knowledge of anything in the universe, fostered atheism by propounding the notion that belief in the gods is illogical—but their arguments are largely based on verbal gymnastics rather than empirical reasoning. Nevertheless, their work—found in the work of such thinkers as Carneades, Clitomachus (who apparently wrote a work *On Atheism*), and Sextus Empiricus—is bracing and ingenious.

But it was Epicurus (341–270 B.C.E.) and his disciples who, even in antiquity, were heralded as closet atheists. This view had much to recommend it. Although Epicurus did assert the existence of gods, his adoption of Democritus' atomic theory compelled him to maintain that the gods were merely made up of very fine atoms not perceptible by human sense organs but directly by the mind; the gods also have no involvement in human affairs but merely exist in the *intermundia* (the spaces between the stars) contemplating their own perfection. One wonders why Epicurus felt the need to envision such entities in the first place; Whitmarsh suggests a fear of persecution such as Diagoras and others had endured. The fact that Epicurus also denied the immortality of the soul—it dissolves into its constituent atoms upon death—did not endear him to theists.

Whitmarsh has little to say of the Romans, whose expertise lay not in abstract philosophical thinking but in running an increasingly large empire. The most acute Roman philosophers were Lucretius (whose magnificent poem *De Rerum Natura* is a comprehensive exposition of Epicurean philosophy) and Seneca the Younger, a Stoic. Whitmarsh does put forth the figure of Lucian of Samosata, a satirist who, like Voltaire centuries later, took great enjoyment from ridiculing the absurdities of religion, including Christianity.

Readers will come away from this book with a renewed appreciation of the dynamism of Greek thought, its fearless treading of ground previously untouched, and its pioneering forays into areas of thought that would not be developed for centuries. It is no accident that the rediscovery of the classics during the Renaissance paved the way for the development of atheism and secularism in the West; for, along with concomitant discoveries in science, the thinkers of classical antiquity laid down a path that ultimately led to the establishment of atheism as a comprehensive and viable philosophy. It is a tragedy that so little work by the Greek philosophers discussed in the book survives except in fragments; but what we have is enough to make us acknowledge them as our intellectual forbears.

In-Your-Face Atheism

Fighting God: An Atheist Manifesto for a Religious World. By David Silverman. New York: St. Martin's Press, 2015. xvi, 284 pp. Hardcover, $26.99.

David Silverman is the president of American Atheists, the group founded by Madalyn Murray O'Hair in 1963. I have previously expressed my skepticism about O'Hair's grasp of philosophy, to say nothing of her ham-fisted prose;[1] but I am second to no one in my admiration for her courage in litigating the court case that led to the Supreme Court's abolition of prayer in public schools in 1963. O'Hair faced years, perhaps decades of abuse and vilification for her brave stance, and all atheists, secularists, and freethinkers owe her a debt of gratitude, whatever one may think of her as a person or as a writer and thinker.

Silverman seems cut very largely from the same cloth—he is an unrepentant, in-your-face atheist who, sadly enough, shares O'Hair's weakness in his grasp of philosophical niceties; and the publisher of this, his first book, has not done him any favors by failing to correct the errors of style, grammar, and syntax that litter it. Nevertheless, one comes away with an admiration for Silverman as one who will step boldly into the fray and challenge the pious boldly, unflinchingly, and at times with profane abuse.

Let me first address Silverman's deficiencies as a thinker. He doesn't spend much time actually debating the truth of atheism or the falsity of religion, since he regards the matter as definitively settled: "all religions are lies, and all believers are victims." At one point he does venture into a discussion of various standard "proofs" of the existence of God (the teleological argument, the cosmological argument, the argument from morality, the ontological argument, and so on); and although his ultimate conclusion—that such "proofs" are "all word games and logical fallacies"—is sound enough, his actual refutations are crude and ill-reasoned. I do not get the sense that Silverman has read the leading atheist philosophers—Bertrand Russell, A. J. Ayer, or even Richard Dawkins, whom he quotes frequently elsewhere and who has provided a blurb for this book—with any diligence or understanding.

Silverman also reveals drawbacks in his understanding of history. He

---

1. See my chapter "Madalyn Murray O'Hair: Prayer out of the Schools," in *The Unbelievers: The Evolution of Modern Atheism* (Amherst, NY: Prometheus Books, 2011).

rightly asserts that science has been a key weapon in the overthrow of religious dogma, but then he curiously dates the "advent of science" to a very specific date and period in history—350 B.C.E. in ancient Greece. He has gained this insight from a website on the history of the scientific method. I have no idea what Silverman could mean by positing such a specific date. He has obviously not read such a work as Benjamin Farrington's *Greek Science* (1953), which pushes the commencement of Greek science back about 250 years before Silverman's date, with anticipations in other cultures centuries before that. Indeed, it is notable that the great majority of the references in Silverman's notes are to websites rather than to actual books or articles. Sometimes one needs to do research in the good old-fashioned way.

Silverman's grasp of modern history seems just as shaky. He rightly criticizes Hinduism for promoting a rigid caste system in India that resulted in untold misery for lower castes (and especially for the "out-castes" or "untouchables") over thousands of years; but he betrays no awareness that Article 15 of the Indian constitution officially abolished the caste system. I am well aware that such an enactment is not likely to change long-standing social and cultural prejudices overnight, but I think the fact ought to have been mentioned.

But these are small points: Silverman is not here to argue as a philosopher. This point is abundantly made in his discussion of the word *atheist*, which he believes ought to be used by all who do not acknowledge the existence of a deity. He heaps endless scorn on those who shy away from this blunt designation in favor of less confrontational terms such as agnostic, freethinker, or secularist. His reason for doing so? Well, you see, the majority of Americans don't really know what those terms mean! As a philosopher, I am troubled by Silverman's willingness to accommodate his vocabulary to the ignorance of his perceived audience; but Silverman puts himself forth not as a philosopher but as an activist.

The overriding question is whether the approach Silverman and American Atheists have adopted is actually effective. He certainly thinks so: "Firebrand atheism works," he states. His proof of this contention is, however, pretty shaky and is largely based on statistics that could very well tell a different story. He feels that Google searches for the word "atheist" over the past decade can be significantly correlated with the actions of his own organization during the same period; but surely it is infinitely more likely that the best-selling books by Dawkins, Sam Harris, Christopher Hitchens, and others have had a great deal more to do with people "outing" themselves as atheists than the work of American Atheists, important in some particulars as that has been. Perhaps Silverman thinks that these "new atheists" are themselves representative of the "firebrand atheism" he practices; but if so, they do so with considerably greater intellectual heft and—especially in the case of Hitchens—dexterity of prose than Silverman can command.

But I do not wish to be too hard on Silverman and his group. He is undoubtedly right that there are probably many more atheists in the United States and the world than are revealed by surveys, since many people still feel shame or even fear in admitting that they have renounced religion. Indeed, one of the most valuable parts of Silverman's book is an appendix in which he discusses this very subject: "On Opening the Atheist 'Closet.'" Here he speaks as a kind of self-help counselor in advocating ways to "come out" in the face of resistance from family members, friends, coworkers, and so on. He recognizes the sensitivity of the issue, but believes (correctly, I think) that the consequences of "coming out" are in fact far less severe than many closeted atheists believe.

The wind, Silverman maintains, is at our backs: the non-religious are, paradoxically, the fasting growing "religious" group in this country, and perhaps around the world. At the very least, we are now at about 20% of the population, and perhaps much higher (Silverman conjectures that, if closeted atheists are counted, the number could reach more than 80 million in the United States). But only a fraction of these are members of any of the numerous atheist, freethought, or humanist organizations in existence. Would our cause be enhanced if more people joined? I daresay; but whether that is a realistic goal is another matter. As Silverman himself would contend, religious people are "joiners" because they are constitutionally inclined toward being part of a group and following orders. It is precisely the chief virtue of atheists that we think for ourselves, and many of us do not feel the need for an "atheist support group" or anything of the sort to maintain our unbelief. We might, therefore, rival cats in being resistant to herding.

I myself am, by temperament, unable to follow Silverman in his *public* confrontations with the pious, even though I am probably more abusive to religion and the religious in print than he is. So I take my hat off to him for fighting the brave fight and refusing to back down. It takes courage to go on Fox News and go toe-to-toe with Bill O'Reilly; it takes courage to wage lawsuits against the erection of Ten Commandments monuments on public grounds; it takes courage to hold a Reason Rally in Washington, D.C.

What Silverman wants is not the elimination of religion, although he feels that that is inevitable; what he wants is the overthrow of the privileged status that religion (and especially Christianity) still retains in all manner of venues, enshrined by laws that are plainly in defiance of the First Amendment's guarantee of freedom of (which also implies freedom *from*) religion. As long as there is a David Silverman out there to fight these battles, we quieter atheists can continue to help the cause less stridently.

Why People Convert

Strange Gods: A Secular History of Conversion. By Susan Jacoby. New York: Pantheon, 2016. xl, 464 pp. Hardcover, $29.95.

This learned, exhaustive, and endlessly engaging book, ten years in the making, is a welcome antidote to the tendentious accounts by religious partisans of the phenomenon of conversion from one faith to the other. Christians in particular have seized upon every noteworthy conversion from some other faith to their own as a testimonial to the "truth" of their religion, asserting without evidence that such conversions are purely a product of an individual conscience voluntarily seeking the light and finding it in Catholic (or Baptist or Presbyterian or Episcopalian or what have you) doctrine. Jacoby keenly points out that, throughout the nearly two thousand years she covers in this book, social, political, psychological, and numerous other factors are always at play when an individual—or, especially, a group—converts from one religion to another. Jacoby writes in her introduction that her book was written "precisely because most histories and personal accounts of conversion have been written by believers in the supernatural, who understandably view changes of faith mainly in terms of their spiritual origins and significance."[1] But Jacoby conclusively establishes otherwise, by a careful analysis of major conversions from as early as Augustine in the fourth and fifth centuries C.E. to Mohammad Ali in the last century. A significant undercurrent of her book is that a great many conversions have been forced upon individuals through threats of ostracism, economic hardship, and death—another inconvenient truth that religions are keen to brush under the rug.

Jacoby deliberately avoids any discussion of the most consequential conversion of them all, at least from the Christian perspective: the moment when

---

1. Jacoby goes on to contrast her approach to that of William James in *Varieties of Religious Experience* (1902), although she remarks charitably that James's treatise "presents a psychological exploration of the conversion experience that holds up well, for the most part." I came to a very different conclusion, finding James so fatally biased in favor of Christian supernaturalism that his accounts are virtually worthless even on a purely psychological basis. See my chapter "The Pragmatical Professor: William James" in *God's Defenders: What They Believe and Why They Are Wrong* (Prometheus Books, 2003).

Saul of Tarsus fell off his horse on the road to Damascus and became the figure we know as St. Paul. This is because "Scripture has little to tell us about the psychological processes by which he was prepared, before his fall off the horse, for his transformation from an enemy of those who followed the prophet Yeshua into the indispensable publicist of the greatest story ever told." Instead, Jacoby begins her account with a dissection of Augustine's *Confessions,* admittedly a remarkable document for which there is no true parallel in classical antiquity for its intimate personal revelations and psychological insight into a troubled soul. But she makes it clear that Augustine was led to his conversion from paganism to Christianity largely by his mother, Monica—and also by what can only be an unnatural, almost perverse, sense of shame and self-loathing in regard to some of his own peccadilloes. In particular, Augustine developed such a loathing of the very act of sex, even in the context of marriage, that he could state that "the good Christian [man] is found . . . to hate the corruptible and mortal conjugal connection and sexual intercourse; that is to love in her what is characteristic of a human being, to hate what belongs to her as a wife." Evidently, for Augustine, it was *not* better to marry than to burn.

Jacoby now backtracks and contextualizes Augustine's conversion by outlining the political and religious disputes of the century preceding him, beginning with the (politically motivated) conversion of the Emperor Constantine to Christianity in the early fourth century. Inevitably, the Emperor Julian, who reigned for only two short years (361–63), comes in for discussion. Jacoby points to Julian's cleverness in attempting by undermine Christianity by extending toleration to all manner of sects that the Christians had already deemed heretical, as well as to Judaism (he tried to rebuild the temple in Jerusalem, destroyed by the Romans in 70 C.E.). His effort failed, of course—and one can only wonder how different the entire history of the West would have been if he had succeeded. Instead, he was succeeded by emperors who found it convenient to embrace the new faith. Theodosius I (r. 379–95), embroiled in a dispute with Ambrose, Bishop of Milan, ultimately capitulated to him, effectively acknowledging the Christian church's superiority to the secular power—a capitulation that resulted in untold bloodshed and misery for the next millennium and a half. Shortly thereafter, Theodosius banned worship at pagan shrines, and Christians took that as a license to destroy pagan temples. In 382 Theodosius made religious heresy a capital offense against the state.

Jacoby focuses on two particular heresies that she regards as of great significance in the early church: Donatism and Pelagianism. Donatists "believed that the validity of the sacraments depended on the sanctity of those administering the sacred rites." Orthodox Christian doctrine, conversely, states that "the validity of the sacraments had nothing to do with the moral probity of priests." A convenient principle, even before widespread revelations of pedophile priests! But, as Jacoby keenly emphasizes, Pelagianism was even more threatening to Christianity by its rejection of original sin. She notes that Pelagianism was in some dim sense a precursor to secularism by decreeing that "Each human being is solely responsible for his virtues and vices." That doctrine could not be allowed to stand, because it essentially denied the role of Jesus' death as atonement for the "curse of Adam." And so it was declared heretical.

Jacoby's account now skips a millennium to focus on the figure of Solomon ha-Levi, a Jewish convert to Christianity who became Paul, Bishop of Bourgos. This conversion allows Jacoby to expatiate on the horrors of forced conversions of Jews and others in Spain during beginning in 1391. Over the next century, things went from bad to worse, not only with the establishment of the Spanish Inquisition in 1478 but with King Ferdinand and Queen Isabella's expulsion of Muslims from Spain in 1492, thereby destroying what had been a thriving and relatively tolerant culture whereby Muslims, Jews, and Christians lived, worked, and intermarried with minimal controversy. The Spanish monarchs also expelled "unconverted Jews" because their mere presence purportedly posed a constant threat to the so-called Conversos (Jewish converts to Christianity), who might be inclined to renounce their conversion or practice their original faith in secrecy.

Jacoby does not fail to emphasize that the Reformation initiated by Martin Luther and others in the early sixteenth century did not result in a diminution of forced conversion but only augmented it; for now both branches of Christianity had a vested interest in holding on to their adherents and grabbing new ones where possible. The sixteenth and seventeenth centuries were awash in a sea of blood, as both Catholics and Protestants used their control of the state to crush troublesome individuals (notably Michael Servetus, executed by John Calvin, who had turned Geneva into a religious totalitarian state) and whole groups of "heretics" (not excluding hundreds of thousands or even millions of "witches," deemed heretical because they purportedly had signed compacts with the Devil; but this is not a subject Jacoby discusses).

Jacoby provides an interesting account of the conversion of Margaret Fell (1614–1702) from "a Calvinist-influenced brand of Puritanism" to the new faith of Quakerism: she was converted by John Fox, founder of the Quaker faith, and later married him. Refreshingly, the Quakers expressed "disdain for state-established churches" and actually sought to make converts based purely by persuasion—what a concept! It is scarcely any wonder that the Puritans in England found Fell a troublesome figure—not least because she was an intelligent and courageous woman unwilling to accept the second-class status imposed on females by both Catholics and Protestants.

Turning her attention to the United States, Jacoby neatly destroys the canard that the nation was founded for the sake of "religious freedom"; for it is easy to establish that the Puritans and others who emigrated here were quick to claim religious freedom for themselves but deny it to others. And yet, the United States is singular in that, from the beginning of the establishment of the colonies, it did not allow forcible conversion—the worst the colonial powers ever did was to exile certain religious undesirables, such as Roger Williams (who, as Jacoby neglects to point out, was the first to establish true religious toleration when he founded the colony of Rhode Island), Anne Hutchinson, and others. There is, however, one immense exception to this policy, and Jacoby devotes some of her most anguished and chilling pages to the issue of African American slavery. "The mass conversion of slaves from paganism or Islam to Christianity, beginning in the late seventeenth century and proceeding as long as new slaves continued to arrive from Africa, is the single example of large-scale forced religious conversion in American history." Even Quakers like William Penn owned slaves. Jacoby goes on to point out how "conversion . . . [was] transformed into an instrument of subjection," as slaves were urged to endure their lot for fancied "freedom" in the afterlife.

Back in Europe, the German poet Heinrich Heine (1797–1856) was born into a Jewish family but converted for "purely utilitarian, worldly purposes" to Christianity—and yet he remained essentially a freethinker. Heine converted in 1825 in the hope that he might secure a position in a law firm—something that would have been denied to him as a Jew. In the end he did not get the job, and both his poetry and his prose make his skepticism regarding Christian doctrine abundantly evident. Then there is the case of Edith Stein (1891–1942), also born into a German Jewish family, who converted to Catholicism in 1922 and eventually became a Carmelite nun. She was later carted off to Auschwitz and died there. Jacoby demolishes the standard Catholic view that she was killed not because she was a Jew but because she was a Christian, and Jacoby also mercilessly exposes the hollowness of the Vatican's claim (expressed in a document written as late as 1998) that the long, sordid history of Christian anti-Semitism played no role in the rise of the Nazis and the holocaust.

While there is a wealth of compelling information in Jacoby's book, I am troubled by what at times can seem a tendency to meander and wander off into tangents. Her introduction—in which she discusses conversions in her own ancestry, mostly from Judaism to various Christian sects, chiefly inspired by the need to establish harmony between spouses of different faiths—is a bit unfocused and self-indulgent. She frequently violates chronology in the earlier sections of the book, as when she discusses the conversion of the English poet John Donne (1572-1631) from Catholicism to Anglicanism, but then goes back a century or so to outline the Catholic-Protestant split caused by the Reformation. Her writing is always luminous,[2] but at times the reader is not entirely clear where Jacoby is heading.

But, minor blemishes aside, this meticulously researched book is bracing and timely. Jacoby, who unabashedly declares herself an atheist, for all that she retains respect for her Jewish ethnicity, can take her place—a place already established by such works as *Freethinkers: A History of American Secularism* (2004)—as a towering and pioneering figure in the secularist movement, and this book will only add to her achievement.

---

2. Although her prose would benefit if she did not consistently make the grammatical error of inserting the supernumerary "of" after "all" (in proper English, one writes "all the time," not "all of the time").

A Fitting Burial

The End of White Christian America. By Robert P. Jones. New York: Simon & Schuster, 2016. 309 pp. Hardcover, $28.00.

Robert P. Jones is (as the dust jacket of this book proclaims) the "founding CEO of the Public Religion Research Institute (PRRI)," an organization that conducts extensive and generally reliable polling on issues relating to religion in the United States. He is, therefore, in a good position to write what is in effect an obituary for White Christian America (which he handily abbreviates as WCA). In Jones's opinion, WCA is already dead—and its death occurred around 2005, or shortly after the re-election of George W. Bush. Strictly in terms of numbers—and that is largely or exclusively what Jones is interested in, and what PRRI is focused on—he is unquestionably right. How much longer the rotting corpse will continue to reek before it is gone for good is a question he prudently refuses to answer.

There are, however, certain ambiguities in Jones's treatise that make it somewhat less valuable as an analysis of contemporary religious trends in this country. Exactly what *is* WCA? He states bluntly that "Throughout this book, I use the term White Christian America to describe the domain of white *Protestants* in America" (Jones's emphasis). He does not clarify this restriction until a little later in his book—especially the question of why white Catholics are not included. He finally explains, plausibly, that his focus on Protestants rests on the obvious fact that it is they who wielded overwhelming social and political power during much of American history, and it is their decline in numbers and influence that he is charting. As for Catholics, he pungently writes: "Many Catholics who would be called 'white' today, even those of northern European descent such as Irish immigrants, found the entry door to White Christian America doubly barred: they were often considered neither white nor authentically Christian." He notes that the temperance movement that led to the passing of the 18th Amendment was clearly motivated by anti-immigrant and anti-Catholic prejudice; and in a sense its repeal in 1933 was the first crack in WCA's armor. That prejudice did doom the candidacy of the Democrat Alfred E. Smith in 1928, but John F. Kennedy happily prevailed in 1960. But even he was forced to declare that he was not under the Pope's thumb, in a speech whose stirring words are more relevant now than when they were delivered:

A Fitting Burial

I believe in an America where the separation of church and state is absolute, where no Catholic prelate would tell the president (should he be Catholic) how to act, and no Protestant minister would tell his parishioners for whom to vote; where no church or church school is granted any public funds or political preference; and where no man is denied public office merely because his religion differs from the president who might appoint him or the people who might elect him.

Jones rightly makes much of the division between mainline Protestants and evangelicals—a division that began at least in the 1940s. He amusingly reports on how, between the years 1947 and 1954, the National Association of Evangelicals engaged in a comic-opera attempt to insert a reference to "Jesus of Nazareth" into the U.S. Constitution, in direct contradiction to the First Amendment. We secularists may have believed that the evangelicals' humiliation in the Scopes trial of 1925 had driven them underground for decades, but they were quietly gaining strength and numbers during that whole period. Their seemingly sudden re-emergence in the 1970s, in the form of the Moral Majority and other manifestations of the religious right, should therefore not have been a surprise.

In the 1990s, evangelicals effected a marriage of convenience with conservative Catholics, since they were united by such issues as "abortion, gay rights, and religion in public schools" (a clumsy formulation, since Jones means that they were opposed to the first two and supported the third). But their real enemies were "the rising tides of secularism and liberalism." The irony, however, is that it was at this very time when the numbers of both evangelicals and Catholics were in decline. Evangelicals spent decades chortling at the dwindling number of mainline Protestant sects (Baptists, Presbyterians, Episcopalians, Methodists, and so on), claiming that it was their fuzzy adherence to biblical "truth" and willingness to sway with the social and political winds that led members to flee them; but this ignores the plain fact that their own numbers were falling also. In one of the several illuminating charts scattered throughout his book, Jones notes how, from 1974 to 2014, the number of Protestants fell from 63% of the population to 47%; the number of Catholics fell from 26% to 22%; while the number of the "unaffiliated" rose from 7% to 22%. In terms of the mainline/evangelical divide, the numbers are just as stark: between the years 1988 and 2014, the former fell from 24% to 14%, while the latter fell from 22% to 18%. White Christians as a proportion of the electorate stood at 73% in 1992, but is expected to fall to 48% in 2024—the first time that WCAs will be a minority in the US population.

What is clearly happening is that young people—even the children of evangelicals—are becoming increasingly secular in their outlook. Today, 27%

of people over the age of 65 are white evangelical Protestants, while 20% are white mainline Protestants; but only 10% of people ages 18–29 belong to each of these groups. Nothing points to this trend more strongly than the varying attitudes toward LGBT rights, specifically same-sex marriage. Jones pungently notes how anti-gay rhetoric on the part of the fossilized leaders of the religious right is a major reason for younger Americans' abandonment of religion. And yet, evangelicals are in a difficult bind:

> Because many conservative right-leaning religious leaders and organizations have self-consciously defined themselves through opposition to gay rights during the heyday of the Christian Right movement, they face thorny choices. To move away from strong opposition to same-sex marriage would spark a profound identity crisis and risk losing support from the current—albeit aging—support base. Refusing to reevaluate, on the other hand, may relegate conservative religious groups to cultural irrelevancy and continued decline, as more and more young people leave church behind.

I'm shedding bitter tears at this dilemma!

Another reason for the decline of WCA was its devil's bargain with the Republican Party. What Jones calls the "White Christian Strategy," stretching from evangelicals' support of Barry Goldwater in 1964 to Mitt Romney in 2012, was an extension of the Republicans' Southern Strategy, whereby lightly coded signals indicated that African Americans, immigrants, and secular liberals all constituted an existential threat to the America they had become familiar with (where, of course, they ruled the roost). That strategy worked, after a fashion, if winning elections is your defining criterion; but what did the evangelicals actually accomplish by putting Reagan, George W. Bush, and others in office? Not much aside from some state laws prohibiting same-sex marriage and the preposterous Office of Faith-Based and Community Initiatives that Bush instituted. One of its earliest leaders, David Kuo, keenly remarked that this office was "a sad charade, to provide political cover to a White House that needed compassion and religion as political tools." The very nomination of John McCain in 2008 and Romney in 2012 (neither of whom were the religious right's preferred candidates) signaled "the end of the White Christian Strategy for presidential elections." As for the evangelicals' current embrace of Donald Trump—well, we can all see what that has done for them.

No discussion of WCA can be complete without a discussion of its attitude toward the central question of race; and here Jones devotes a chapter that, for all its attempt at bland neutrality, is a damning indictment of its self-serving hypocrisy. He tells the familiar story of how the Southern Baptists split from the Baptist church in 1845 precisely because it wished to defend the institution of slavery; and Jones's account emphatically demonstrates that Christian churches in general continue to foster and augment the racial segregation found in American society at large. As for evangelicals, Jones does not mince words: "No segment of White Christian America has been more complicit in the nation's fraught racial history than white evangelical Protestants."

Some WCAs are belatedly attempting to make amends on the issue. In 1995, around the time of the 150th anniversary of the founding of the Southern Baptist Convention, the group issued a "sober apology to African Americans for the role slavery played in the convention's founding and for its consistent failure to support civil rights." But this mea culpa was confounded two decades later when the odious Richard Land, head of the SBC's Ethics and Religious Liberty Commission, defended George Zimmerman, the vigilante who killed the unarmed black youth Trayvon Martin, in Florida. Land went on to claim outrageously that a black man is "statistically more likely to do you harm than a white man." Mercifully, Land was replaced by Russell Moore, a younger and more tolerant Southern Baptist who has actually endorsed the Black Lives Matter movement and urged the desegregation of both black and white Christian congregations.

Jones's final chapter is a lengthy "Eulogy for White Christian America," and he applies the five stages of grief propounded by Elisabeth Kübler-Ross—denial, anger, bargaining, depression, and acceptance—to the corpse of WCA. Were he not such a soberly humorless fellow, I would suspect Jones of writing satire here, but he tells his story with deadpan seriousness. As he dryly notes, "Anger has come naturally to white evangelicals," and they are now waging furious rearguard actions on several fronts—from denying that their numbers are falling and their congregations are aging to making deceitful and unconstitutional pleas for "religious freedom" as an excuse to discriminate against LGBTs to a grotesque attempt in Mississippi to make the Bible the "state book." Others feel that separation from the horrors of a liberal, secular, tolerant society and a retreat into the safety of fundamentalist enclaves are their only recourse. I for one would be happy to see them cast themselves out of American society, but it does not seem as if they will do so in any great numbers.

It is difficult to get a read on where Jones himself stands on the issues he discusses. He has adopted an attitude of scrupulous even-handedness, generally using poll numbers to make his arguments rather than addressing such fundamental issues as whether there is any truth to the claims of WCA or whether its imminent demise is a good or bad thing. I think he has done a disservice to readers in not revealing his own inclinations; but some hints of his biases do appear almost in spite of himself. He refers in passing to right-wing attempts to delegitimize President Obama by claiming he was not born in the United States—but then maintains that this conspiracy theory "had its roots in emails from Hillary Clinton's supporters, sent as her campaign was faltering in the spring of 2008." This claim—which Donald J. Trump repeated in his slimy acknowledgment of the falsity of the "birther" myth—was deemed by every responsible news organization as preposterously false, but Jones repeats it with a straight face.

Late in his book Jones devotes some pages to us atheists who have cheered the demise of WCA, trotting out the standard array of "New Atheists"—Harris, Dawkins, Dennett, and Hichens. But he goes on to assert that we have uncharitably refused to acknowledge that "many of our nation's achievements and critical moments in our history such as the civil rights movement may have been stillborn without their religious DNA," and also asserts that several atheists, in attacking Muslims, have themselves become intolerant fascists. Let me say that I believe Jones to be in error on both counts. No fair-minded atheist has denied the "good" things that religion has done over the centuries, even though a fair number of these things have been tainted by a great many bad things, chief of which is the brainwashing of helpless children into patently false religious dogma. And atheists' attitudes toward Muslims are very diverse: I suspect a majority of them do not follow the tendentiousness of Sam Harris on this issue.

Much of Robert P. Jones's book will not be new to anyone who has kept abreast of current events over the past several decades, but it is useful to have all this information in one place, with unequivocal numbers supporting it. If Jones seeks to give White Christian America a fitting burial, I for one will shed few tears at its grave.

Trump and the Religious Right

One of the more peculiar aspects of the most bizarre presidential campaign in American history is the extent to which religious conservatives embraced the candidacy of Donald J. Trump. On the face of it, this association was not at all intuitively obvious. In the past, the religious right was enamored of candidates who, however hopeless their chances in the general election or even in the Republican primaries, hewed to its principles by an outward show of piety and orthodoxy. Remember Mike Huckabee, Rick Santorum, and their ilk? Trump, on the other hand, seems pretty devoid of what could by any reasonable standard be called religious sentiment. He has frankly admitted that he rarely goes to church, has never sought forgiveness for his sins (presumably because, in his cocksure way, he doesn't feel as if he has committed any), and also made the amusing gaffe of referring to 2 Corinthians as "two Corinthians" instead of "Second Corinthians." On top of which, Trump is a thrice-married and twice-divorced man who has openly committed adultery and who has crudely stated his desire to grope women's private parts. A fine Christian, he!

But many conservative Christian leaders were apparently able to put aside their reservations for this "flawed" individual and support him. Why? The obvious answer is that they feel that, regardless of his personal peccadilloes, he will toe their party line. His choice of the extreme social conservative Mike Pence was an obvious bone he threw in their direction. It is true that Trump's ascendancy has to some degree split religious conservatives, especially younger ones. After the election, Andy Crouch, executive editor of *Christianity Today*, wrote that the religious right's support of Trump "gives our neighbors ample reason to doubt that we believe Jesus is Lord. They see that some of us are so self-interested, and so self-protective, that we will ally ourselves with someone who violates all that is sacred to us."

But the religious right's hopes for Trump rest on their using him as a tool to secure their Holy Grail—the abolition of abortion, or at the very least the overturning of *Roe v. Wade* by a newly constituted Supreme Court, which would return the legality of abortion to individual states. Let it pass that Trump was apparently both a Democrat and a supporter of abortion rights in the past; he has made it clear that he will in fact nominate an extreme conservative to fill the seat of the late unlamented Antonin Scalia. This nomination alone—assuming it is approved by the Senate—will not in itself change the calculus of the court, which still has five members who support abortion rights. One of these justices would have to resign or die, and yet another conservative justice, would have to take a seat before *Roe v. Wade* could be dealt a true body blow. But the chances of that happening are strong, given the fact that Anthony Kennedy is eighty, Ruth Bader Ginsburg is eighty-three, and Stephen Breyer is seventy-eight. Can they survive even a single Trump term? It is anyone's guess.

The religious right is certainly fired up on the abortion issue. Many of them, in the wake of Trump's unexpected victory (and, more significantly, the expansion of their majorities in state legislatures), are gearing up for further assaults on abortion rights. Trump himself has crassly declared that, if *Roe v. Wade* is overturned, women wanting abortions in states that would then outlaw the practice could just travel to some other state. What this suggests is that there will emerge a kind of new underground railroad whereby women who live in such benighted places as Alabama or Idaho will be compelled to take "abortion vacations" to a neighboring state. How poor women could afford to do this is not entirely clear.

But religious conservatives have been disappointed on this issue before, and they are likely to be disappointed again. In the first place, the Supreme Court ruled last term that certain restrictions on abortion rights are unconstitutional, and the likelihood is that some of these restrictions will fall by the wayside and new restrictions passed by conservative legislatures will similarly bite the dust.

But there is much more to the religious right's support of Trump than abortion. He has openly endorsed so-called religious liberty legislation—legislation, in other words, that would allow for-profit businesses to deny services to gays, the transgendered, and other groups they despise, and, more pertinently for megachurch leaders like Franklin Graham, legislation that would make it legal for churches to engage in direct political action without fear of having their tax-exempt status withdrawn. This last point is particularly insidious. As it is, many far-right pastors have been deliberately provoking the IRS by sending tapes of themselves making public endorsements of a given candidate, in defiance of current law. The IRS has taken no action on the matter, but the pastors clearly hope that a sympathetic Supreme Court will allow them to have their cake and eat it too, so that they can continue to rake in the shekels without paying taxes while offering full-throated support of the political figures who lick their boots.

Then there is the matter of gay and transgender rights. A lesser Holy Grail for the religious right is the overturning of the recent Supreme Court decision legalizing same-sex marriage. In the unlikely event that that occurs, there would still be at least thirty-six states that had previously legalized the practice, so that only certain deep-red states in the South and elsewhere would reinstitute a ban on gay marriage, leading to all manner of confusion and litigation if legally married same-sex couples from other states moved to these dark havens of prejudice. As for laws stipulating that the transgendered must use bathroom facilities based on their sex at birth—well, things haven't worked out so well. The governor of North Carolina, Pat McCrory, who led his state legislature in passing such a law, found himself losing narrowly to his Democratic opponent, Roy S. Cooper, in an election that otherwise saw North Carolina Republicans emerge triumphant.

There is one more area where religious conservatives hope to prevail: education. Not that they have the slightest interest in improving educational standards, since they well know that increasing education correlates strongly with decreasing religious belief. Rather, the focus of their fear and horror is the public school system. Why? The reason is obvious: thanks to Madalyn Murray O'Hair, prayer in public schools has been banned for more than a half-century. This is why the religious right was thrilled at Trump's nomination of the wealthy businesswoman Betsy DeVos for secretary of education. DeVos is a rabid devotee of charter schools and school vouchers. Even though she made a perfect mess of the Detroit schools when she was in charge of them, she sees in charter schools and vouchers a means of shifting tax dollars from public schools to largely religious schools. In 2001 she stated that this kind of school "reform" would "advance God's kingdom." Her family—which includes Richard DeVos, Sr., the co-founder of Amway—is one of many on the religious right that openly advocates the total elimination of the public school system. Back in 1986 Jerry Falwell looked forward to the day when there wouldn't be "any public schools—the churches have taken them over and Christians will be running them." The likelihood that DeVos could do much to foster this goal is fairly slim—but I suspect she will give it a go.

It is difficult to know what Donald Trump actually believes on these issues—there seems to me a strong probability that he has given them little thought at all. But he has allowed himself to be led by his far-right consultants to advocate policies and put forth nominations that could result in a further theocratization of America. Regardless of what one may think of Trump on other issues, this alone would be enough for all secularists to oppose him tooth and nail.

Atheism and Women

Women Beyond Belief: Discovering Life without Religion. Edited by Karen L. Garst, PhD. Raleigh, NC: Pitchstone Publishing, 2016. 264 pp. Paperback, $16.95.

There is a reason why Richard Dawkins, Sam Harris, Daniel Dennett, and Christopher Hitchens are called the Four Horsemen of the New Atheist movement: they are all men. In spite of the fact that women, ranging from Elizabeth Cady Stanton to Ayn Rand to Madalyn Murray O'Hair, were pioneering atheists (and, as this book makes clear, so are such celebrities as Katherine Hepburn and Emma Thompson), their voices have generally not been heard in the rising tide of atheism, agnosticism, and freethought that we have witnessed over the past few decades. Karen L. Garst, former executive director of the Oregon Community College Association and the Oregon State Bar, has sought to change that. In this extraordinarily compelling volume, she has assembled essays by twenty-two women of many different professions attesting to their gradual deconversion from the beliefs in which they were raised. Every single essay is vivid and perspicacious, as the authors not only reveal keen self-awareness of their own shifting religious and anti-religious sentiments but are frank and open in acknowledging the profound personal difficulties associated with the abandonment of their faith.

Garst has gathered contributors from several different Christian denominations (Catholic, fundamentalist Christian, Seventh-Day Adventist, Methodist, Southern Baptist, Lutheran) as well as from other belief systems such as Mormonism, Judaism, and Jehovah's Witness. The contributors also range geographically from the United States to Europe to Africa. Even if there is in some regards a certain uniformity in these women's progression from belief to unbelief, the details of this progression are fascinating in their diversity and the impact it had on themselves and their families.

It would be a crude stereotype to think that personal or familial events were central in impelling these women to shed their religions: no doubt such events have had similar impacts on men, and most of the contributors also attest that it was academic investigation of the truth-claims of their religions that ultimately led them to cast off their faiths for good. Still, it is striking to see how some dramatic personal traumas played a vital role in the process. One of the most searing accounts in the book is by Michelle DeBord (raised as a Mormon), who was appalled when her beloved thirteen-year-old sister was taken away from the family for having sex with the bishop's son: no penalty was inflicted upon the boy or his family, and DeBord writes that "I will never forget the heartache the doctrine caused in my family or the huge rift it created between all the people I loved." On a lighter note, Ceal Wright (raised as a Jehovah's Witness) tells of how she learned of the pleasures of masturbation from a five-times-married great-aunt. When she started dating a non–Jehovah's Witness, she literally had to "hide" him from scrutiny by her family and her community. But the elders of the faith found out about the relationship and declared the poor fellow a tool of Satan!

Karen Brotzman was raised as a Methodist and married a Lutheran; but he proved to be abusive, so she fled with her children and later converted to Mormonism, remaining in that faith for more than thirty years. But trips to Israel shook her belief in the veracity of early Christian history, and an atheist group pointed out the logical fallacies in the entire Christian system. Jackie Burgett had been fascinated by occult phenomena as an adolescent and actually held a séance in her barn—but nothing happened! Later, a college class on "Critical Thinking: Science and the Occult" turned her into a skeptic. One of the more unusual accounts is by Robin Stafford, a Southern Baptist who had an odd experience as a child in which she thought she saw a demon in her room; this led her to become a Wiccan, and a subsequent car accident led her toward a "reality-based life."

Matilde Reyes writes distinctively as a Catholic born and raised in Peru. Aside from providing curious information on Spanish tarot cards, she tells how she became involved with Opus Dei at her school. But when her cousin died of cancer at the age of fifteen, her faith was shaken: "In those few months I went from believer, to doubter, to hater." Emma Graham, raised as a Catholic, was horrified when a friend took her to a Pentecostal service, noting keenly: "Religion is a difficult drug to give up."

Ruth Marimo was born in Zimbabwe, which had become thoroughly Christianized by European colonists. She pungently attests the brainwashing she underwent: "I had not been given a choice about Christianity as a child." She further acknowledges how rare it is for an African woman to walk away from religion. This leads directly to the account of Taressa Straughter, an African American raised in the Pentecostal faith. But she strikingly announces that she had become a full-fledged atheist at the age of fourteen, adding that Christianity was a key tool in perpetuating slavery: "Religion in general has not done much good for society, but Christianity of all religions should be the last one a black person pursues."

It is no accident that the misogyny at the heart of Christianity and other religions was a central force in motivating some women to abandon their

111

faith. Ann Wilcox, raised as a fundamentalist Christian, writes bitterly that "I could not escape the feeling that this religion had tried to kill me." Marsha Abelman was raised in the Church of Christ sect in Texas but was increasingly bothered by the restrictions imposed on girls and women but not on boys and men. When both she and her husband left the faith together, she was predictably shunned by their friends. Garst herself, raised as a Lutheran, found that the church was the center of her social life as an adolescent, but she too was so disturbed by the church's attitude toward women that she abandoned it.

Anna Rankin's essay details how she was led by her early interest in heavy metal music to think that "god had somehow abandoned his people on Earth." Later she was pressured by her family to become a Mormon, even though she felt that "these people were from another planet." She had had a lesbian relationship as a young woman, but in accordance with the Mormon belief that people should be (heterosexually) married in order to enjoy the full fruits of the afterlife, she married an older Mormon man and had two children by him. But she reached the end of her rope—and faith—when, after several troubled years of marriage, he chastised her by saying, "Why will you not just submit?"

Religion, and religious differences, were the cause of discord in numerous families, as attested by several gripping accounts. (The editor writes that several contributors are using pseudonyms in order to avoid ostracism from their families or their communities.) Taylor Duty, a Seventh-Day Adventist, did find that her faith inculcated a respect for animals—a belief augmented by a trip to India, which inclined her toward Hinduism. But of course Christianity preaches that this religion is wrong and misguided, and that was the beginning of the end of her belief in it. Gil Brennan, an Englishwoman, was raised secular and married a secular man; but when his sister suddenly became a born-again Christian, a rift developed in the family—"all because of this God thing." Moving to the United States, Brennan was regaled by multiple instances of hypocrisy among the Christians of her acquaintance. Lilindra Ra is, distinctively, the daughter of a Vietnamese woman (Catholic) and an American man (Baptist). Given that each faith decrees that the adherents of the other will end up in hell, her sloughing off of both of them seems inevitable.

Some contributions are a bit less personal, presenting the intellectual factors that led their authors to shed their faith. Kay Pullen's sane and temperate essay speaks eloquently about how "My path to atheism was pretty much a quiet and steady falling away." Sylvia Benner's essay provocatively suggests that religion is a kind of fantasy narrative not entirely different from those by Tolkien and other writers; but the critical difference is that *it allows you to be a part of it,* and that is why it is so hard to give up. Benner herself now finds more interest in the reality-based cosmic sweep of the universe from the Big Bang to the present. Nancy J. Wolf admits that, although she is no longer a believer, she has not come all the way to atheism. It was, ironically, at a Christian college that she realized she was no longer a Christian: "But what was I? Had I a faith in anything?" She wants God to exist, but doesn't think it is very likely; and she marshals a cogent series of arguments as to why belief in the biblical narrative is unwarranted.

Many of these accounts testify to the crippling of young minds by religious indoctrination, the pain of withdrawing from a faith that is the center of so many ties to family and community, and the confluence of personal trauma and intellectual endeavor that led these women to renounce their religion. We need more books like this—by men and women, by Americans and Europeans and Africans and Asians—to paint a broader picture of how religion is a blight on humanity and how its discarding can lead to a richer, more fulfilling life.

Throwing In the Towel

The Benedict Option: A Strategy for Christians in a Post-Christian Nation. By Rod Dreher. New York: Sentinel/Penguin Random House, 2017. 262 pp. Hard-cover, $25.00.

This book is a scream. Every atheist, agnostic, secularist, and freethinker will find much merriment in it—at the author's expense, it is true. For in this treatise—a bizarre mix of lugubrious lamentation, petulant whine at his perceived enemies, and grotesque self-help manual—Rod Dreher has thrown in the towel for Christianity in America and Europe. It is his contention that we are already living in a post-Christian age, and his only solution is for true Christians to withdraw into their own homogeneous communities and find what sanctuary they can.

Dreher—both a religious conservative and a political conservative (he is a senior editor at the *American Conservative*)—is convinced that the barbarians have taken over in the United States. That would be us—i.e., the proponents of "liberal secularism," who are now causing persecuted Christians to retreat into their shells because some of them are being dragged them into court for exercising their "religious freedom" (i.e., for continuing their bigotry and discrimination, mostly against the LGBT community). Indeed, these horrible liberal secularists are "robbing us and future generations of our religious beliefs, moral values and cultural memory, and making us pawns of forces beyond our control." Exactly how we are performing this remarkable feat is not quite clear; perhaps our mere existence is bringing it about.

All this may come as a surprise to those of us who think that Christians still have an outsize—and unconstitutional—place in American society, ranging from the motto "In God We Trust" on our currency to tax exemption for churches to tax dollars being used to support parochial schools. But Dreher believes that his religion is doomed as far as American society as a whole is concerned. He speaks in apocalyptic terms on the matter: "The light of Christianity is flickering out all over the West. There are people alive today who may live to see the effective death of Christianity within our civilization." Would that it were true! Evidently the legalization of same-sex marriage "was the Waterloo of religious conservatism." Dreher hears death-knells all over the place: when the states of Indiana, Arkansas, and even Kansas either failed to pass "religious freedom" bills that would allow discrimination against LGBTs or were forced to back-track in the wake of immense opposition from the business community, it was a sure sign for Dreher that his side had definitively lost the culture wars.

I was initially puzzled why Dreher is so fixated on LGBTs. He assumes without question that for-profit business such as bakers and photographers who deny services to such lamentable people are simply exercising their "religious freedom," but he never once presents any coherent arguments to defend such practices. The closest he comes is in his passing remark that Christians should be allowed the "First Amendment right to be wrong." But surely there is more going on here than that. This denial of service is surely an instance of religious *coercion:* that baker is not merely defending her right to practice her religion, but is *forcing others to abide by its tenets.* That is the very thing that the Establishment Clause of the First Amendment was designed to prevent. Moreover, because the baker is not performing a specifically religious function but running a for-profit business, "religious freedom" claims cannot possibly be said to apply.

Dreher's frenetic chapter on sex provides some clarification. Although early in his book he presents a simple-minded account of the progress of science and culture in the West, from the Renaissance to the present day, which led many intellectuals to shed their religious beliefs, it is the Sexual Revolution (always capitalized by Dreher) that was the final nail in Christianity's coffin. To Dreher, who believes that the only way for a "traditional Christian" to practice sex is "within marriage between one man and one woman," same-sex marriage and transgenderism are morally out of bounds because they "deny complimentarity." Ah, yes! The famous "argument from plumbing"! You see, because the private parts of same-sex couples don't (in Dreher's understanding) fit together very well, any such relationships must be unnatural. Indeed, he maintains that transgenderism, homosexuality, and bisexuality are all "forms of disordered sexuality." After all, the Bible has "clear teaching" on these subjects.

Well, maybe not so clear. Although Dreher presents himself as a learned scholar on the history of Christianity, he is obviously unaware of—or unconvinced by—some quite cogent recent arguments that the Bible does not unequivocally condemn same-sex relationships.[1] In an ecstasy of fear Dreher states that acknowledging anything but heterosexuality within marriage will lead inexorably to "the deconstruction of any obstructions, in law or in custom, to freely chosen polygamous arrangements." But wait a minute. Wasn't there a person named Solomon who had a thousand wives (300 of whom were concubines)? Dreher cannot resort to the ineffective dodge that this is just a part of the bad Old Testament; he himself draws upon the line "male and female created He them" from Genesis to justify his position, so he is the last person to jettison the Old Testament as theologically invalid.

And yet, Dreher is on to something here. The sexual revolution of the 1960s really did lead to women's liberation, gay liberation, and an increasing acknowledgment of the rights of the transgendered. And Dreher may well be right that these things "signify the final triumph of the Sexual Revolution and the dethroning of Christianity." What Dreher refuses to understand is that every religion has tried to control sex, and every religion has failed. He blandly states, "If Christianity is a true story, then the story the world tells about sexual freedom is a grand deception. It's fake." But what if the converse is true? If Christianity is bogus (as seems overwhelmingly likely), then the story *it* tells about sex must be correspondingly fake.

What is Dreher's solution to this lamentable state of affairs? It is the Benedict Option. We are asked to believe that this fellow, repulsed at the "vice and corruption" of the Roman society of his time (late fifth and early sixth centuries CE), lived as a hermit for three years and then established a series of small communities that allow their adherents to preserve their faith and incidentally "evangelize barbarian peoples." Understandably, Dreher rhapsodizes about the medieval age, when "religion was everywhere . . . as a matter not merely of belief but of experience." Ah, my heart bleeds for such a paradise lost! Dreher has been to Benedictine monasteries here and there and urges fellow Christians to set up similar communities to shield themselves from the horrors of liberal secularism. Indeed, he explicitly states that you should make your home a "domestic monastery"!

Some of Dreher's prescriptions are astoundingly radical. He well understands that brainwashing is the key to preserving what remnants of his faith can be preserved. He will never call it that, but that is what it comes down to. "Tradition," he says, "frees [Christians] from the burden of having to make things up as they go along." Indeed! In other words, it frees them from the burden of thinking. He is appalled that many purported Christians don't even teach their children the rudiments of Christian doctrine; recent surveys indicate not only that more than one-third of Millennials are unchurched, but that many of them do not even know what Christianity is. And so Dreher does not mince words on what he sees as the only viable solution: "It is time for all [sic] Christians to pull their children out of the public school system." Yes, that's right: *all* Christians must shun the public schools as anathema!

But many avowedly Christian schools don't meet Dreher's strict criteria, and so he recommends something called "classical Christian education," a new movement that apparently makes use of both Greco-Roman and Christian texts with the purpose of providing "education that is rightly ordered— that is, one based on the premise that there is a God-given, unified structure to reality and that it is discoverable." But Dreher's account of such schools does not inspire confidence that they are very big on science. And I don't imagine they would allow reading the lascivious Catullus or the *De Rerum Natura* of Lucretius, the poetic disciple of Epicurus. And I imagine they would have to tread rather lightly on the pederasty that was a recognized element of ancient Greek educational practice.

Dreher insists that you have to teach your children Scripture, and he is dismayed that even Evangelicals and Catholics don't make their kids read the Bible. But *which* parts of Scripture, my dear man? The parts that advocate the death penalty for "witches," Sabbath-violators, and gays? The parts that state unequivocally that the earth is flat and that the sun revolves around the earth? The parts that welcome slavery as a fundamental component of society? Dreher curiously fails to mention any of these things.

He is also big on cutting oneself off from television, the Internet, and any other things that might corrupt Christian youth. Smartphones are very bad because they allow easy access to the unlimited porn on the Internet. But he fails to note that the political party he professes to espouse is the very one that has promoted rampant capitalism and consumerism in American society—although to his credit he expresses doubt that even Republicans in the (very short-lived) age of Trump are likely to stem the tide of liberal secularism.

One wonders how plausible any of Dreher's recommendations for his diminishing flock really are. The likelihood that any significant number of Christians ("traditional" or otherwise) will follow him seems to me vanishingly small. David Brooks, one of the token conservative columnists for the *New York Times*, has referred to this book as "already the most discussed and most important religious book of the decade."[2] Well, I guess I don't travel in the right circles, for I've heard nary a peep about it. But in all honesty it warms my heart that Dreher feels so persecuted. A passing comment that Christians are now facing "internal exile from a country we thought was our own" inadvertently gets to the heart of the matter. What Dreher is really complaining about is that Christians—and especially white Christian men—can no longer lord it over gays or blacks or Hispanics or women or atheists or Muslims or any other groups they have long disfavored. It is entirely to be expected that he interprets growing equality for these groups as a baleful sign of the subjugation of his own. And although Dreher denies that he is trying to turn back the clock, that is exactly what he hopes to do. He holds out the pitiable hope that his knots of Christian faithful can ride out the new Dark Age and someday resume control once civilization has collapsed entirely. To which all I can say is: Good luck with that.

Notes

1. See my "The Bible and Gays," *American Rationalist* 61, No. 5 (September/October 2015): 11–12 (a review of two books on the subject).
2. David Brooks, "The Benedict Option," *New York Times* (14 March 2017).

The "Cake Artist" and His Bigotry

Jack Phillips is an *artiste*. Well, okay, he doesn't use the French term, but he does call himself an artist. Phillips is the charming fellow in Colorado who, as a self-styled "cake artist," refused to make a wedding cake for a gay couple who wished to marry. The couple sued, and the Colorado Court of Appeals ruled against him. In a fit of pique, Phillips, instead of going ahead and making the cake for the gay couple, refused to make wedding cakes for anyone. And, predictably, the usual alliance of bigots and religious fanatics (such as the Alliance Defending Freedom) has argued that it is the hapless "artist" who is being punished for the expression of his religion. Curiously, however, Phillips's legal team is arguing that his right to discriminate rests not upon the "free exercise" clause of the First Amendment ("Congress shall make no law . . . prohibiting the free exercise [of religion]"), but the more basic "freedom of speech" clause.

The claim seems, on the face of it, quite bizarre. "Artists" generally do not get to choose the audience for their art. I am not aware that Picasso opened a storefront to sell his wares, nor that he or his agents conducted an interrogation into the social and political views of his potential buyers before selling them a painting. It does not appear that the renowned violin virtuoso Jascha Heifetz demanded that concertgoers fill out a questionnaire stipulating their religious or cultural beliefs before being allowed to listen to him. And yet, Mr. Phillips maintains that "I'm being forced to use my creativity, my talents and my art for an event—a significant religious event—that violates my religious faith." (Let it pass that weddings are not always "religious events," and it is an open question whether the same-sex wedding in question would have been one. Would Mr. Phillips have discriminated against a couple of whatever sort who frankly stated to him that their wedding was going to be conducted by a justice of the peace rather than by some cleric? Or, paradoxically, would this pious artist have waved aside his reservations because the ceremony in question would not involve a church?)

Mr. Phillips magnanimously declares, "I have no problem serving anybody—gay, straight, Muslim, Hindu. Everybody that comes in my door is welcome here, and any of the products I normally sell I'm glad to sell to anybody." Any products, that is, except wedding cakes. But before we lavish praise on the "cake artist" for his open-mindedness, let us pause a moment over exactly what he is saying. He is a fervent Christian—and yet, he is prepared to sell his wares (and here it is unclear whether this includes wedding cakes or not) to people of all faiths, and perhaps even to lowly atheists! Well, he can't be a very good Christian in that case. I mean, doesn't the First Commandment say, "Thou shalt have no other gods before me" (Exodus 20:3)? And yet, this guy is happy to give Muslims and Hindus the sugar rush they so crave! Something doesn't seem quite right here.

Isn't it clear what is going on? Federal and state laws prohibit discrimination on the basis of race, religion, and gender, and neither the "free exercise" of religion nor "freedom of speech" can be used to justify such discrimination. But sexual orientation is not (yet) a protected category, so bigots in certain jurisdictions are free to thumb their noses at gay people in any way they choose.

But the supporters of Mr. Phillips do not quite realize what a can of worms they are opening—nor how the tables could be turned on them in certain situations. If sexual orientation is not a protected category, then political preference certainly isn't. So what is to prevent anyone (whether he is an "artist" or not) from refusing service, say, to Republicans? Indeed, since the Trump administration has recently proposed new rules permitting corporations and other entities to deny free contraception to their workers if they have not merely "religious" but even "moral" objections, why shouldn't those individuals—and there are many of us—who have moral objections to the very existence of Republicans engage in similar discrimination? I am mightily inclined to open a shop for the sole purpose of hanging a sign prominently in the window declaring, "NO REPUBLICANS WILL BE SERVED." (I live in a famously liberal city, so I would not expect to suffer financial harm from such prejudice; indeed, my customer base might actually expand as delighted liberals rush to support me.) This would all be perfectly legal, and there is nothing that Republicans could do about it.

I am writing this column before Mr. Phillips's case is scheduled to be argued at the Supreme Court in December 2017, but there is hope that sanity will prevail. In spite of the recent appointment of the fake justice Neil Gorsuch, the deciding vote is likely to be cast by Anthony Kennedy, who has been more and more forthright in his opposition to prejudice against gay people. I also hope that at least some of the more conservative justices recognize the incredible mischief that would result if discrimination of the sort that Mr. Phillips wishes to practice is sanctioned by the court. We really don't want to live in a society where every shop we go into will require us to state our preferences on a wide variety of subjects and to be summarily denied service if any of those preferences happen to offend the delicate sensibilities of the shop owner.

The Party of Traitors

The question of the day is: How have we reached the stage where an entire political party in this country has in effect descended into treason?

I refer, of course, to the current incarnation of the G.O.P. Let it not be thought that I am echoing a longstanding Republican ploy of demonizing my antagonists by attributing treasonous motivations to mere political differences. Republicans have admittedly perfected this technique, lambasting support for abortion rights, gun control, and even the raising of the minimum wage as some kind of lèse-majesté against truth, justice, and the American way. On the contrary, I am speaking of a party that has gone out of its way to subvert American law and American ideals in ways that could, if it were successful (which, in fact, it won't be), lead us down the road to autocracy.

Let us consider, first, the ineffable Roy S. Moore. To everyone's surprise (especially his own), this "judge," who had twice been thrown off the Alabama Supreme Court for sundry offenses, lost narrowly to a Democrat, Doug Jones, in a special election on December 12 for the U.S. Senate seat vacated by our current "attorney general," Jeff Sessions. I am not interested in the credible accusations from at least nine women that Moore dated and, in at least one instance, molested them when they were underage; these allegations may reveal Moore's despicable character, but not his violations of constitutional law. It is these latter—his refusal to acknowledge the separation of church and state and his truculent denial of the legality of same-sex marriage—that make him such a dangerous figure.

And yet, Moore lost the election by fewer than 22,000 votes. Okay, we're talking about Alabama; and I suppose we should be grateful that at least a certain number of Republicans (including, incredibly, Alabama's other senator, Richard Shelby) refused to support him. But his support remained unwavering among evangelicals in that state. Is it any wonder that Mark Galli, editor of *Christianity Today*, remarked ruefully on the day of the election that "there is already one loser: Christian faith"? The moral uprightness of evangelicals—always a canard except in their own minds—has now been seen as the hollow sham that it is, given the devil's bargain they have made with the Republican party. The short-term political gains they may or may not achieve will be massively outweighed by the long-term harm they will suffer as their hypocrisy and corruption become increasingly evident.

Let us now turn our attention to the action that the Republicans fondly wish will save them from electoral decimation in 2018: the passage of the Frankenstein's monster of a tax "reform" bill at the end of 2017. I refer not to the specifics of the bill, although those are bad enough: the deliberate targeting of "blue" states by capping state and local taxes; the many and numerous gifts to the wealthy, whether it be a lower income tax rate for the super-rich or drastically lower corporate taxes or a virtual elimination of the estate tax; the appalling injustice inherent in the fact that the corporate tax reduction is permanent while the (minimal) tax reductions for the lower and middle class are temporary.

All that is, as I say, bad enough from a policy perspective—and the blatant lies about the bill that were uttered by all manner of special pleaders, from the treasury secretary on down, are worse. The question becomes: how could a majority of G.O.P. members of Congress vote for a bill that was demonstrably unpopular even with their own constituents? One Republican congressman, Chris Collins of New York, inadvertently let the cat out of the bag when he said: "My donors are basically saying get it done or don't ever call me again." Strange: I always thought that politicians were supposed to serve their constitutents, not their wealthy donors. Silly me!

But the rot that afflicts the G.O.P. begins at the tip and filters all the way down to the rank and file. I refer, of course, to our esteemed "president," whose many and various derelictions—growing evidence of his campaign's collusion with the Russian government; his own obstruction of justice in the investigation of that matter; his sexual assaults on dozens of women; his barefaced and unrepentant enrichment of himself by virtue of his office; his reckless and irresponsible tweets, which could easily trigger wars around the world, nuclear or otherwise—are drearily familiar. These issues, any one of which would be grounds for impeachment, are bad enough; transcending them in loathsomeness is the vile toadying of Mr. Trump by nearly every member of the Republican party. The comment by the doddering senator Orrin G. Hatch—who in recent years has systematically destroyed whatever standing as a statesman he once had—is typical: "We are going to make this the greatest presidency we have seen, not only in generations, but maybe ever." Yeah, right. (Oh, wait—I forgot to mention how that eminent historian Mike Huckabee has compared Mr. Trump favorably to Winston Churchill.) Here again, in exchange for certain short-term gains the G.O.P. is happy to become bootlickers and lickspittles of what his own advisers have called a "dope" (or is that an "idiot" or a "moron"?). Well, we'll see how far that gets them.

So what is to be done? Short of carrying out the standard punishment for traitors, an elegantly simple solution presents itself: go out and vote. What could be more satisfying than to give this motley crew of hypocrites, time-servers, dogmatists, and defiers of the public will the gift of a comfortable life as private citizens? That is exactly what will happen to a good many of them before the year is over.

Whether the Republicans' descent into permanent minority status will chasten them and compel them to conduct any kind of introspective assessment of their irremediable corruption is anyone's guess. I, for one, tend to doubt it.

II. The Stupidity Watch

[July/August 2011]

In 1932, one Walter B. Pitkin published *A Short Introduction to the History of Human Stupidity,* a work that is more relevant to our times than to his own. That the widespread stupidity, individually and collectively, of the human race goes far in accounting for the manifold woes of this groaning planet seems evident; H. L. Mencken believed that the number of genuinely intelligent people on this earth amounted to about one-eighth of one percent of the population. But Pitkin emphasizes that the phenomenon of stupidity, seemingly straightforward and even banal, is one of infinite complexity. He writes:

"Stupidity can easily be proved the supreme Social Evil. Three factors combine to establish it as such. First and foremost, the number of stupid people is legion. Secondly, most of the power in business, finance, diplomacy and politics is in the hands of more or less stupid individuals. Finally, high abilities are often linked with serious stupidity, and in such a manner that the abilities shine before all the world while the stupid trait lurks in deep shadow and is discerned only by intimates or by prying newspaper reporters."

That last comment is of relevance in this context, for I hope to present in this column the wondrously diverse instances and ramifications of human stupidity, especially in the areas of religion and politics. My own schedule permits me to read only the *New York Times* daily; and, while I daresay I could cull many more instances of stupidity from other venues—the editorial page of the *Wall Street Journal,* for example, or Fox News, or *Christianity Today*—the *Times* provides a surprisingly rich treasure-trove of imbecility, often presented with a deadpan sobriety that renders it all the more piquant. Without further ado, therefore, let me see what the last several months of idiocy have revealed.

Cappie Poindexter is a twenty-eight-year-old professional basketball player for the New York Liberty, a team in the WNBA. I suppose it is unreasonable to expect intelligent statements, especially on matters of religion and politics, from athletes, but her recent utterance on Twitter, in the aftermath of the devastating earthquake and tsunami in Japan, is worth citing: "What if God was tired of the way they [the Japanese] treated their own people in there [*sic*] own country! Idk guys he makes no mistakes." Elaborating on this utterance, Poindexter later wrote: "u just never knw [*sic*]! They did pearl harbor so u can't expect anything less."

Let me see if I get this straight. Because Japan was responsible for the attack on Pearl Harbor (an attack that killed approximately 2400 people, mostly members of the military), God has punished them seventy years after the fact with a deadly earthquake and tsunami. The United States, on the other hand, even though it killed 120,000 people (mostly civilians) in its atomic attack on Hiroshima and Nagasaki, has apparently been spared God's wrath, although certain people in Louisiana, Alabama, and Missouri might take issue with that point. No doubt this is because we are a "Christian nation"!

It is reported that a federal appeals court has thrown out an earlier ruling that the National Day of Prayer—instituted in 1952 (two years before "under God" was inserted into the Pledge of Allegiance and three years before "In God We Trust" was affixed to every form of U.S. currency) as part of this country's un-remitting attack on "godless" communism—is unconstitutional because the party bringing the suit, the Freedom from Religion Foundation, did not have standing to sue because the proclamation had not caused them any harm. In the learned words of the appeals court, "Hurt feelings differ from legal inju-ry." If an organization that is expressly devoted to ridding the public sphere from impermissible intrusions of religion, in accordance with the First Amendment and other relevant laws, does not have "standing" in this case, it is difficult to decide who does. And as for hurt feelings—I have no particular feelings, hurt or otherwise, about the "In God We Trust" motto I carry on my dwindling supply of currency—but I certainly feel that it is an infringement of my right to be free of religious coercion.

The one genuine conservative on the *New York Times*'s Op-Ed page, a young man named Ross Douthat, provides many moments of unwitting comic relief in an otherwise ponderous section of the paper—which is no doubt why the *Times* hired him. Lately, Douthat ventured into an owlish discussion of hell—specifically, why the belief in and fear of it has declined, and why this is a bad thing. Partly quoting Anthony Esolen (a translator of Dante), Douthat asserts that "the idea of hell is crucial to Western humanism. It's a way of asserting that 'things have meaning'—that earthly life is more than just a series of un-important events, and that 'the use of one man's free will, at one moment, can mean life or death . . . salvation or damnation.'" It doesn't seem to occur to Douthat to ponder the numerous paradoxes of the hell concept, e.g., *eter-nal* punishment (a very long time, indeed) for mere lack of belief in a given deity or belief in the "wrong" deity. And, of course, the notion that neither heaven nor hell exist except in the brainwashed fantasies of the devout is something Douthat can never bring himself to countenance.

In my eternally relevant, and apparently unanswerable, query, "Why are con-servatives such twits?," some fragments of an answer may come from the recrudescence of the ineffable Newt Gingrich, who is attempting to resurrect his none too fragrant political career by running for president—and, to boot, as a devoted family man and Family Values protector. Inspired by his most recent mistress-turned-wife, Gingrich proclaims himself a Roman Catholic. Along the way he makes no secret of where his religious prejudices lie. He accuses President Obama and others of leading a "secular socialist machine"; he maintains that gays and lesbians are determined to impose a "gay and secular fascism" upon this country; and so on and so forth. The use of the word "secular" is curious, given that it is obviously a code-word—indeed, a euphemism—for "atheist"; and one would think that branding his perceived opponents as frank atheists (in politics, it hardly matters whether such accusations are true or not) would be even more effective propaganda, since atheists are—more than gays, Mormons, and Muslims—the most suspected minorities in this putatively secular republic.

[*September/October 2011*]

When I am not being a professional atheist, I am a critic of supernatural fiction. This is not as paradoxical as it seems, for few writers, readers, and critics of supernatural fiction actually believe in the supernatural, which is used largely for metaphorical or symbolic purposes. One of the most popular writers of today, surpassing even the phenomenal Stephen King, is one Dean R. Koontz. While King is in general a good liberal (although he doesn't like abortion), Koontz is very much on the right wing of the spectrum, both politically and religiously. He converted to Roman Catholicism in college because it gave him answers to his questions about the purpose of life and because of its "intellectual rigor"!

I recently had the dubious privilege of reading Koontz's bestseller *Phantoms* (1983). In this novel, Koontz posits an age-old entity who is not actually Satan himself, but who may perhaps have given rise to the myth of Satan and other such "evil" creatures. Koontz's moralizing in this novel is singularly inept. First he makes the extraordinary assertion that "There's evil in nature," referring to "the blind maliciousness of earthquakes" and "the uncaring evil of cancer"—as if "evil" could somehow be manifested by entities other than human beings, who are the only creatures within our purview who have a (socially constructed) sense of right and wrong. Then, after various maunderings about whether the creature is actually the Devil or merely the source of the legend of the Devil, a character learnedly opines: "If the shape-changer *was* the Satan of mythology, perhaps the evil in human beings isn't a reflection of the Devil; perhaps the Devil is only a reflection of the savagery and brutality of our own kind. Maybe what we've done is . . . create the Devil in our own image." If Koontz expects this epitome of the obvious to pass as profound philosophical disquisition, then perhaps he is underestimating even the admittedly low intelligence of his chosen audience.

In the final frenetic days before the passage of a gay marriage law by the New York State Legislature, the fulminations against the bill reached epic, and ludicrous, proportions. One learned legislator (a Democrat, surprisingly enough), Dov Hikind, waved a copy of the Hebrew Bible and shouted, "You want to tell God he doesn't know what he's talking about?" Hikind would probably have greater success as a straight man in a comedy routine, for it would be difficult to find a juicier set-up line than this. So God is never wrong, eh, Dov? Well, aside from the fact that, to my knowledge, there is not a single passage in the Hebrew Bible mandating marriage solely between a man and a woman, we have such other dicta as the death penalty for violating the Sabbath (Exod. 31:15, Num. 15:35), the death penalty for practicing homosexuals (Lev. 20:13), the ownership of wives by their husbands (the Tenth Commandment: Exod. 20:17), the bland acknowledgment of slavery as a normal feature of human society (the Fourth and Tenth Commandments: Exod. 20:10, 17), the belief that the sun revolves around the earth (Josh. 10:12–13), and so on and so forth. Aside from the minor caveat that the constitution and laws of this country are not based on the Bible, Hebrew or Christian, one should ask Mr. Hikind how many of the above tenets he would like to see enacted into law.

The Catholic Church of course became embroiled in the controversy, the ineffable Archbishop Timothy M. Dolan not hesitating to state that the homosexual lifestyle was "immoral." But—as he was forced to declare when he was criticized for the remark—he didn't mean to offend anyone! Surely we have long passed the stage when the Catholic Church can lecture anyone on morality.

The ineffability of the current crop of Republican candidates for president—which now includes Gov. Rick "Hallelujah!" Perry—is indicated by Mitt Romney's recent remark, in the face of a heckler who demanded higher taxes on corporations, that "Corporations are people, my friend." The comment reminds us of a celebrated passage in one of Robert G. Ingersoll's essays arguing against the notion that the United States is a "Christian nation": "A nation is a corporation. To repeat a familiar saying, 'It has no soul.' There can be no such thing as a Christian corporation. Several Christians may form a corporation, but it can hardly be said that the corporation thus formed was included in the atonement." One would have thought that this line of reasoning would appeal to the Mormon Romney.

On a somewhat related subject, that of polygamy (which, contrary to current usage, should and must mean both a man with multiple wives and a woman with multiple husbands, or any other combination imaginable), I note that a man in Utah with four "wives" (to only one of whom is legally married) and sixteen children is suing the state to be left alone to pursue his lifestyle as he (and, presumably, his wives) wish. An editorialist in the *New York Times* unearthed Supreme Court Justice Antonin Scalia's celebrated remark (made when the court, in 2003, overturned a Texas law that criminalized sodomy) that the court was now paving the way toward legalization of "bigamy, same-sex marriage, adult incest, prostitution, masturbation, adultery, fornication, bestiality and obscenity." This is a rather odd "parade of horribles." Can Scalia, for all his saturation in Catholic doctrine, really find masturbation and fornication so dreadful? The latter term has become so antiquated that it can only be used today for comic purposes. Even adultery is an act that the state can have no legitimate purpose in criminalizing, and the few states that retain adultery as a criminal act rarely prosecute it. What century is Scalia living in? As for polygamy, I echo the comments of Ambrose Bierce, who repeatedly said that, until it becomes mandatory, he had no objection to people having as many wives or husbands as they choose—so long, of course, as the choice is genuinely and freely made.

For all that this column is devoted to the exposure and ridicule of the widespread and multifarious phenomenon of stupidity, we should now and again pause to acknowledge those individuals, few as they may be, who struggle against intellectual darkness—what might be called the "up from stupidity" syndrome. We are now presented with two shining examples of the practice. About a decade ago, one Bethany Patchin, then an eighteen-year-old college student, wrote an article in an evangelical Web magazine that Christians should not kiss before marriage. (Yes, that's *kiss*—meaning, *a fortiori*, that cuddling, necking, and still more obscene acts, up to and including the dreaded "fornication," are also outlawed.) As luck would have it, Bethany met a like-minded young man, Sam Torode, who initially opposed the smooching ban (it would "drive young Christian men mad with desire" [!], he wrote in a letter to the editor), but ultimately came to agree with her. He and Bethany met, courted each other, and married. Then they wrote a treatise, *Open Embrace: A Protestant Couple Rethinks Contraception.*

The thrust of this book is that all forms of "artificial" contraception should be rejected in favor of what used to be called the rhythm method—tracking carefully a woman's ovulation and limiting sexual intercourse to days when she is not fertile. (Why this practice is to be considered any less "artificial" than any other is not apparent.) The book became something of a best-seller, feeding into a growing anti-contraception movement among conservative Protestants. But lo and behold!—a miracle occurred. By 2006 the couple declared that they no longer believed in this "natural" contraception, and by 2009 they were divorced. Bethany now uses birth control and even voted for Barack Obama for president.

What happened? If I may paraphrase the stale old joke of political conservatives, a non-fundamentalist is one who has been mugged by reality. Bethany came to realize that her anti-contraception stance in youth was a conservative rebellion against her "middle-ground evangelical" parents (I have to take her word for it that there are such people). In her book, she also stated that "having children (or adopting them) brings husbands and wives closer together and expands the community of love"—something that marriage-boosters have stated for centuries without a scintilla of proof. More pertinently, the couple realized that "natural family planning" is radically opposed to the human body's natural sexual rhythms, both male and female; indeed, they have daringly stated that it is "a theological attack on women to always require that abstinence during the time of the wife's peak sexual desire (ovulation) for the entire duration of her fertile life, except for the handful of times when she conceives."

Both Bethany and Sam attend "liberal" Christian churches, which from our perspective might be considered a small mercy. Bethany has gone so far as to say that she is a "secular Christian," whatever that may be. Sam, for his part, has gone into comedy writing—and his latest work is a charming little treatise called *The Dirty Parts of the Bible!*

[November/December 2011]

Iain Banks is a Scottish writer whose first novel, *The Wasp Factory* (1984), contains this illuminating passage, referring to a character named (I kid you not) Leviticus, who was "a person of such weapons-grade stupidity his mental faculties would probably have improved with the onset of senile dementia." This remark has struck me with especial force as I watch in amazement the antics of the current batch of hopeless hopefuls vying for the Republican nomination for president.

The hapless Michele Bachmann is perhaps too easy a target for this column, but her notorious comment, in regard to Governor Rick Perry's plan (never put into effect) that teenage girls be vaccinated against cervical cancer, that the vaccine may be dangerous has been widely reported. Evidently she came to this view—entirely refuted by medical science—by talking to a single person, a mother whose daughter purportedly developed mental retardation after taking the vaccine. (It must be evident that the poor girl was only heeding the inexorable call of heredity. The apple does not, after all, fall very far from the tree.) Bachmann then compounded her folly at another presidential debate. When Perry claimed he was "offended" at accusations that he signed the executive order on the vaccine to bring in revenue to a campaign donor who made the vaccine, Bachmann shot back: "I'm offended for all the little girls and the parents that didn't have a choice." She apparently didn't catch on to the fact that the Texas Legislature rescinded the order before it could be put into effect. Perry, for his part, compounded his own buffoonery by later apologizing for the executive order—the one sensible thing he has done in his undistinguished governorship.

The shock waves following New York State's passing of a gay marriage law continue to reverberate in amusing ways. We are now faced with a town clerk in upstate New York, one Rose Marie Belforti, a devout Christian who refuses to issue a marriage license to a lesbian couple. The *New York Times* noted that Ms. Belforti read to a reporter "a passage from the first chapter of Romans, which she says condemns homosexual activity, offering it as an explanation for her stance." The passage in question is no doubt this one, referring to various unspecified but clearly unsavory characters: "For this cause God gave them up unto vile affections: for even their women did change the natural use into that which is against nature" (Romans 1:26). It does not seem that Ms. Belforti knows what a can of worms she is opening. If United States law really were based on the Bible, then we would have to institute (or re-institute) the death penalty for Sabbath-violators (Exod. 31:15), the death penalty for practicing homosexuals (Lev. 20:13), and, in general, the institution of slavery (Exod. 20:17 and many other passages). Possibly that would be acceptable to Ms. Belforti—who, incidentally, has the gall to say about her case, "This is about religious freedom. This is not about trashing gay people."

Jim Daly, president of the right-wing "family values" group Focus on the Family, protests that gay activists are asking Microsoft and other major corporations to cease its association with "hate" groups. Daly maintains that his group's opposition to gay rights (including gay marriage) is strictly a result of "a deeply held belief that God's design for human sexuality lies within the lifelong context of one-man, one-woman marriage." (We've all seen how well that has worked out.) Not long after this luminous remark, one Bryan Fischer, chief spokesman for the Family Research Council, was in the news because on his radio show he likened gay rights advocates to domestic terrorists, going on to say (in the words of the *New York Times*) that "gay men and lesbians should be barred from public office and repeating the discredited theory that homosexuals built the Nazi party." On top of this, the learned Mr. Fischer devised the novel view that Mormons, Muslims, and others (no doubt including atheists) should not enjoy First Amendment protections because these are reserved only for Christians! But of course the Family Research Council is not a "hate" group. Maybe it would best be identified as a "strongly dislike" group.

I thought it might be refreshing to provide a non-political instance of stupidity, since the widespread prevalence of political ninnies is at times too depressing to contemplate. We go (where else?) to Florida, where a psychic has been arrested for absconding with some $40 million (yes, that's $40,000,000) in cash, goods, and property from various clients. And what service did she provide? Evidently she persuaded these bright people to give them all their money so that it could "wash away" curses, cure health problems, and change their fortunes. (Well, it certainly did that.) A good half of this money came from a single person—one Jude Deveraux, a woman who made her fortune by writing romance novels! As a struggling writer I find it hard to imagine how anyone can make $20 million by this method. Her ability to please legions of morons must be regarded as something of a gift—but then, it takes one to know one.

And to conclude with some laugh-out-loud imbecilities:

Nikki R. Haley, Republican governor of South Carolina, has required state workers to answer phones with the following purportedly cheerful message: "It's a great day in South Carolina." I am sorry to report that it's never a great day if one is forced to live in South Carolina.

An evangelical pastor, in reference to Mitt Romney, has declared Mormonism a "cult." A more pungent instance of the pot calling the kettle black would be difficult to find.

[January/February 2012]

Some time ago the *New York Times* published a lengthy op-ed piece by Karl W. Giberson (a former professor of physics) and Randall J. Stephens (an associate professor of history), both of them employed at some institution of higher [sic] learning called Eastern Nazarene College. They are the authors of a treatise called *The Anointed: Evangelical Truth* [sic] *in a Secular Age*. All this does not sound very promising, but the title of the article is of interest: "The Evangelical Rejection of Reason." Sadly, the article does not quite live up to the provocativeness of its title.

The authors' main contention—"the rejection of science seems to be part of a politically monolithic red-state fundamentalism, textbook evidence of an unyielding ignorance on the part of the religious." In the end, the authors hope (and, no doubt, pray) that the insularity and anti-intellectualism of evangelicals can fade and that they can come to accept at least some phases of "secular" knowledge, somehow managing to incorporate it into their overarching theology. They contend that some evangelicals do manage to "recognize that the Bible does not condemn evolution and says next to nothing about gay marriage."

This view that the Bible can somehow accommodate evolution—a view embraced by the Catholic Church—requires somewhat greater intellectual contortions than might be evident on the surface. The idea is that God somehow either fostered or "allowed" evolution to take place. Let it pass that there is not the slightest shred of evidence for such an assertion. The notion, even if it is accepted, falls squarely into the fallacy identified by Occam's razor: one must not multiply causation needlessly. If evolution by natural selection is in itself a sufficient cause for the phenomena it seeks to explain (and it is, otherwise it would not have been posited), then the idea that God "allowed" evolution to occur creates an extra level of causation that must, by the principle of Occam's razor, be cut away. No doubt Mr. Occam, a very pious medieval gent, would be horrified that God is the greatest casualty of his logical razor, but such I fear is the case.

Crockett Keller, a gun instructor in (where else?) Texas, recently made news by declaring that he would refuse to teach anyone who was either a "socialist liberal" [sic] or a "non-Christian Arab or Muslim." Far be it from me to dictate to Mr. Keller whom he can teach, but his charming selectivity raises some interesting questions.

Let us suppose we live in the Bizarro World and I am a gun instructor. I might feel obliged not to accept Christian Caucasians in my class. Was not Timothy McVeigh a Caucasian and a Christian (raised, indeed, as a devout Catholic)? One must not allow such people to have weapons. . . .

One Daniel Avila, who is a lawyer and policy adviser for the United States Conference of Roman Catholic Bishops, asserted in a recent issue of the official newspaper of the Roman Catholic diocese of Boston, *The Pilot*, that homosexuality may be caused by the Devil. In the learned words of Mr. Avila, "the scientific evidence of how same-sex attraction most likely may be created provides a credible basis for a spiritual explanation that indicts the devil." (Incidentally, what's with the non-capitalization of "the devil"? It seems to me vaguely disrespectful. As Ambrose Bierce once noted, "The Devil is a sacred personage (the Fourth Person of the Trinity, as an Irishman might say) and his name must not be taken in vain.")

The paper quickly apologized for the article, stating that the church "does not have a definitive theory on the origins of same-sex attraction." What a relief! One might otherwise be compelled to believe that the Catholic Church itself is one of the safest havens for the Adversary of Souls.

The legions of anti-abortionists in this country, ever determined to find novel ways to turn every fertile woman into an incubator, are now proposing something they call a "heartbeat bill." The idea is to outlaw abortion whenever a heartbeat is detectable in the fetus—something that usually occurs six to eight weeks into a pregnancy. The result would be the effective banning of 80 to 90 percent of all abortions. Such a bill is about to be brought before the Ohio state legislature, and plans are afoot to take it to other states as well. (The bill, even if passed, is likely to be ruled unconstitutional by most federal courts; the thinking is that the Supreme Court will take up the matter and thereby overturn *Roe v. Wade*.)

Our right-to-life friends, who seem so concerned with fetal life but somewhat less so with the undoubtedly living, breathing existences of pregnant women, death-row inmates, and other contemptibles, are lucky that they are not advocating what I might call a "brain-scan bill." If one's life were to be dependent on brain activity, I fear that the abortion and capital punishment rates would skyrocket.

Rick Santorum is a pious and humble man. Some months ago he declared that his 1994 election as senator from Pennsylvania was guided by a divine hand: "And I really felt blessed that I knew at that moment, when I won, I had a constituency of One."

There is a refreshing candor in this frank admission that Santorum was not planning to heed the wishes of those who actually elected him, but that is a small point. A moderator at one of the recent Republican presidential debates, no doubt inspired by the Devil, proceeded to ask Santorum what message God was sending him when he lost a re-election bid in 2006.

Santorum could not come up with an answer.

[*March/April 2012*]

It is well known that, in spite of the Supreme Court's ban on prayer in public schools, the prohibition is widely flouted, especially in the South. A "traveling evangelist" named Christian Chapman recently opined that non-Christians should not object to such prayers, since it is no worse than Christians being forced to hear about evolution every day. I don't think Mr. Chapman realizes the can of worms he is opening. The theory of evolution may or may not be heretical, but another doctrine—the heliocentric theory—most definitely is, as it specifically contradicts a passage in Joshua (10:12–13) that clearly indicates that the sun revolves around the earth. Doesn't Mr. Chapman know that the heliocentric theory was deemed heretical by the Catholic church up to the year 1822? (Imagine, incidentally, the discomfiture of Catholics at that time. One day it was heresy to believe that the earth revolved around the sun; the next day it was heresy to believe the converse. And the change was necessitated, not by the accumulation of new evidence, but by the fiat of a man in a funny hat!)

The two conservative columnists on the *New York Times* regularly provide much amusement at their own expense. David Brooks frequently places a dunce-cap on his head by attempting to be a philosopher, economist, or sociologist without the slightest expertise in any of these disciplines. (Contrast the *Times*'s leading liberal columnist, Paul Krugman, who won the Nobel Prize for economics.) A young man named Ross Douthat, taking over after William Kristol's stint as resident buffoon was abruptly terminated, is also engagingly fatuous. Recently he protested President Obama's refusal to grant exemptions to a wide array of religious institutions—hospitals, schools, and charities—that would have allowed them to refuse to provide contraception and other services mandated by the new health care law. Douthat, like the Catholic Church, sees this as an infringement of their religious liberty; but in fact it is a striking blow for the religious freedom of any of those non-Catholics who are obliged to use the services in question. Why should such people, who may have no option but to go to a Catholic hospital, be forced to accept Catholic doctrine on contraception and other issues as the price for being served? It was exactly this kind of religious coercion that our laws were designed to prevent.

A brave teenager in Cranston, R.I., sixteen-year-old Jessica Ahlquist, has protested the existence of an eight-foot-high plaque—I kid you not, eight feet high!—in her public school addressed to "Our Heavenly Father" and concluding with "Amen," the intervening prayer containing such pearls of worldly wisdom as "Grant us each day the desire to do our best." Ahlquist, an atheist, rightly contended that the plaque was a violation of the Establishment Clause of the First Amendment, and a federal judge agreed with her, so the plaque has been covered with a tarpaulin. Predictably, Ahlquist has been the target of an unconscionable campaign of hatred and abuse in this Roman Catholic city, with predictable death threats directed at her—how typical for a faith that proclaims itself a religion of love and mercy! One recent graduate of the high school, Brittany Lanni, shot back with this bit of luminosity: "If you don't believe in that [prayer], take all the money out of your pocket, because every dollar bill says, 'In God We Trust.'" Exactly, my dear girl! (Can anyone come up with a counter-example of any person named Brittany—or Britney—not being an intellectual dwarf?) Will any of us live to see the day when this offensive and transparently unconstitutional motto is eliminated from our currency?

I'm no particular fan of Fidel Castro, although one has to have a grudging admiration for his ability to be such a thorn in the side of the United States for more than half a century. Lately he uttered some words about the Republican presidential campaign, as follows: "The selection of a Republican candidate for the presidency of this globalized and expansive empire is—and I mean this seriously—the greatest competition of idiocy and ignorance that has ever been."

To this there's not much to add. Any chance of a show for Fidel on CNN?

One of my inveterate vices is a rabid interest in professional sports. I suspect that even those unfamiliar with the notable players of the National Football League have heard of one Tim Tebow, the quarterback of the Denver Broncos—a man who has become celebrated for wearing his piety on his jersey. Indeed, so inspirational has he become that, in a recent poll, 43% of Americans believe that God assisted him in some of his come-from-behind victories during the regular season and playoffs.

We are, then, faced with a delicate theological conundrum in witnessing Mr. Tebow's humiliating loss to the New England Patriots, by the score of 45–10, in a playoff game that ended the Broncos' season. How are we to account for this defeat? Surely it cannot be said that the Patriots were inspired by Satan, for that would mean that Satan is more powerful than God (or, at a minimum, knows how to call better plays on the football field). Are we to take away some kind of lesson—say, in humility? Or must we resort to the old "God works in mysterious ways" dodge?

I, for one, have some hope that we have made a few grudging skeptics out of that benighted 43%.

In a debate in early January, Newt Gingrich declared that the "sanctity of marriage" must be preserved.

I don't think there is anything I can add to this.

[*May/June 2012*]

It is, perhaps, too easy to attack Rick Santorum for both his political and his religious views—there is really no sport in it. In spite of his recent withdrawal from the campaign to secure the Republican nomination for president, he is worth discussing because he so perfectly symbolizes how the entire

Republican party, and in particular its religious/conservative wing, appears to have gone collectively insane.

I am not sure many prospective voters grasp quite how bizarre Santorum's views are. For example, he announced in a speech to students of Ava Maria University in Florida that "Satan has his sights on the United States of America." Lest one think that he was speaking metaphorically, the rest of his remarks make it evident that he believes literally in the Devil: "Satan is attacking the great institutions of America, using those great vices of pride, vanity and sensuality as the root to attack all of the strong plants that has [sic] so deeply rooted in the American tradition. . . . The Father of Lies has his sights on what you would think the Father of Lies would have his sights on: a good, decent, powerful, influential country—the United States of America."

This nostalgia for a fancied golden age of morality and decency in this country is popular among conservatives, and especially religious conservatives, who are infuriated that they can no longer force Christianity upon the rest of us through prayer in public schools and much else besides. That golden age certainly was one for a tiny fraction of white males—not so good, though, if you were a woman (who couldn't vote until 1920), an African American (considered three-fifths of a human being until 1865), a gay person, or a member of many other disfavored groups, among whom atheists are always high on the list. The incredible thing, for the devout Catholic Santorum, is how ignorant he is that his own sect was for many decades the object of extreme prejudice by the evangelical Protestants whom he hopes to whip up into a frenzy.

As for the present, Santorum sees dangers all around. Protestantism, in his view, "is in shambles. It is gone from the world of Christianity as I see it." This might come as a surprise to those of us who are aware that one-quarter of the American population identifies itself as fundamentalist. But the pinnacle of Santorum's sage analysis of contemporary culture is his attack on President Obama and liberals in general (let it pass that Obama is in no sense a liberal—you'll never convince any Republican of that): "They are taking faith and crushing it. Why? When you marginalize faith in America, when you remove the pillar of God-given rights, then what's left is the French Revolution. What's left is a government that gives you rights. What's left are no unalienable rights. What's left is a government that will tell you who you are, what you'll do and when you'll do it. What's left in France became the guillotine."

Ah, now we're getting to the heart of the matter! Santorum fears that his head, and the heads of all the other pious citizens in this country, will be lopped off by crazed liberals! And yet, you'd think there would be a certain economy in such a procedure, since all those heads are clearly not being used to any purpose.

I have never owned a gun. I have—in spite of having lived for seventeen years in the New York City area—never seen a gun carried by anyone but a police officer, or ever seen one fired. It was, therefore, illuminating for me to read an op-ed piece by one Seamus McGraw, who maintains that it is somehow more humane and sporting to kill a deer using a flintlock rifle rather than with ordinary weapons. For you see, deer in his part of the country (he lives in rural Pennsylvania) no longer have any predators and are overrunning the region, causing untold environmental damage. It does not occur to McGraw that the chief culprits of environmental degradation are the species called *Homo sapiens*. I would be happy to hunt Mr. McGraw, with a flintlock rifle or any other weapon of his choosing, so long as he himself has none, just like the deer he kills so regretfully. A judicious culling of the human race does seem to be in order.

Wendy E. Long is one of several individuals vying to run against Kirsten E. Gillibrand, the Democratic senator from New York. Long is described as a staunch (is there any other kind?) social conservative. She is much enamored of the "slippery slope" argument, being opposed to gay marriage because, in her judgment, it could open the door to humans marrying animals.

Let us consider this prospect for a moment. Given the dismal state of human marriage, where one in two unions end in divorce, I imagine you could do far worse than tying the knot with Fido or Snowball. At least one would avert the possibility of inadvertently marrying a Wall Street broker, a televangelist, or a Republican.

The Catholic Church is taking the novel and morally upright stance of going after various victims' support groups that formed after the sexual abuse scandal that has rocked the church for a decade. William Donohue, president of the Catholic League for Religious and Civil Rights, noted keenly: "There's a growing consensus on the part of the bishops that they had better toughen up and go out and buy some good lawyers to get tough. We don't need altar boys."

But of course the church does need them—for another purpose.

[July/August 2012]

Bill Donohue, the loudmouth president of the Catholic League for Religious and Civil Rights, has submitted to the humiliation of purchasing space on the *New York Times*' op-ed page for a screed that could not have found acceptance as an actual submission. He has further brought ridicule upon himself by the subject of his miniature treatise. He has protested Jon Stewart's "making fun of Fox News" for not addressing the Republican Party's "war on women."

Stewart went on to say: "Maybe women could protect their reproductive organs from unwanted medical intrusions with vagina mangers." The humorless Donohue soberly opined: "How ironic that in the name of defending women, he grossly degraded them, while also insulting Christian sensibilities."

Donohue should learn that you cannot win against satirists. In the first place, it is plain to anyone (including myself, who did not see Stewart's presentation) that the true object of satire is the hypocrisy and phony piety of Republican politicians (not to mention the religious demagogues, like Donohue, who support them), who loudly trumpet their devotion to Christian dogma but behave in ways that would have made Jesus seethe with righteous indignation. In the second place, Donohue seems unaware that satire is *meant* to be offensive—that is its very purpose and *raison d'être*. Donohue pleaded for a boycott against Stewart on the part of his advertisers, but it has been as successful as most such pleas tend to be.

In the wake of North Carolina voters' regrettable approval of a constitutional amendment outlawing gay marriage, some amusing theological buffooneries emerged. The Rev. Billy Graham (who, in all honesty, I had thought had already departed this life and drifted into the comfort of virgins and flowing wine—oops! wrong religion) took out an ad in several North Carolina newspapers several days before the vote, thundering: "At 93, I never thought we would have to debate the definition of marriage. The Bible is clear—God's definition of marriage is between a man and a woman."

Well, I fear it is not so clear as all that, my dear sir. Surely we all recall the biblical stories of King Solomon with his thousand wives (300 of whom were concubines)? And what of King David? It would seem that he had eight wives and any number of concubines, with several of whom he had children. The point seems to be of particular relevance, now that we have a Mormon as a presidential candidate. And surely there must be no little eyebrow-raising over David's unusual friendship with Jonathan, the son of Saul, who is explicitly stated to have "loved" David (1 Samuel 18:1 etc.)? I guess I'd better not go there. . . .

And now we are regaled with a hysterical sermon by one Charles L. Worley, pastor of the Providence Road Baptist Church in Maiden, N.C., who declared: "Build a great, big, large fence—150 or 100 mile [sic] long—put all the lesbians in there. . . . Do the same thing for the queers and the homosexuals and have that fence electrified so they can't get out. . . . And you know what? In a few years they'll die out . . . do you know why? They can't reproduce!" Let us bypass the legal and moral niceties of this scenario; one has to wonder at the learned pastor's grasp of simple biology. How does he think gays and lesbians came to be in the first place? By reproducing *with each other*? Is it not plain that gay and lesbian children are born to heterosexual parents every day of the year? It would seem that the only infallible way to nip the dreaded homosexual plague in the bud is for the entire human race to cease procreating altogether—a consummation devoutly to be wished, if the average specimen of humanity in any sense resembles the Rev. Mr. Worley.

On the other side of the political spectrum there is also a bit of folly. One Susan Schneider, pastor of a Lutheran church in Madison, Wis., admitted that "The Bible has some nasty things to say about homosexuality," but she went on to add: "As Lutherans, we don't give each part of the Bible equal weight. Luther described the Bible as 'the cradle of Christ.' The whole book contains the story of God, but some parts touch the baby more closely than others." This is precisely the kind of "cafeteria Christianity" (picking and choosing what one wants to believe out of a text that is presumably divinely inspired) that has brought such ridicule to even liberal Christianity. Why is it that it is exactly those parts of the Bible (e.g., those advocating slavery, subjugation of women, and the death penalty for homosexuals, Sabbath-violators, and sundry other heretics) that cannot be reconciled with the tenets of modern civilized society that are now seen to be somehow less "inspired" than others? What is the *authority* for brushing these passages under the rug aside from preventing embarrassment?

We now learn that the United Methodist Church has voted against changing its longstanding policy stating that homosexuality is "incompatible with Christian teaching." One of the debaters at the Methodist convention in Tampa, Fla., was an African delegate who stated in Swahili that saying a homosexual was created by God was like saying that "God created me to live with animals." As a cat lover, I resemble that remark. After more than half a century of existence in this vale of tears, I would much prefer the company of animals than of almost any human being I can think of. I suppose the learned African can be excused for his ignorance of the fact that his countrymen were, for centuries, regarded as little better than animals when they were brought over against their will to this land of freedom and liberty.

[*September/October 2012*]

Is it possible to have a rational discussion about guns?

Evidently not, at least on the side of gun rights advocates, who apparently feel that even the slightest concession in the direction of gun control amounts to a humiliating capitulation. The gun nuts, you see, are valiant patriots who are amassing a formidable arsenal to guard against the very high probability that jack-booted thugs from the federal government will come to take them away. I'm sorry to report that these charming people are indulging in a slight elevation of their sociopolitical importance: why the government, amidst all its other worries, would have the slightest interest in these people is more than I can fathom.

My interest in this issue has been renewed by a series of disturbing events. First there was a news report in June in which the tactic of "microstamping" (the process of stamping a numeric code on shell casings so that the gun they were fired from can be identified) has been predictably opposed by the National Rifle Association. As always, the NRA and like-minded groups are engaging in lies and distortion to make their case. The National Shooting Sports Foundation claims that microstamping would increase the cost of a firearm by more than $200; in fact, the added cost would come to about $12.

Then there was the horrific shooting of dozens of people in a Colorado movie theatre by a gunman armed with multiple weapons, including an assault rifle. It was only the jamming of that rifle that prevented the killing of even more people. And yet, the NRA has resolutely argued against the renewal of the ban on assault weapons. In my grotesque ignorance, I fail to see why anyone would want an assault rifle. Surely one cannot use it for hunting. (And don't tell me that I'm obliged to "respect" the rights of hunters: the idea of respecting anyone who kills a defenseless creature *for sport* is, in all honesty, obscene.) Do you want to practice shooting an assault weapon on a rifle range? Well, why not have the range stock the weapons and rent them out?

Isn't it time we considered the NRA a terrorist organization? Isn't it in the forefront of the inconceivable opposition to banning the sale of assault weapons even to those on the terrorism watch list? If this isn't "material support for terrorism" (now a federal offense), I don't know what is. (Incidentally, 82% of NRA members actually support such a ban, meaning that the NRA leadership is not only an enabler of terrorists but anti-democratic to boot.)

The absurdity continues. At the Republican national convention in Tampa, the local police will not be allowed to ban concealed handguns for those with legal permits, but will be allowed to ban . . . squirt guns. Maybe, like the Wicked Witch of the West, Republicans are allergic to water. And we now hear of a man in Maryland who owned twenty-five (25) guns, along with a T-shirt with the charming emblem "Guns don't kill people, I do." Mercifully, this patriot was arrested before he could act on his fantasies.

The paranoia of gun supporters appears to no know bounds. Right-wingers (but no one else) are fixated on the botched "Fast and Furious" program by the ATF, which allowed American-bought guns to cross the border into Mexico. Some see a crafty and despicable plot behind this very failure. The sage chief executive of the NRA, Wayne LaPierre, opined: "There's a belief among a lot of people—and I believe it, too—that Fast and Furious was a political attack on the Second Amendment and that the Justice Department facilitated a crime to further their gun control political agenda."

Americans' obsession with guns is about as close to insanity as anything I can imagine—and, to my mind, it is worse and more harmful than their obsession with religion. Indeed, Americans embrace gun ownership as if it were a religion, with all the dogmatism, intolerance, and irrationality that religions foster.

I suppose it is unfair to pick on Ross Douthat, the one genuinely conservative member of the *New York Times*'s op-ed page. Whereas his fellow (moderate) conservative, David Brooks, is merely an intellectual cipher, repeatedly engaging in vapid discussions of subjects on which he has no expertise, Douthat can be actively offensive in his ignorance. He naturally took the side of Dan Cathy, the president of the fast-food chain Chick-fil-A, who unequivocally declared his support of "the biblical definition of the family unit" (which one?—the polygamy plainly advocated by the Old Testament or the monogamy decreed by Jesus Christ?) and his resolute opposition to same-sex marriage. In response, according to Douthat, "mayors and an alderman in several American cities threatened to prevent the delicious [!] chicken chain from opening new outlets." In the first place, this is factually false: none of these people made any such threat, but merely suggested that Chick-fil-A would not be welcome if it practiced discrimination against its clientele. Douthat sees all this as an issue in the "free exercise" of religion, and so it is. No one is denying Mr. Cathy the "free exercise" of his religion in advocating his views, but Douthat would seemingly want to muzzle those who oppose him from the "free exercise" of their own views. Freedom of religion does not mean freedom from criticism.

In the wake of the Supreme Court's surprising upholding of most of the provisions of the Affordable Care Act, Republican presidential candidate Mitt Romney stated, in reference to the so-called individual mandate (the requirement that all uninsured persons secure health insurance or suffer a monetary penalty): "The Supreme Court is the highest court in the nation, and it said that it's a tax, so it's a tax."

On this reasoning, Mr. Romney is presumably a supporter of abortion rights, since the Supreme Court has repeatedly stated since 1973 that abortion is legal. This returns him to a position he once held in his saner days.

[*November/December 2012*]

I am writing this in early October, in the sublime confidence that President Barack Obama will cruise to victory when the first Tuesday after the first Monday in November rolls around. He will do so in spite of one of the most incredibly deceitful and despicable campaigns ever conducted by the Republican party—and that's saying something. The deliberate and shameless lies mouthed by Mitt Romney and his lapdog Paul D. Ryan; the bare-faced voter suppression laws passed by Republican governors and their stooges in state legislatures; and the millions of dollars of campaign money offered by casino magnates, hedge fund managers, and other deep-pocketed reactionaries hoping to profit from Republican policies—all these things will go for naught. We may still be plagued with a conservative Supreme Court and a Tea Party–dominated House of Representatives for some time, but that is a cross we must all bear.

But I come to you today, my friends, to say that liberation is at hand. Hallelujah! For the plain fact of the matter is that the Republican Party, in its current incarnation, is overwhelmingly white, male, old, and fat—not a good combination! The demographics are all against them. There will come a time, perhaps within the next thirty years, when whites will be a statistical minority in this country. With due apologies to all those Caucasians out there, this election—regardless of its outcome—appears to be the last futile stand of the American white man. When Texas flips to the Democrats, as it will in due course of time, Republicans will become unelectable on the national stage. There may still be pockets of conservatism here and there, especially in Southern states (ah, why couldn't we have let them secede when we had the chance?), but they will be a minor nuisance. At that point we can finally say, "Free at last! Free at last! Thank John Boehner, I'm free at last!"

But, you say, what about the legions of religious conservatives out there? Even for this benighted community there is hope. For there is clear evidence that the children of fundamentalists and evangelicals are slipping away from the fold in droves, so once again the numbers are against them. Atheists, agnostics, secularists, and the nebulous band of "spiritual but non-religious" people are the fastest growing "religious" groups in this country. I'm not predicting a permanent Utopia of liberal, religion-free rule here—it never pays to underestimate the inspissated ignorance of Americans—but time of our liberation from trickle-down economics and "legitimate rape" is at hand.

One must, of course, express a certain rueful sympathy toward Mitt Romney, who ran one of the most incompetent campaigns in presidential history. His verbal gaffes alone ("I like firing people"; "I don't care about the poor") would fill a volume. The revelation of his "inelegant" remarks about the 47% of Americans who don't pay federal income taxes and are, in essence, little better than moochers was the final nail in his coffin. My feeling is that he would have fared better had he undertaken a novel approach to campaigning: The Mute Candidate! Why not take a page from Silent Cal Coolidge and quite literally *say nothing* on the campaign trail? When opening one's mouth leads to such manifest embarrassments, the obvious strategy is to do the reverse.

Well, the Muslims have done it again. Incited by an ineffably crude trailer for a film, *Innocence of Muslims,* that probably doesn't exist, a small handful of Muslims in Libya, Egypt, Pakistan, and elsewhere have resorted to violence—extending to the murder of the U.S. ambassador to Libya—in retaliation for this "insult" to their prophet, Mohammad. Taking into account that the violence has deeper sociopolitical roots than merely religious umbrage, and that the protesters constitute a tiny proportion of the billion or so Muslims in the world, we still have to wonder why this religion continues to engender this kind of violence when other religions do not. Did anyone die when Martin Scorsese released the supposedly blasphemous *The Last Temptation of Christ*? Or when Andres Sarrano displayed the notorious "Piss Christ"? Or when Dan Brown published his trashy potboiler *The Da Vinci Code*?

What is even more troubling is the number of Arab leaders who are now calling for curbs on free speech only where religion is concerned. A leader of the Muslim Brotherhood, the party now running Egypt, has called for the "criminalizing of assaults on the sanctities of all heavenly religions." President Asif A. Zardari of Pakistan stated at the United Nations: "The international community . . . should criminalize such acts that destroy the peace of the world and endanger world security by misusing freedom of speech." This would take us right back to the bad old days when "blasphemy" was still a criminal offense in the West, as it still is in the benighted Middle East.

We are told that we crass Westerners are insufficiently attuned to the cultural sensitivities of Muslims, who apparently revere Mohammad and all his works even more than Christians revere Jesus. But cultural sensitivity is a two-way street, isn't it? Where is Muslims' appreciation of the long Western tradition of irreverent satire, extending back two millennia and a half to the days of Aristophanes and Juvenal?

My own feeling is that, until Islam has its Enlightenment, incidents of the sort we have seen in Libya and elsewhere will only continue. That Enlightenment cannot come fast enough.

The recent discovery of a fourth-century papyrus fragment in which Jesus apparently mentions "my wife" is certainly of interest. This discovery would appear to shed some light on another papyrus fragment of contemporaneous date, in which Jesus makes an otherwise inexplicable reference to a "ball and chain."

[January/February 2013]

What is it with Republicans and rape? In two separate cases during the last election, Republican senatorial candidates made embarrassing remarks that caused them to lose, materially helping the Democrats retain control of the Senate. In both cases, religion had much to do with the matter.

The most notorious case was that of Todd Akin, vying against Senator Claire McCaskill of Missouri. She was, at the outset, declared virtually a dead duck in a state that has become increasingly conservative. But the Republicans of that state made a tactical error by nominating Akin in the primary over a somewhat less fanatical candidate. Akin did not disappoint: during a television interview, he made a curious argument that in cases of "legitimate rape," the woman has a miraculous ability to prevent conception, so that the idea of granting exceptions to abortion in cases of rape is needless.

I imagine the remark was widely misunderstood. In defense of Akin, what he meant by "legitimate rape" was, apparently, that some women lie about being raped simply in order to get an abortion. This is bad enough, but it at least does not convict him of believing that some rapes are somehow acceptable. Let us discount the preposterous pseudo-science of the remark: this is just what one would expect from a person who has gained a master's degree in divinity from some place called Covenant Theological Seminary in Missouri. According to an associate, Akin was so convinced of the rightness of his stance ("God called me to run") that "he thinks it's his destiny, and so you're going to have to get somebody pretty high up there—or, in his mind, pretty close to God—to push him out." I'm by no means convinced that the voters of Missouri are particularly close to a non-existent God, but they seem to have done the trick well enough.

Then there is the case of Richard Mourdock, the Republican candidate from Indiana. Take it from me, who lived in that benighted state for seven years: it is hard for a Republican to lose in Indiana; one has to be especially gifted in buffoonery to do so. But Mourdock performed this miracle when he remarked that, when a woman was impregnated by a rapist, "God intended" the conception to happen.

Once again, let us consider the full context of Mourdock's comment: "I've struggled with it myself for a long time, but I came to realize that life is that gift from God. And even when life begins in that horrible situation of rape, it is something that God intended to happen." Here the misconception rests with all those Republican (and presumably religious) supporters who found the remark repugnant. For the fact of the matter is that Mourdock was regurgitating fairly orthodox Christian theology: *If God is omnipotent, he must be responsible for everything that happens, both the "good" and the 'bad."* One cannot simply attribute all the "good" things that happen in the world to God and all the bad things to . . . whom? Satan? In that case, Satan would presumably be equal in power to God, or perhaps even more powerful, if God couldn't prevent the bad things from happening. So what is one to do? One must either give up the belief that God is omnipotent or that he is benevolent; one cannot have both. Some Christian theologians, such as Hans Küng, have done exactly that, maintaining that a non-omnipotent God is just doing the best he can in an imperfect world. Well, I suppose that is a solution around the difficulty . . . but since the difficulty is purely a result of an absurd definition of God in the first place, surely it is better simply to jettison the belief and liberate oneself from theism altogether.

Ross Douthat, the dunce-cap conservative columnist for the *New York Times*, takes umbrage at the "liberal gloating" that has gone on in the weeks and months after the re-election of President Obama, saying dourly that this victory masks some "unpleasant truths." One of these, apparently, is that the increasing numbers of secular voters, who tend significantly toward Democrats, are a symptom of the failure of the church and other social institutions to "foster stability, encourage solidarity and make mobility possible." Why should this be "unpleasant"? The role of the church as a kind of "social glue" has been on the wane for decades, and it is only conservatives of the Douthat sort that thinks this is some kind of tragedy to be lamented rather than a step forward to be welcomed.

It is reported that Pope Benedict XVI has activated a Twitter account. I myself have not adopted this new-fangled technology, just as I am not on Facebook. I understand that Twitter messages are restricted to 140 characters, and my inveterate loquacity would seem to mitigate against success in this compressed medium. If I were to send the Pope a message, it might read as follows: *Give it up, guy. Your religion is finished and your quest to halt the world's inexorable move toward secularism is doomed.* That is 122 characters, and I didn't even have to resort to incomprehensible abbreviations!

A judge in Oklahoma has sentenced a young man convicted of DUI manslaughter to mandatory church attendance (a Christian church, naturally). He was puzzled at the outcry and was not convinced that his sentence violated the

First Amendment. I suspect this learned jurist received his legal training at the late unlamented Jerry Falwell's Liberty University.

In the wake of my triumphant success in predicting President Obama's re-election in my last column, I'll go out on a limb even more daringly and make the following prediction: *The world will not end on December 21, 2012.* Check back here next time to see if I'm right!

[*March/April 2013*]

Pity the lot of persecuted gun owners!

These worthy gentry are feeling the heat after yet another gunman mowed down yet another bevy of innocent people—this time a group of twenty kindergarteners and six teachers in the small community of Newtown, Connecticut. In an age and a country so numbed to gun violence as ours, it is passing strange that this incident is finally inciting political leaders to take a serious look at our obsession with guns and do something about it.

Of course, the gun nuts are reacting with their typical hysteria and paranoia. Senator Lindsey Graham of South Carolina reported that some of his constituents came up to him with the plangent plea: "Please don't let the government take my guns away!" It begins to seem as if President Obama's much-derided comment that persons of a certain intellectual level "cling to guns and religion" is accurate after all.

The opposition to sensible gun control measures is taking typical form. The gun nuts among us are fond of making a distinction between "law-abiding gun owners" and "criminals," as if these are essential and inflexible attributes. But many of our recent gunmen were "law-abiding gun owners" . . . until they weren't. The focus on mental health issues has some justification, but it is notoriously hard to determine whether such mentally disturbed persons will or will not take out their aggression with a semiautomatic. (It did not escape our attention that, on the very same day as the Newtown killing, an apparently crazy person in China stabbed twenty-three children—but none of those children died. A more emphatic refutation of the tired canard "Guns don't kill, people do" couldn't be asked for.)

Of course, the NRA, our resident domestic terrorist organization, is of no use at all. Its chief executive, Wayne LaPierre, delivered one of the more amusing press conferences in recent history on the subject. Looking a bit like a crazed gunman himself, he blamed everyone and everything he could possibly blame except guns and gun owners: violent video games, "gun-free schools" (!), the mental health industry, and so forth. (His comments were, at least, not quite so moronic as those of the ineffable Mike Huckabee, who blamed the Newtown massacre on the absence of prayer in schools. Figure that out if you can, my friends!)

LaPierre's comment that "The only thing that stops a bad guy with a gun is a good guy with a gun," and his suggestion that every school in the nation—all 100,000 of them—have armed guards have provoked much derision at his expense. Still, let us examine this idea a bit more carefully. In the first place, we are faced with the age-old query voiced two millennia ago by Juvenal: "Who will guard the guards?" Who, in short, will protect us from our protectors? Aside from the fact that armed guards were unable to prevent the carnage in Columbine, Colorado, in 1999, the question becomes: What if these guards themselves "snap" and open fire on their charges? Being faced, day after day, with little hellions poking fun at their bald pates and expanding paunches, one never knows what our valiant, gun-toting guards will do. . . . And there is the inconvenient fact that gun deaths have occurred in many other places than schools: so are we to have armed guards in every mall, movie theatre, and any other place where people congregate?

The arguments of the gun nuts are so weak as to be beyond contempt. When queried about the possibility of a ban on assault weapons, a woman in the benighted commonwealth of Kentucky quickly replied: "That's the beginning of the slippery slope." What rubbish! It is already illegal for private individuals to possess bazookas and rocket-propelled grenades and nuclear weapons—even the NRA has not (yet) lobbied for the legalization of these armaments. Where was the "slippery slope" argument when these things were banned?

Meanwhile, sales of guns and ammunition have predictably shot up all over the country—not to mention the alarming growth of "patriot" groups who are determined to battle the "tyranny" of the federal government by stocking up on weapons. The only tyranny here is the tyranny of a gun culture that blandly shrugs its collective shoulders at the eighty people who die in this country *every day* from gun violence (murder, accident, suicide). If the gun nuts did nothing more than kill themselves or one another, I would happily get out the popcorn and enjoy the amusing spectacle. It is when these despicable people kill others who don't share their insane obsession that my blood boils.

It is also reported that many sheriffs—especially in rural parts of the country—are declaring their outright refusal to carry out any federal gun-control legislation that may be passed, even in the seemingly uncontroversial matter of universal background checks. It is refreshing to see these defenders of the law be so forthright in expressing their treason.

I repeat what I've said before: *gun ownership has become a religion*—and, like every religion, it is impervious to facts and evidence. Fact: In a household with a gun, it is *twelve times more likely* that a member of the *household itself* will die rather than an intruder. Fact: It is *three times more likely* that a suicide will occur in a household that has a gun than in one that doesn't.

In my more cynical moments I often wonder whether any sensible or meaningful gun control legislation will ever be passed in this country. Maybe something might happen if several dozen (Republican) members of Congress were similarly mowed down—not to mention the entire executive board of the NRA.

I am, of course, speaking only hypothetically.

[*May/June 2013*]

We may have reached a tipping-point. I am referring to recent surveys showing that the number of "nones" (i.e., those persons who acknowledge no affiliation to an established church) is now greater than the number of Christian fundamentalists in this country. Recent polls show the "nones" constituting about 30% of the population, while the fundies are down to 25%—and the numbers are growing for the former and declining for the latter. Of course, not all the "nones" could be considered atheists, or even agnostics; but the numbers are intriguing.

The *New York Times* has for weeks been filled with articles showing an inexorable decline in religious belief: Catholic schools are closing at an alarming rate (alarming, at least, to some Catholics); contemporary novels are increasingly abandoning religion as a subject for discussion; and the *Times* even allowed a full-fledged atheist, Susan Jacoby, to write an op-ed piece, "The Blessings of Atheism," in its January 5 issue (a Sunday, be it noted).

To counteract this lamentable tendency toward secularism, a British commentator—Jonathan Sacks, a rabbi and member of the House of Lords—came back with a confused article maintaining that Darwin's theory of evolution supported religious belief! This is only the latest in a string of feeble attempts, stretching back decades or even centuries, to enlist science in bolstering religion. Sacks takes the novel approach of maintaining that, since recent findings support the notion that altruistic behavior among animals can be favorable from an evolutionary standpoint, therefore religion has a place in society. I suppose there is no need to point out the howling logical errors in this argument. Even if we ignore the howls of the Randians and acknowledge that altruism is an evolutionary benefit, it is child's play to establish that altruism is not intrinsically religious in nature; indeed, the very fact that animals practice it (assuming they do) is fatal to Sacks's argument, since we are surely not to assume that the animal kingdom must now be regarded as budding Christians or Muslims or Buddhists or Hindus or whatever.

More follies from the gun nuts!

I am tickled to note the existence of a gun lobby that is even more extreme than the NRA, something I didn't think possible. This is a relatively tiny organization called Gun Owners of America, whose führer—er, leader—is one Larry Pratt. This individual believes that no restrictions of any kind on gun ownership should be in effect, including *any background checks on anyone at any time.* Why? All he can do is evoke the tired "slippery slope" argument; or, in his own words, "We have opposed them [background checks] from the beginning, because there will be mission creep." As for penalties for straw purchases—purchases of guns by legal individuals, who then promptly sell them to those who cannot pass background checks—the learned Mr. Pratt opposes these also: "There would be no straw purchasing if there were no limits on who can carry a gun." Bravo! Since background checks have already stopped nearly 2 million criminals, terrorists, and other undesirables from securing firearms, it would seem that Mr. Pratt is entirely happy with these gentlefolk obtaining weapons for whatever purpose they wish.

It also happens that Mr. Pratt is a deeply religious man—where guns are concerned. He opines: "When we're talking about firearms, we're not really talking about a right but an obligation, as creatures of God, to protect the life that was given them." So the right to bear arms must be in the Bible! Even though I've read that windy tract from kiver to kiver, I seem to have overlooked the passage in question. Silly me!

The state legislatures of Arkansas and North Dakota have gone off the deep end. (Did I mention that these august bodies are controlled by Republicans?) They have both passed severe anti-abortion laws, prohibiting abortion after as little as 12 weeks, and in some cases before that. These measures are so fragrantly unconstitutional that they will no doubt be shot down by the courts with relish, and I will greatly enjoy the spectacle.

The standard anti-abortion position is full of paradoxes and absurdities. Most of those who prate that abortion creates a "culture of death" are also among those who slaver rabidly to execute as many prisoners on death row as they can, regardless of whether the wretches actually committed the crimes for which they were convicted. And those who shed bitter tears at the fate of the aborted fetus usually have not the slightest concern with the fate of the actually born baby, especially if that baby is of the wrong color or class; they whine plaintively about "welfare mothers" sucking up the valuable and limited resources of the nation, and so on and so forth.

But the greatest paradox is that the anti-abortionists are also those who fervently wish "limited government": "Get the government off our backs!"

they shriek. But it is hard to imagine a more intrusive invasion of government into the most intimate aspects of human life than what would be necessitated by a ban on abortion.

Until a fetus is viable outside the womb, it must be considered a part of the mother, to do with as she sees fit. Anything else is intolerable tyranny. In urging the "humanity" of the fetus, the opponents of abortion deny humanity and moral agency to the mother—she becomes, from the moment of conception, nothing more than an incubator, and a ward of the state.

If the opponents of abortion really want the government to poke its figurative nose between the legs of every pregnant woman, they are welcome to do so. I doubt they will have many supporters on their side.

[*July/August 2013*]

If Michele Bachmann didn't exist, it would be necessary to invent her. She so perfectly embodies the inveterate ignorance, irrationality, hypocrisy, and buffoonery of the current Republican party that she becomes a symbol for why that party, in its current incarnation, is doomed to irrelevance and perhaps outright extinction. One of her more priceless statements came recently, when she strove—cleverly enough, from her perspective—to link conservatives' detestation of the Affordable Care Act (i.e., Obamacare) and the current kerfuffle over the IRS's investigation of Tea Party activists (many or most of whom do not in fact deserve tax-exempt status, since they are clearly political organizations) by remarking as follows, according to a news report:

"Since the I.R.S. also is the chief enforcer of Obamacare requirements, she [Bachmann] asked whether the I.R.S.'s admission means it 'will deny or delay access to health care' for conservatives. At this point, she said, that 'is a reasonable question to ask.'"

Well, maybe not so reasonable. It is not clear (a) how the IRS could ascertain whether any given person is a conservative or not; and (b) how the IRS could "deny or delay" health care access to such unfortunates. Given the fact that a substantial proportion of conservatives are white, old, male, angry, and fat (a dangerous combination, indeed!), one suspects they need all the health care they can get!

But, of course, we shall no longer have Michele Bachmann to kick around anymore. In a surprising move (or perhaps not so surprising, given numerous investigations of campaign finance shenanigans relating to her comic-opera run for president in 2012), she announced her retirement from politics after her current term is over. In a predictable whine against her opponents, she declared that the "mainstream liberal media . . . always seemed to attempt to find a dishonest way to disparage me." If quoting the words that directly came out of her mouth is "dishonest," well, so be it.

Bill Donohue, president of the Catholic League, has once again succumbed to the ignominy of having to purchase ad space in the op-ed page of the *New York Times*. This time he has written a love letter to the new pope, Francis I. It is a most interesting document—assuming, for the nonce, that imbecility is ever interesting. It is predictable that Donahue would condemn the inexorable march of secularism throughout the world, especially in Europe and the United States, but he does so in a curious way. I quote:

"In Europe and in the Americas, the ascent of radical secularism has taken a heavy toll. Seductive in its appeal, the secular option alone ignores the hand of God in the everyday world. Core institutions such as marriage and the family are under assault from those who embrace an ethics of radical individualism. Similarly, life, from the time of conception to natural death, is threatened not by tyrants, but by those who speak the language of compassion."

Very clever! Well, perhaps not. Donohue fancies that merely dropping the adjective *radical* into his discussion will somehow clinch his argument; but it is such an obviously hollow tactic that one suspects even he sees its absurdity and is merely hoping against hope that his more foolish readers will be taken in. Isn't this always how the Catholic Church has functioned?

I am writing this in early June, a few weeks before the Supreme Court is expected to hand down its decision on two same-sex marriage cases that were argued before the court in March. The accepted wisdom is that the court will declare the Defense of Marriage Act, prohibiting federal benefits to same-sex couples who are legally married, unconstitutional, but that the court will suffer a predictable spasm of cowardice and fail to make same-sex marriage constitutional throughout the nation, as a ruling in the other case (California's referendum outlawing such marriages) could allow. I imagine this is a correct reading of the situation.

What is so interesting is the continued opposition of conservatives on the issue, even in the wake of polls that show an ever-increasing acceptance of same-sex marriage by a wide segment of the American public. Even more interesting is the incredibly inept arguments offered by conservatives in defense of "traditional" marriage, whatever that may be. A youngster, the thirty-one-year-old Ryan T. Anderson, a fellow of the Heritage Foundation (where else?), has opined: "In redefining marriage to include same-sex couples, what you're doing is you're excluding the norm of sexual complementarity. Once you exclude that norm, the three other norms—which are monogamy, sexual exclusivity, and permanency—become optional as well."

Um, pardon my ignorance, but has "traditional" (i.e., heterosexual) marriage been a resounding success in advocating or exemplifying "monogamy, sexual exclusivity, and permanency"? Most forms of polygamy of which I am aware are resolutely heterosexual; and given that one out of every two heterosexual marriages end in divorce, it does not seem plausible that permanency is a very high objective or result in such marriages either. Ryan's comment is of course nothing more than a pseudo-academic slur against the purported sexual proclivities of gay men, who in conservatives' minds continue to thirst for as many sex partners as possible—ignoring the countless numbers of committed gay and lesbian unions and the equally countless numbers of heterosexual philanderers in our midst.

The bad news is that a fire in a factory in Bangladesh killed eight people.

The good news is that—unlike an earlier building collapse that killed more than 1100 workers, most of them women—this fire killed only the management of the factory, including its owner.

Behind every dark cloud there is a silver lining.

[*September/October 2013*]

Atheists continue to speak out aggressively on issues important to them, in particular the separation of church and state. No longer are we on the defensive; the numbers—and the issues—are on our side, and so we are sticking it to the pious. On July 4, the Freedom from Religion Foundation took out a full-page ad, in color, in the *New York Times* with portraits of several of the leading Founding Fathers and pungent quotations attached attesting to their belief that America is not a Christian nation, and so on and so forth. Bravo! Meanwhile, our friends the American Atheists have received a substantial donation from an unnamed party to erect a series of public monuments to secularism. The idea is that such monuments, placed next to monuments proclaiming the Ten Commandments, will incite others to demand that monuments proclaiming their faith (or lack of it)—ranging from pagans to Satanists—will in effect cause public officials to take down all the monuments in question. I am no particular advocate of Satanism, which is only marginally less foolish than the Christianity it apes and parodies, but as a refreshing diversion it may have its uses. After all, prisoners can now practice it, so why can't the rest of us?

A pious resident of the Tennessee town where the American Atheists' monument went up made the following pitiable lament: "This is something we thought we would never experience in a small town. It points out how many people don't believe in God, and have different opinions." My heart bleeds for you, friend. The idea that people have different opinions from your own must be a tough pill to swallow.

On a somewhat more serious note, it does occur to me that a clever ad campaign getting the atheist point of view across—on buses, bumper stickers, and the like—might be amusing. Something like: "Freedom from religion . . . what a blessing!"

The piety of the Republican Party appears to be wondrously embodied in the figure of Stephen Fincher, a representative from Tennessee. In a recent series of votes, Fincher voted in support of additional farm subsidies (especially to cotton farmers) but no money at all for food stamps. Fincher said indignantly of the latter proposal, "The role of citizens, of Christians, of humanity, is to take care of each other. But not for Washington to steal money from those in the country and give it to others in the country." Who could object to that? Well, the issue is perhaps not as straightforward as it seems. When Juan Vargas, a Democrat from California, in protesting the denial of food stamps to the hungry, quoted Jesus' statement that "Whatever you did for one of the least of these brothers and sisters of mine, you did for me" [Matt. 25:40], Fincher shot back with the following biblical aphorism: "The one who is unwilling to work shall not eat" [2 Thess. 3:10]. I suppose it is a small point that this utterance is found in one of Paul's epistles and is not attributed to Jesus. One imagines that Fincher could have quoted a much more celebrated utterance that actually is put in Jesus' mouth: "For ye have the poor always with you; but me ye have not always" (Matt. 26:11), a charmingly frank admission of Jesus' utter lack of concern with the less fortunate.

But Fincher is in a rather curious position himself. It turns out that he is a cotton farmer and has himself received $3.5 million in farm subsidies over the years. (By my calculations, this is equivalent to food stamps for more than 2000 people for a year.) I have no idea exactly how much farming he has done in that period of time, but his current occupation in the House of Representatives (on the Republican side) would seem to constitute just about the perfect embodiment of "unwillingness to work" as any I can think of.

In a recent vote in Congress, Republicans voted to ban abortions after twenty-two weeks. Among the several novel arguments justifying the vote, the most piquant came from Michael C. Burgess, a representative from Texas, who apparently maintained that fetuses of that age are capable of all manner of human acts—including masturbation. I quote directly: "They [the fetuses] stroke their face. If they're a male baby, they may have their hand between their legs. I mean, they feel pleasure, why is it so hard to think that they could feel pain?" *Touché!* I am all for allowing people to masturbate as often as possible, although I fail to see why female fetuses, who also are presumably able to place their hands between their legs, could not enjoy the same procedure.

Before the fall of President Morsi and the Muslim Brotherhood in Egypt, there was a substantial increase in prosecutions for blasphemy. After all, said one outraged politician, "Contempt for religion, any religion, is a crime, not a form of expression." Well, O.K., if you really feel that way about it. As a matter of fact, the prosecutors went on to proclaim that putting the luckless blasphemers in prison was actually a delicate mark of consideration for them—because otherwise they would simply have been lynched by pious Muslims. In regard to one such blasphemer, a particularly devout Muslim was heard to say: "They should have cut his throat for it." I guess I won't be visiting Egypt anytime soon.

Russia, under the influence of the Russian Orthodox Church, has passed a law prohibiting "homosexual propaganda" under pain of criminal prosecution. It is not specified exactly what "homosexual propaganda" actually is, but that is a small matter. The leader of the Russian Orthodox Church, Patriarch Kirill I, has referred to the legalization of same-sex marriage as "a very dangerous symptom of the apocalypse."

Kirill, old chap, don't you *want* the apocalypse to occur? And the sooner the better? O.K., folks, let's get down to all the propagandizing we can—for the Rapture is upon us!

[*November/December 2013*]

We have been regaled in the past few months by some entertaining buffoonery emerging from the benighted state of Missouri. (Did I mention that this state's government is now almost entirely in the hands of Republicans?) Some time ago the legislature attempted to pass a bill nullifying all gun laws passed by the federal government and, moreover, making it a crime for federal agents to enforce them in the state. This flagrantly unconstitutional measure was vetoed by Governor Jay Nixon (a Democrat, in spite of his dubious surname), and the only question was whether Republicans would succeed in overriding the veto. They had the numbers to do so, but when the vote came, a single sane Republican (let's assume for the moment that that phrase is not an oxymoron) prevented the override.

This comic-opera incident is actually worth some further study, for its display of Republican thinking (if it can be called that) on this matter exactly parallels the thinking of many Christians in regard to their scripture. Just as Christians happily brush under the rug those parts of their sacred text that

155

they now find embarrassing (the death penalty for gays and Sabbath-violators; the proposition that the earth is flat or that the sun revolves around the earth; the endorsement of slavery), so Republicans seem delighted to embrace the Tenth Amendment ("The powers not delegated to the United States by the Constitution, nor prohibited by it to the States, are reserved to the States respectively, or to the people"), but aren't so keen on another part of this storied document, namely Article VI, Clause 2 ("This Constitution, and the Laws of the United States which shall be made in pursuance thereof . . . shall be the supreme law of the land; and the judges in every state shall be bound thereby, anything in the constitution or laws of any state to the contrary notwithstanding"). In other words, federal law trumps state law.

The fact that so few Republicans in Missouri can grasp this elementary fact is a bit disturbing. And more than disturbing—a good case can be made that it is in fact treasonous. Resolutely opposed to the death penalty as I am, my understanding is that treason is still a capital offense. One can engage in delightful mind-pictures of some particularly piquant manner of exacting this penalty—maybe by firing squad?

Meanwhile, the horrific toll of gun violence continues—one of the latest and most egregious being a shooting in, of all places, the Navy Yard in Washington, D.C., where a gunman who confessed to "hearing voices" mowed down a dozen people before being mowed down himself. But of course, even this incident did little to change the stone-faced resistance of gun nuts for sensible gun control. We hear them prating bombastically about their "rights." What about my right not to be blown away by a maniac?

There needs to be a change in the gun culture in this country—and the onus of that change rests entirely in the hands (and minds) of gun owners. So long as they resist any and all attempts to control gun violence, however reasonable (such as universal background checks for gun sales), on flimsy or paranoid grounds (e.g., that a gun registry will inevitably lead to confiscation: cars are registered, but how many non-criminals have had their cars confiscated?), then they are part of the problem, not part of the solution. They are implicitly condoning gun violence; more, they are the enablers and active encouragers of that violence, and as such are complicit in it just as if they had pulled the trigger themselves. To repeat a hackneyed axiom, "With rights come responsibilities." If sane gun owners (assuming there are any such) refuse to acknowledge that a significant minority of their number do not use guns responsibly, then they are abdicating their own responsibility to society as a whole and thereby forfeiting any "right" they may have to firearms.

156

The Republicans in the House of Representatives have performed what I thought was an impossibility: they have proved that they are simultaneously stupid, crazy, and evil. How so?

One would have to be stupid not to know basic arithmetic. The House Republicans appear to believe that they (constituting a body of one) can override the Senate (controlled by Democrats) and President Obama (making a total of two) in the catastrophic standoff that has led to the shutdown of the government and an imminent national default.

They are crazy for thinking that their antics can somehow stop or delay the implementation of the Affordable Care Act. Don't take my word for it. Michael Horowitz, general counsel under Ronald Reagan, stated recently: "For Congress to ask for a shutdown when the opposite political party is in charge of the White House is my definition of insanity."

And they are evil for refusing to fund food stamps for the poor when they are happy to supply handouts to corporate farmers who are making record profits and defense contractors building weapons that will never be used.

But there is a deeper problem here. While it may be amusing to see Speaker of the House John Boehner, like a scared rabbit, running in terror from the relatively small number of Tea Party anarchists, one has to remember that these backbenchers leading us toward the apocalypse have sworn—like all other members of the executive and legislative branches of government—to uphold the U.S. Constitution. But in the most fundamental way, they are violating that oath by denying the basic principle of democracy—the rule of the majority. There is good reason to think that these despicable lunatics are traitors to their country.

Remind me again—what is the punishment for treason?

[January/February 2014]

It is hard to fathom how Supreme Court Justice Antonin Scalia could have gained a reputation for erudition and cleverness, for to my mind he is one of the prime dunces in a court that is in no way deficient in folly. In recent months, however, his imbecility has become embarrassingly evident. He ought to be grateful that stupidity is not a capital offense.

Consider his remarks in a case challenging overall limits to direct campaign contributions from individuals to candidates. Given that the Scalia-led court has already shredded many sensible campaign contribution limits in its catastrophic Citizens United decision (during which Justice Anthony Kennedy joined the ranks of the morons by declaring that unlimited corporate contributions do not even create the "appearance" of corruption!), it was to be expected that Scalia would lead the way to more money infiltrating the political system. Justice Ruth Bader Ginsberg stated, "By having these limits, you are promoting democratic participation. Then the little people will count some and you won't have the super-affluent as the speakers that will control the elections." To this, Scalia replied acidly that he assumed "a law that only prohibits the speech of 2 percent of the country is O.K."

Let us pause a while over this assertion. Exactly how is a wealthy person's freedom of speech being infringed upon by campaign contribution limits? There is nothing stopping such a person from supporting a particular candidate by way of a billboard or a television commercial or a full-page ad in a newspaper or any other of a thousand different methods. What is being prohibited is a specific activity that, in the past, has undeniably led to political corruption and (*pace* Kennedy) is surely doing so at this moment, at all levels of government.

Let me state my view of this issue in simple-minded terms that even Scalia, John Roberts, and Clarence Thomas can understand. Money is not speech; money is money, and speech is speech. Money may facilitate speech, but that is a very different thing from saying that money *is* speech. Only in a nation so besotted by capitalism as ours can this false equivalency ever have gained traction.

Then there was the matter of Scalia's learned comment when a case was brought before the court challenging a "non-sectarian prayer" (can there ever be such a thing?) that habitually preceded a legislative session in a small town in New York. Scalia, after asking a reasonably sensible question as to whether such a prayer could ever satisfy atheists, went on to ask, in reference to a prayer that began "To the Almighty": "What about devil worshippers?" I am touched by Scalia's tender solicitude toward Satanists, but the lawyer defending the town had a clever retort: "Well, if devil worshippers believe the devil is almighty, they might be okay." Bravo!

Among the many silly and frivolous court cases being launched, in a kind of futile frenzy, against the Affordable Care Act, the lawsuit by one David Klemencic of Ellenboro, West Virginia, takes the prize for nincompoopery. This fearless and self-reliant individual declares that he has (in the words of the *New York Times*) "deep, philosophical objections to any effort by the government to require him to purchase insurance, and would refuse to accept a subsidy even if eligible."

Well, friend, I myself have deep philosophical objections to a single penny of my tax dollars going to the Defense Department—but there's not a great deal I can do about the situation, is there? If everyone who had deep philosophical objections to this or that government policy engaged in litigation, we would be in a pretty pickle. Mr. Klemencic went on to say: "I go to the doctor now, I go to the dentist now, I take my checkbook and I pay for it." Bully for you, old son! "If I'm forced into some sort of program where it's subsidized by the government, I won't see a doctor." I don't care to contemplate the spectacle of Mr. Klemencic sitting in his home with all his teeth fallen out and dying of some preventable illness, all for some "deep philosophical objection." One wonders, however, exactly how happy he would be to pay a six-figure hospital bill in the event of a serious illness. He won't be grinning much then (assuming he has the teeth to do so)!

I would never have thought that I would agree with anything that a Tea Party Republican says, but lo and behold! It has happened. And my partner proves to be none other than one Dean Young, a real estate developer in the benighted state of Alabama, who was running for Congress in a solidly Republican district. This learned gentleman, in the course of a campaign stop, uttered the immortal words: "We are witnessing the end of a Western Christian empire."

Shake, pal! I'm with ya! It appears, however, that Mr. Young (who was lamentably defeated by a Republican candidate not quite as extremist as himself) was bemoaning this state of affairs, whereas I welcome it. Still, I must give a tip of the hat to Mr. Young for his historical perspicuity.

Stop the presses! The House of Representatives has passed gun control legislation! Well, on second thought, keep those presses rolling. The measure—extending a law banning firearms that can pass undetected through airport X-ray machines—was passed in a cowardly voice vote so that individual votes could not be tallied and therefore be subject to enraged NRA opposition; and the measure is noticeably weak in certain particulars. It remains inconceivable that Republicans in Congress will pass any serious or significant gun control measures, even in the wake of 30,000 deaths or injuries every year from gun violence. So much for the "pro-life" party!

[*March/April 2014*]

Let's talk about gay rights, shall we?

It is remarkable what progress has been made since 2004, when Massachusetts became the first state to legalize same-sex marriage. Within ten years, sixteen or seventeen more states, as well as the District of Columbia, have followed suit. In 2012, my own state, Washington, was one of three that voted in support of referendums on the issue—the first time that had happened. (Previously, same-sex marriage had been legalized by state judges or legislative action.) Last summer the Supreme Court shot down California's Proposition

8 prohibiting such marriages as well as the 1996 Defense of Marriage Act, and it is only a matter of time that it makes same-sex marriage legal throughout the nation.

That same-sex marriage was ruled legal (briefly) even in the deep-red states of Utah (yes, Utah!) and Oklahoma, and that it is currently being debated in other bastions of bigotry as Indiana and Virginia, is an ominous sign for those defenders of "traditional marriage" who are increasingly losing battle after battle. The increasing absurdity and desperation of their arguments—think of the horror of flower shops forced to sell to same-sex couples!—tell a sad story of how people cling to irrationality to the bitter end.

Around the world, however, the situation is not so sanguine. Several African nations have passed stringent measures making same-sex relations of any kind illegal, and now the Supreme Court in India has reinstituted a barbaric 1861 law criminalizing sodomy. Most of the time I am proud of being an Indian-American. On rare occasions—as, for example, when I contemplate the continued existence of Deepak Chopra and Dinesh D'Souza—my pride turns to shame. I am covered in shame at this moment.

Not to be outdone, Russia has passed a bizarre law prohibiting the dissemination of "homosexual propaganda" among the young. The law conveniently fails to specify exactly what "homosexual propaganda" is. And can anyone point to a single individual, young or old, who has been influenced by such "propaganda" to suddenly turn gay? It is to laugh.

Russia's dictator—er, that is, president—Vladimir Putin recently put his foot in his mouth by declaring that, after all, homosexuality itself is not illegal in Russia, and that all such people are welcome to come and spend their money at the Winter Olympics in Sochi (assuming, of course, they can dodge terrorist bombings), so long as they "leave our children in peace"! I'm sure gays will make heroic efforts to restrain themselves.

Then, of course, there is the exquisite buffoonery of Phil Peterson of the television show *Duck Dynasty*. Not being particularly current on pop culture, I had to do considerable research to determine exactly what *Duck Dynasty* was. From the title alone I naively inferred that this might be some kind of sci-fi scenario whereby our quacking friends take over the world; in fact, the show is about a family-run business that produces duck-hunting merchandise. Mr. Peterson gave an interview in *GQ* (of all places) declaring that homosexuality in some mysterious way leads to "bestiality, sleeping around with this woman or that woman" [is that something a gay man would do?] "and these men." He concludes ominously that all such degenerates "won't inherit the kingdom of God."

Well! This comment led A&E to suspend Mr. Peterson from the show, although he was soon brought back by inexplicable popular demand. And the usual assortment of Religious Right demagogues screamed about the First Amendment and the scorn and abuse that religious expression receives from us horrible liberals. But what was never pointed out is that Mr. Peterson does not in fact reflect true biblical teaching on the subject. It is not merely that gays will not inherit the kingdom of God; it is that they must be summarily executed. Let us recall Leviticus 20:13: "If a man also lie with mankind, as he lieth with a woman, both of them have committed an abomination: they shall surely be put to death; their blood shall be upon them." Come on, Phil, why aren't you advocating the death penalty for gay men? Stand up for what you believe in! (The biblical passage curiously omits any mention of lesbians. Perhaps the authors of the Bible didn't believe in the existence of lesbians.)

What was also left unanswered by this whole kerfuffle is why anyone should take seriously the maunderings of a grotesque troglodyte like Phil Peterson.

Jeff Sessions, Senator from Alabama, said recently: "Like the frog in the warming water, we do not realize we are being cooked and that the freedoms of Americans are being cooked." Omigod! Stop the presses! Can a Republican actually be pointing out the dangers of global warming? . . . Oh, wait a minute: Sessions was actually complaining about the Democrats' revision of the filibuster rule in the Senate as a result of Republicans' insane opposition to every judicial and executive nominee President Obama puts forward. For a moment I thought a Republican was actually seeing the light. I'll not make that mistake again.

Governor Chris Christie of New Jersey maintains that he had no knowledge of the closing of several traffic lanes in the town of Fort Lee leading to the George Washington Bridge, evidently a payback for the mayor of Fort Lee's refusal to endorse Christie in his re-election campaign. The lane closings were evidently ordered and executed by his deputy chief of staff (Bridget Anne Kelly), two chosen appointees at the Port Authority of New York and New Jersey (David Wildstein and Bill Baroni), and his campaign manager (Bill Stepien). In spite of all this, Gov. Christie protests his ignorance.

To which all I can say is: Fat chance. If you catch my meaning.

[May/June 2014]

There is such a thing as feeling sorry for bigots.

For many months now, the forces of anti-gay bigotry have been suffering one painful defeat after another. In Indiana—hardly a bastion of liberalism, as

I can attest from personal experience—the fire-eating state legislators suddenly underwent an anomalous spasm of cowardice, diluting a constitutional amendment prohibiting same-sex marriage. Because the amendment was significantly different from an amendment passed two years ago, the whole process must start all over again; and even if the measure does pass, it would likely by then have already been unconstitutional by the Supreme Court. A bill that would have allowed individuals to refuse business to same-sex couples in Kansas went down to humiliating defeat.

Consider now the exquisite misery of conservatives in Arizona. There, a law even stricter than the aborted Kansas law was passed by the state legislature. After several days of waffling, Governor Jan Brewer—whom one would not exactly consider a bleeding-heart liberal—vetoed the bill, on the recommendation of the state Chamber of Commerce and other entities of presumably unimpeachable conservative credentials.

The most instructive case occurred in Michigan, where a same-sex (lesbian) couple was seeking to achieve legal adoption of their children in the face of the state's ban on same-sex marriage. Their opponents marshalled what seemed to be impressive sociologists and other "scientists" who averred that children raised in same-sex households suffered all manner of ills as opposed to those raised by heterosexual couples. The only hitch in all this is that this "research" was bogus. Indeed, the chief witness—one Mark Regnerus, of the University of Texas—endured the humiliation of being repudiated by his own university, and his credibility was further damaged when it was learned that he had received the sum of $785,000 from the Heritage Foundation (who else?) and the Bradley Foundation to conduct his research. The judge in the case, ruling in favor of the same-sex couple, found the arguments of Regnerus and his colleagues "unbelievable."

What is remarkable about this whole business is that the bigots revealed no inkling of the dangerous tendencies of their arguments. Even if it could be established that children are somehow "harmed" by being raised by same-sex couples, the very same thing could much more convincingly be established for single-parent families, divorced couples, and so on. Does this mean that these undesirables shouldn't be allowed to raise children either?

Bans against same-sex marriage are being struck down in state after state, but most of these bans will remain in force until federal appeals courts and/or the Supreme Court rules; but the overwhelming likelihood is that the Supreme Court will finally gain the courage to make same-sex marriage legal throughout the nation. When such a ban was struck down in Texas (a state that has become the Cloudcuckooland of American politics), a learned state legislator, Todd Staples, opined: "I will change my definition of marriage when God changes his." Alas, my friend, God has already done so! Are you not aware that polygamy was manifestly legal throughout the Old Testament, as evidenced by King David's eight wives and King Solomon's thousand (300 of whom were concubines)? True, Jesus did enunciate the one man/one woman principle, if the Gospels are to be believed; but no one could possibly deny that there are multiple definitions of marriage in the Bible. And why would United States civil law be determined by the Bible anyway?

The bigots are now banking on the Supreme Court to come to their aid in a related case—the notorious attempt of clearly secular, for-profit businesses to refuse to provide free contraception to their employees on religious grounds. Incredibly, the conservative members of the court actually seemed tentatively receptive to this astounding argument, although they are likely to approve it only for private, not public, corporations. This might allow for some denial-of-service cases to pass muster, but that would be a thin reed for them to rest on.

As a grotesque pendant to this whole situation, we learn of the death of Fred Phelps, a virulently antigay preacher in Kansas who ran a tiny congregation that protested at military funerals as a way of showing how America had gone to the devil because of its approval of gay rights. And yet, this repugnant individual did exhibit more courage in his religious convictions than many, as witness his resounding utterance: "You can't believe the Bible without believing that God hates people. It's pure nonsense to say that God loves the sinner but hates the sin. He hates the sin, and he hates the sinner. He sends them to hell. Do you think he loves the people in hell?" Amen to that, brother!

I suppose there is no real sport in kicking the butt of Ted Nugent. Shooting fish in a barrel is a more difficult enterprise. Recently, this forthright musician, cozying up to the likely Republican candidate for governor of Texas, Greg Abbott, declared that President Obama was a "Communist-raised, Communist-educated, Communist-nurtured subhuman mongrel." I would have thought those last two words would have applied more accurately to Nugent himself. Nugent, who seems to have a fatal addiction to underage girls, was also the one who declared, in April 2012, "I will either be dead or in jail by this time next year." Much as I would have liked to have seen either branch (especially the former) of this prediction fulfilled, I think it is better for this brave patriot to remain in freedom, so that he can continue to cast disrepute upon the whole gang of Texas Republicans and, by extension, the Republican Party in general.

Oh, and did I mention that Nugent's comment on Obama was uttered during an interview on Guns.com? Why am I not surprised?

[July/August 2014]

The matter of the resignation of Brendan Eich, chief executive of the Silicon Valley technology company Mozilla, because of his professed opposition to same-sex marriage has died down in recent months, but it raises certain broader issues that are worth dwelling upon. Eich contributed $1000 to Proposition 8, the California measure that banned same-sex marriage in 2008, but was later overturned by the Supreme Court. Once Eich's contribution became known, he faced a tidal wave of criticism and promptly resigned.

Our friends on the right had a field day over the matter, alleging that Eich had been the victim of a vicious campaign of what has been called "liberal fascism" whereby dissenting views on hallowed subjects are impermissible. The *New York Times*'s resident dunce—er, that is, conservative—opined that the whole contretemps demonstrated "a serious moral defect at the heart of elite culture in America." How so?

Let Douthat explain in his own words: "The defect, crucially, is not this culture's bias against social conservatives . . . Rather, it's the refusal to admit—to others, and to itself—that these biases fundamentally trump the commitment to 'free expression' or 'diversity' affirmed in mission statements and news releases."

Well, that doesn't sound good at all! But let's examine exactly what is at stake here. Let it pass that, at the very minimum, this is a priceless case of the pot calling the kettle black: where, in Republican circles, is there any respect paid to the expression of support for, say, abortion rights or immigration reform or raising the minimum wage or the reality of global warming—or, forsooth, the admittedly incredible notion that an atheist might actually be a morally sound person fit for higher office?

But the matter goes well beyond this kind of hypocrisy. In fact, Eich was felled not by some liberal conspiracy that sought to muzzle him. He withdrew of his own accord, and after a surprisingly feeble fight, when *others* expressed *their* right to "free expression." For example, a letter appeared on the online dating site OkCupid (which uses Firefox, manufactured by Mozilla), stating the plain fact that "Mozilla's new CEO, Brendan Eich, is an opponent of equal rights for gay couples" and going on to say: "We would therefore prefer that our users not use Mozilla software to access OkCupid."

What Douthat and other conservative dogmatists apparently want to see is the expression of *their own* point of view but not any point of view opposing it. In other words, "free expression" only extends to the view they support, and any attempt by opponents to express an opinion of their own is ludicrously interpreted as some kind of censorship of the other opinion. Everyone is entitled to "free expression"; what no one is entitled to is freedom from criticism. In my view, this stance is a pale-pink holdover from the time when religion could express—and enforce—its dogmas without fear of rebuke; indeed, when it could severely punish opposing views, by excommunication, exile, or death. Those times are long over, and good riddance to them.

We are informed by two separate scientific studies that a large section of the ice sheet in West Antarctica has begun falling apart, and its melting now appears unstoppable. This gives new meaning to that old French expression *Après moi, le déluge!* Other recent reports declare that global warming is a concern of the present, not of the near or distant future. And yet, our Republican friends continue to bury their heads in the sand. (One wonders how much longer there will be any sand left for them to bury their heads in.) The continued blusterings of Senator James M. Inhofe of Oklahoma, who has publicly gone on record to declare global warming a hoax, have been a tad fatiguing, like the party guest who remains blissfully unaware that he is telling the same old joke (which was never very funny to begin with) over and over again to the same people. But one would have thought that other Republicans less dependent on the largesse of the oil industry would be a bit more rational on the subject.

Republicans being rational? What could I be thinking? Here is the learned opinion of Senator Marco Rubio of Florida, who stated on national television: "I do not believe that human activity is causing these dramatic changes to our climate the way these scientists are portraying it." Rubio, who had earlier declared languidly that "I'm not a scientist, man," now suddenly believes he has superior knowledge than the 97% of climate scientists who confirm the reality of global warming. Remind me what college you went to, Marco?

It is of course plain why Rubio has taken this position. He is well aware that, in a party that has fallen into the classic tail-wagging-the-dog dilemma whereby the morons of the Tea Party (especially relishing their toppling of Majority Leader Eric Cantor in a primary for being—get this—insufficiently conservative) must be placated in Republican primaries, a stance that even faintly inclines toward the acceptance of science and reason on this issue is a sure-fire death-knell to any presidential hopes. So we have reached the stage where one of our two major political parties is now governed by proud Know-Nothings to whom all potential candidates for national and, in some cases, local office must kowtow in self-abasing sycophancy. This same self-imposed ignorance was on display in Wyoming (where else?), when the state legislature rejected national science standards for schools, since those standards make reference to global warming and its largely human causation. "See No Truth, Hear No Truth, Speak No Truth!" would now appear to be the motto of the G.O.P.

[*September/October 2014*]

If there is any doubt that the five conservative justices of the Supreme Court—all male and all Catholic—are now nothing but an offshoot of the Republican party, their controlling decision in the Hobby Lobby case should dispense with that doubt once and for all. This family-owned for-profit company explicitly labels itself a "Christian" corporation and objected to the provision in the Affordable Care Act mandating that the insurance companies it uses to provide health care to its 13,000 employees provide free contraception coverage. Hobby Lobby magnanimously asserted that it did not object to all forms of contraception, only to certain forms that they claim (falsely, it appears) is tantamount to abortion.

The ruling was so wrongheaded on so many fronts that it is difficult to enumerate all the mischief it will cause. First and foremost, it would seem to allow corporations (and not just "closely held" ones, as the majority of the justices contend) to control the reproductive lives of their employees. Given the ferocity of Republicans' customary objections to government's heavy hand over its citizens, it is bizarre that they seem content to allow corporations to engage in this kind of paternalism.

But the critical issue is over the precise legal meaning of the notion (embodied in the Religious Freedom Restoration Act of 1993) of what constitutes a "substantial legal burden" upon an individual (or, as the Supreme Court has increasingly ruled, a corporation—for it now appears that corporations are full-fledged human beings with all the rights thereto) in the practice of his or her religion. Hobby Lobby claims that even allowing a third party (i.e., an insurance company) to dole out contraceptives to its employees would make it complicit in "sin." It is astounding that the family that owns Hobby Lobby (which, incidentally, does a brisk business in China, a country that still maintains the practice of forced abortions) cannot see that it has now descended to fascism. The definition of fascism is that you are not content to do (or not to do) something yourself; you are only satisfied if *everyone* does (or doesn't do) that thing. It is not Hobby Lobby's call to say what is a "sin" or not a "sin" on behalf of its employees.

What is more, the scope of the ruling could theoretically extend far beyond the issue of contraception. There could theoretically be an infinite number of "religious" objections to all manner of medical procedures—what of a for-profit company owned by Jehovah's Witnesses, which objects to blood transfusions?—and to other issues well outside the medical arena. Justice Ruth Bader Ginsburg pointedly exposed the dangers of the ruling in a subsequent statement: "There was no way to read that decision narrowly. . . . What of the employer whose religious faith teaches that it's sinful to employ a single woman without her father's consent or a married woman without her husband's consent?" What, indeed.

I recently undertook an entertaining road trip through the states of Montana, Wyoming, and Colorado. The natural landscape was spectacular, although I am forced to admit that the non-human denizens of these states (deer, elk, buffalo, bears) seemed considerably more interesting than the human inhabitants. But the experience reminded me of the exquisite farce of Mr. Ted—er, that is, Cliven—Bundy. This priceless chap has dropped out of the news lately, but you will recall that this Nevada rancher has been mooching off of government land (that is, land owned by you and me) to graze a herd of 500 cattle for years. When the Bureau of Land Management attempted to evict him for owing millions of dollars in fees and taxes, Bundy managed to round up a motley crew of fifty like-minded thugs to drive the federal marshals away.

What puzzles me most about this issue is the degree to which our Republican friends—who are usually so vociferous in railing against lazy (and usually dark-skinned) welfare addicts—are so enamored of this bare-faced deadbeat who refuses to pay the (extremely modest) grazing fees that most other ranchers on public land pay. The matter turned wondrously comical when the learned Mr. Bundy opined on race relations in this country. Referring to African Americans, Bundy pondered, "Are they happier now under this government subsidy system than they were when they were slaves, when they was [sic] able to have their family structure together" [Bundy evidently is unaware that many slave families were torn apart mercilessly for financial gain] "and the chickens and a garden, and the people had something to do?" Can't you just hear the strains of "Mammy" played on the old family ukelele? These comments caused many high-profile Republicans to flee from Mr. Bundy as if he were the plague. So far, he remains on his illegal ranch—but the clock is ticking against him.

I am sorry to report that, in my estimation, the recent war between Israel and Hamas has all but destroyed Israel's legitimacy. The utter disregard for civilian casualties caused by Israel's repeated shelling of schools, hospitals, and other purported "safe areas" creates the disturbing impression that there is little moral difference between the two sides. If Hamas is a terrorist organization, Israel has become a rogue state.

I am well aware of the standard rebuttal by Israel's supporters: "Anti-

Semite!" But surely they must realize that this knee-jerk slur makes reasoned discussion of the subject impossible. If no possible criticism of the Israeli government or the Israeli Defense Forces is allowed, then presumably that nation could engage (as, indeed, it appears to have done in a half-hearted manner) in a complete genocide of the Palestinian people without incurring any moral or political censure.

That does not seem sensible to me.

[*November/December 2014*]

We are regaled by reports that the Supreme Court's favorite "person" (i.e., family-owned corporation), Hobby Lobby, is planning to build a Bible museum just two blocks away from the National Mall in Washington, D.C. Such an institution would, in the words of Steve Green, president of Hobby Lobby, serve a most edifying institution. "The nation is in danger because of its ignorance of what God has taught. There are lessons in the past that we can learn from, the dangers of ignorance of this book. We need to know it. If we don't, our future is going to be very scary."

Shake, pal! I'm with ya 110 percent!

No, dear friends, I have not converted to Christian fundamentalism. I wholeheartedly recommend the teaching of the Bible—to Christians.

For it is they—as survey after survey has found—who know far less of their scripture than we atheists, agnostics, and secularists do. It is certainly not commonly known, I daresay, that the Bible proclaims that the sun revolves around the earth (Joshua 10:12–13), that slavery is a morally sound institution (Exodus 20:10), that wives are the property of their husbands (Exodus 20:17), that violators of the Sabbath should be put to death (Exodus 31:15, Numbers 15:35), that practicing homosexuals should be put to death (Leviticus 30:13), and so on and so forth. I greatly look forward to displays on all these points in the Hobby Lobby Bible Museum!

And as for forgetting the "lessons in the past," I think it is certainly advisable to remember the millions of "witches" killed because of a single sentence in the Bible (Exodus 22:18), not to mention the killing of millions of "heretics" and "infidels," the forced conversion of Jews, Muslims, and other undesirables, and the centuries-long persecutions of the Inquisition.

"Discovery after discovery supports the accuracy of this book," opines Mr. Green. "The book we have is a reliable historical document." Hear, hear!

Given the current makeup of the Supreme Court, it is sometimes more of a blessing when it does nothing than when it actually renders a verdict. Such is the case with its recent decision to let stand appeals courts' rulings that had effectively shot down statutes in five states prohibiting same-sex marriage, with the result that such marriages were immediately legal in Indiana, Oklahoma, Utah (!), Virginia, and Wisconsin, and are likely to become legal in as many as nine additional states.

Some officials in these latter states (Republicans, *naturellement*) are suffering spasms of apoplexy and are continuing to resist the tidal wave. Kraig Powell, a state representative in Utah, whimsically suggested that same-sex unions be referred to as "pairages," on the following illuminating grounds: "The differences between a same-sex relationship and an opposite-sex relationship are large enough that maybe we ought to recognize the difference between them." Yeah, maybe. But in a sign that sanity is not entirely absent in the Mormon state, we hear a state senator, Jim Dabakis, state that such a proposal would establish "apartheid marriage."

Gayle Ruzicka, president of the ineffable Eagle Forum, brought up the issue of states' rights in a heated comment. "The bottom line of course is religious liberty—we need to pass legislation to protect Utah's religious liberty." Ah, so now states as well as individuals have religious liberty! What a wonderful development of our constitutional law!

But a certain sense of resignation is setting in even among the most furious opponents of same-sex marriage. Officials in Idaho, in pleading for the Supreme Court to maintain its temporary stay of the appeals court ruling that would have legalized same-sex marriage in that state, declared: "If the court wishes to signal that its recent denials of various marriage-related petitions was intended to finally and conclusively resolve the constitutionality of state laws defining marriage as a union of [a] man and a woman, the court should deny Idaho's application." A few hours later, the stay was lifted.

Scott Walker, current (and, one hopes, soon to be ex-)governor of Wisconsin, put it more bluntly: "It's over."

Some Republicans, as is now well known, are opposed to contraception for women. How such a primitive and fascistic policy could have gained currency is beyond my understanding, but at least we find one Republican who has bravely come out in support of contraception—for certain people, at any rate. Russell Pearce, a former state senator in Arizona who gained notoriety for shepherding stringent anti-immigrant laws through the state's legislature (many of which were subsequently overturned on appeal), recently stated that he advocated mandatory birth control for Medicaid recipients. In his own imperishable words: "You put me in charge of Medicaid, the first thing I'd do is get Norplant, birth-control implants or tubal ligations." I daresay it struck Mr. Pearce as a bit unjust that the kerfuffle over his remarks forced him to step down as the state Republican Party's vice chairman—but such are the fruits of all fearless advocates of truth and justice!

In the ongoing battle between Amazon.com and the Hachette publishing group over the pricing of e-books, Amazon has resorted to delaying the delivery of thousands of titles by Hachette authors in an attempt to strong-arm Hachette into caving in to its demands. But it is making prompt delivery of at least one title by a Hachette author—none other than *The Way Forward* by Republican congressman and "thinker" (I use the term loosely) Paul D. Ryan. But, alas, a book strongly critical of the conservative Koch brothers, after briefly reaching the bestseller lists, fell off the list after Amazon delayed delivery by a full five weeks.

So it appears that, while all Hachette authors are equal, some are more equal than others.

[January/February 2015]

Amidst all the crowing by Republicans over their perceived electoral victory (a victory that, I daresay, will prove very short-lived indeed), there were a few flies in the ointment. As is so typical, some members of that "party of Lincoln" ended up putting their feet in their mouths and being forced to retreat into ignominy. One of the most pungent is Ira Hansen, who had just become the speaker-elect of the Nevada state legislature. He was forced to abandon his new position even before he filled it by revelations of a succession of derogatory remarks directed toward various disfavored groups as found in newspaper columns, radio talks, and so forth. The one comment that seemed to turn the tide was Hansen's characterization of the relationship between African Americans and the Democrats whom they overwhelmingly favor: "The relationship between Negroes [sic] and Democrats is truly a master-slave relationship, with the benevolent master knowing what's best for his simple minded darkies."

But I deny with all the strength of my being that Ira Hansen practices discrimination; he seems to disdain all manner of people quite uniformly (except maybe white males), as witness his comments on women ("The truth is, women do not belong in the Army or Navy or Marine Corps, except in certain limited fields"), Hispanics ("You cannot read a story about criminals or watch a news report locally without noticing a grossly disproportionate amount of Hispanic involvement"), and gays ("Male homosexuals are grossly disproportionate in child molestation cases").

Needless to say, Mr. Hansen has strongly protested the unearthing of these unfortunate statements, saying it is part of an orchestrated plan of "character assassination." It seems to me that Mr. Hansen has done a splendid job of assassinating his character all by himself.

I had an engaging conversation the other day with a longtime friend who, although endowed with many virtues, happens to be a gun nut. Well, nobody's perfect. The discussion became a bit heated at times, in the course of which—as I discovered only later—my friend spouted any number of falsehoods on the issue. For example:

- In my friend's opinion, the percentage of households owning guns in the United States stands at 45%. In fact, it is about 32%. (I had supplied the figure of 20%—taken from Michael Waldman's *The Second Amendment: A Biography*—and, although my figure was too low, it was minimally closer to the truth than my friend's.)
- According to a source my friend quoted, the number of burglaries or break-ins foiled by gun-toting householders was estimated to be 800,000 to 1.2 million *a year*. This figure struck me as inordinately high—and, in fact, it was. According to the Violence Policy Center, the figure stands at about 67,000 a year—quite a difference! (My friend's statistics came from something called the Institute for Justice, which he asserted was a branch of the Justice Department. In my naïveté I accepted the claim—until I found out that the Institute for Justice is some crazy right-wing organization.)

But my friend's inaccuracies—as one can charitably call them—is the least of the difficulties. When I asked him why he was so passionate about the gun issue, he replied with an entirely straight face: "Because gun owners are free and everyone else is a slave."

Let us consider this statement more carefully. The idea appears to go back to the putative "original" meaning or function of the Second Amendment, which was thought to be a bulwark against the "tyranny" of a "standing army" led by the federal government. Evidently, in my friend's opinion, one must always be vigilant against the ever-present threat of "enslavement" by our government.

I was so stunned at this comment that I did not have the intellectual wherewithal to make some obvious replies:

- Exactly *how* could a federal (or state or municipal) government, which cannot consist of more than a few hundred thousand people (not counting the Army), "enslave" an American populace that must now number about 325 million?
- *Why* would the federal (or state or municipal) government *want* to enslave us? What would it stand to gain by such a procedure? The gov-

ernment can already levy taxes and force us to accept such heinous infringements on our liberties as wearing seat belts and not playing a boombox in public at 3 in the morning.

• Most significant of all, how could a relatively small band of gun owners, with their pea-shooter weapons, stand up against the strength of the U.S. Army?

Let us assume, for the sake of argument, the truth of the paranoid fantasy that the government is trying to enslave us. Would taking up arms against it be the best defense? Surely it would be more effective to take the government to court (as our Republican friends are doing in response to certain executive actions by President Obama) on the grounds that the measures in question are unconstitutional; or to arouse public opinion in opposition to the measures; or—in a worst-case scenario—to persuade the Army to defect from a tyrannous government. All these actions would seem to lead to far better results. But the moment you admit that, the ultimate premise for gun ownership (at least as espoused by my friend and those who think like him) falls to the ground.

But there is a more serious issue behind this ridiculous argument, and that is this: *How do you argue rationally with someone who holds such insane beliefs?* What course of reasoning can you adduce against someone who thinks that not owning a gun makes you a slave? For my part, I give up on reason—and resort to my old friends, satire and ridicule.

[*March/April 2015*]

We are faced with the engaging spectacle of a state supreme court judge defying the instructions of federal courts, including the Supreme Court. No, we are not talking about Southern opposition to desegregation in the 1960s, although we are indeed in the South. I refer to Roy S. Moore, the saintly chief justice of the Alabama Supreme Court, who issued a directive to probate judges that they are not obliged to fill out marriage certificates to gay couples after a federal judge decreed that the state's prohibition of such marriages was unconstitutional.

You will recall, of course, that it was Moore who set up in a building in Montgomery a 5000-pound concrete monument featuring the Ten Commandments. When he defied an order by a federal judge (those pesky federal judges again!) stipulating that the monument be removed, he himself was removed from his office—as was his monument. It is strange enough that Moore would seek to bolster his Christian credentials by means of a monument recording words from the Judaic part of the Bible; it is even stranger (or perhaps, on second thought, it isn't) that Moore would be so oblivious of the fact that the text in question advocates slavery and the ownership of wives by their husbands. Moore, after all, is a Baptist, and I suspect these principles are entirely acceptable to his primitive faith.

The benighted voters of Alabama returned Moore to office in 2012. Well, they re-elected George Wallace several times, didn't they? The current contretemps is made more amusing by ludicrous assertions on the part of Moore's partisans. One county probate judge, Nick Williams, maintained that he would "only issue marriage licenses and solemnize ceremonies consistent with Alabama law and the U.S. Constitution; namely, between one man and one woman, so help me God." Bully for you! Too bad the U.S. Constitution devotes not one word to marriage.

Moore himself has stated that "state courts are not bound by the judicial opinions of federal district or appeals court on questions of federal constitutional law." Study that statement deeply, my friends, and see if there is the slightest bit of sense or reason in it.

I am heartened by such plain indications that Judge Moore has committed treason. The only question is the method of his punishment in this capital crime. Given his state's fondness for guns, I recommend a firing squad.

Speaking of guns, one cannot help bypassing the exquisite case of the two-year-old boy who, while he was sitting placidly in a shopping cart at a Walmart in Idaho, reached into his mother's purse, pulled out her loaded gun, and blew her away.

I can't help feeling that this little boy should be a poster child for the NRA. After all, don't they believe in getting firearms training from the earliest possible age? And surely the mother had it coming to her: What was she doing shopping at the Evil Empire anyway?

The outbreak of measles in numerous states has brought to the fore the issue of parents' "philosophical" or religious objections to vaccination. These individuals comprise not only religious fundamentalists and right-wingers hostile to anything that smacks of government "intrusion" into their lives but also the wealthy (and mostly liberal) inhabitants in such places as Santa Monica, California—which only goes to prove the old adage that extremism on both the right and the left eventually fuses into a confused mass of ignorance and irrationality.

Certain parents are now feeling the weight of public pressure and condemnation, but are sticking to their guns. Putting aside the nitwits who still maintain a connection between vaccination and autism—a claim first put forth in a scientific paper in 1998 but subsequently debunked many times over—we are faced with absurdities like the following from one Crystal McDonald, a parent in Palm Desert. In the words of a *New York Times* reporter, "She said they [her family] ate well and had never been to the doctor" [which is of course a guarantee that they would never need health care of any kind], "and insisted that her daughter was healthier than many classmates" [which of course assures us that she will remain so for the duration of her time in school]. One Kelly McMenimin avers that she doesn't want "so many toxins" in her child. Too bad there are no toxins in vaccines!

The most amusing reactions have been from politicians (Republicans, needless to say). Governor Chris Christie of New Jersey opined: "It's more important what you think as a parent than what you think as a public official. [Huh?] I also understand that parents need to have some measure of choice in things as well." Choice, eh? Well, would Mr. Christie endorse the "choice" of a Christian Science parent to withhold medical treatment to a child, leading to the child's death?

Then there is Senator Rand Paul of Kentucky, the darling of the libertarian set. He first asserted that he was aware of "many tragic cases of walking, talking, normal children who wound up with profound mental disorders after vaccines." He was quickly forced to backtrack, saying (plainly falsely) that he did not "allege causation" in the matter. Things became still more embarrassing for Mr. Paul when it was discovered that he was a longtime member of a radical group, the Association of American Physicians and Surgeons, that is not only hostile to vaccination but advocates the exploded theory of a connection between abortions and higher rates of breast cancer, not to mention that great white whale of right-wing crackpots, the "murder" of Vincent Foster (by Bill and/or Hillary Clinton?). It is unlikely that Paul's hasty receipt of a Hepatitus C vaccine will relieve people's worries over how much of a wingnut he is.

[May/June 2015]

To paraphrase the Bible, there is a time for every purpose under heaven (turn, turn, turn!). A time to be subdued, and a time to gloat.

Today, my friends, it is time to gloat—if, that is, one is an atheist, a supporter of gay rights, and a civilized person.

I refer, of course, to the exquisite farce that we recently witnessed in the legislatures of the benighted states of Indiana and Arkansas, where the attempt to enact legislation allowing for-profit companies (including major corporations) to refuse service to gay and lesbians (especially those who are evilly attempting to subvert traditional marriage by tying the knot) by claiming a "religious freedom" exemption to do so. No doubt these legislatures thought they were being clever by attempting to expand upon the 1993 Religious Freedom Restoration Act (RFRA) to protect the put-upon merchants whose moral sensibilities are gravely endangered by having to cater to gay couples.

(Who knew that florists, photographers, and wedding planners had such lobbying clout?) But RFRA was designed to protect religious *minorities* against undue infringement of their religious practices by the *government* (although the state legislators also tried to rely on the Supreme Court's colossal error in allowing the corporation Hobby Lobby to opt out of providing free contraception for its employees, in accordance with the Affordable Care Act).

The end result for the startled legislators was, however, a furious backlash—not just by gays but by anyone who believes in equal treatment of individuals in the commercial sphere. Even though David C. Long, president pro tem of the Indiana State Senate, piously affirmed that "It is not the intent of the law to discriminate against anyone, and it will not be allowed to discriminate against anyone," it was obvious to everyone that that was the exact intent of the law. The uproar forced both states to amend their laws to make it clear that such discrimination was prohibited.

This whole incident has given a huge black eye to religious conservatives throughout the nation, and for that we can only be grateful. The contretemps could easily have been avoided if our devout friends had only followed one of their own avowed principles—that is, the Golden Rule. Imagine yourself being a member of a persecuted minority and being denied service at a for-profit business that otherwise serves everyone. What if I set up a shop that refused to serve members of the Tea Party? This would be perfectly legal, because political affiliation is not a protected category, as race, religion, and gender are. If these laws had been sustained in their original form, would we eventually reach the stage where every merchant asks every potential customer to fill out a questionnaire specifying the political, social, religious, and cultural issues that the merchant might find offensive and therefore trigger a denial of service? It is all too ridiculous. The sooner these fundamentalist troglodytes crawl back under the rocks from which they emerged a few decades ago, the better it will be for the civilized world.

It's time to pop open the champagne, people! Haven't you heard? Benjamin Netanyahu has succeeded in his bid to be re-elected as prime minister of Israel. Whoo-hoo!

No, I have not suddenly converted into a right-wing supporter of Likud. Instead, I see Netanyahu's re-election as the final nail in the coffin of Israel's international reputation. Here we have a purported world leader who, in the days before the election on March 17, frankly repudiated the promise of Palestinian statehood that he had (no doubt insincerely) endorsed in 2009, stating that no Palestinian state would ever be established during his term in office. Then, two days after the election, he blandly reversed himself—thereby joining the company of Vladimir Putin and Bashar al-Assad as one of the most hypocritical and duplicitous politicians on the planet. A noteworthy achievement indeed, given the number of viable candidates for the position!

On top of which, Netanyahu frankly and unashamedly made a crudely racist appeal to his base by warning of the threat of a flood of Israeli Arabs rushing to vote. To quote: "The right-wing government is in danger. Arab voters are heading to the polling stations in droves." Imagine the furor if a politician on this side of the water said something similar! Well, it is in fact sadly plausible to hear such a person of the Republican persuasion say: "The right-wing control of the House of Representatives is in danger. Black and Hispanic voters are heading to the polling stations in droves." Republicans have, in effect, been saying exactly that for a generation or more—and acting upon it through voter suppression laws. Netanyahu later made a smarmy "apology" on this point also. I'm surprised he didn't admit with pride that some of his best friends were Israeli Arabs.

If any further evidence is needed that Netanyahu (and the millions of Is-raelis who support him) believe that Arabs on either side of the 1967 border are not quite human, this must be it. And if any evidence is needed that Israel has now definitively become an apartheid state, we need look no further than to the fact that the 350,000 settlers in the occupied territories can vote, whereas the millions of Palestinians there cannot. So can we please end all this blather about Israel being the only "democracy" in the Middle East?

Those who equate a refusal to support an Israeli leader—no matter who he or she is, and no matter what policies he or she advocates—with anti-Semitism may be in a somewhat more uncomfortable position now. If a Grand Wizard of the KKK became president of the United States, would it be "anti-American" to oppose and condemn him?

[July/August 2015]

Ya gotta love this Pope!

Since his elevation to the papacy a little more than two years ago, Pope Francis has ruffled not a few feathers in his own church by refusing to con-demn homosexuals ("Who am I to judge?"), suggesting that devout Catholics should give up the practice of "breeding like rabbits," and even having kind words about nonbelievers: "We also sense our closeness to all those men and women who, although not identifying themselves as followers of any religious tradition, are nonetheless searching for truth, goodness, and beauty." He once went so far as to say that "even atheists" can get to heaven—a remark that was quickly repudiated by the Vatican hierarchy. Well, Frank, thanks but no thanks: the privilege of an atheist entering the Christian heaven is a dubious one indeed.

Now Francis is creating consternation among conservatives by refusing to bury his head in the sand about climate change. He recently held what the *New York Times* called a "high-level workshop . . . on the moral dimensions of climate change," in advance of a significant encyclical on this topic. He said on Twitter: "We need to care for the earth so that it may continue, as God willed, to be a source of life for the entire human family." That last remark is sadly in conformity with standard Catholic doctrine that appears to express concern only for human life (for, of course, animals do not have "souls")—but let that pass.

The response by opponents of the overwhelming scientific consensus on climate change—including those benighted legislators in our own Congress who think it some kind of liberal hoax—was characteristically vicious and disrespectful. Maureen Mullarkey (yes, folks, that really is her name) said in the conservative journal *First Things*: "Francis sullies his office by using demagogic formulations to bully the populace into reflexive climate action with no more substantive guide than theologized propaganda." My, my! Such language! Joseph Bast, president of something called the Heartland Institute (a libertarian group sponsored by—who else?—the Koch brothers), was only a little less restrained: "Though Pope Francis's heart is surely in the right place, he would do his flock and the world a disservice by putting his moral authority behind the United Nations' unscientific agenda."

Now John Boehner, Speaker of the House, has invited the Pope to address Congress. As a reporter for the *National Catholic Reporter* stated, "I think Boehner was out of his mind to invite the pope to speak to Congress. Can you imagine what the Republicans will do when he says, 'You've got to do something about global warming'?" Stay tuned!

It will be readily apparent that I enjoy poking fun at the crazy right (although these days it seems the entire Republican party has gone crazy)—but I am in no way blind to the existence of a crazy left, politically and culturally insignificant though it may be. A recent event, however, crystallized some of the exquisite buffooneries that such leftists can engender. I refer to the bizarre protest against the PEN American Center's decision to award a "Free Expression Courage Award" to the editors of the Paris satirical magazine *Charlie Hebdo*, who were gunned down by fanatical Muslims last January.

Garry Trudeau, creator of *Doonesbury*, began the follies by all but accusing the editors of *Charlie Hebdo* of causing their own deaths. You see, by ridiculing Islam the paper was "punching downward . . . attacking a powerless, disenfranchised minority" (referring to the millions of Muslims who now live in France). Trudeau went on to say that "ridiculing the non-privileged is almost never funny—it's just mean." I trust the multiple levels of stupidity embodied in this utterance are evident to all. Firstly, the paper is not directly ridiculing individual Muslims (whether in France or elsewhere) but the religion as a religion. Secondly, *Charlie Hebdo* is an ecumenical satirist, and evidence shows that it has much more vigorously lampooned Christianity than Islam. Thirdly, I would suggest that the resulting deaths of the editors make it fairly clear that Muslims in France aren't exactly "powerless."

The whole notion that satire must be polite and tactful and only attack the "privileged" reveals a catastrophic failure to understand the very nature and purpose of satire—the more astounding from one who has practiced the art so assiduously over a lifetime. Satire is *meant* to be rude, impolite, deliberately offensive—this is how it provokes thought and reflection. And even attacking the "non-privileged" can serve its uses. Ambrose Bierce was criticized for directing his barbs upon such insignificant nobodies, but he replied vigorously: "In satirizing real persons I follow the example of *all* satirists who succeed. It does not at all matter how obscure, or how anything-else, the persons satirized may be; the merit is *in the satire*. Do you suppose that the merit of Heine's, or Pope's, or Byron's attacks on *persons* has any relation to the personality of the objects of it. The merit is *intrinsic*."

And yet, a letter signed by 145 prominent writers protesting the PEN award made the breathtaking claim that the award is "valorizing selectively offensive material: material that intensifies the anti-Islamic, anti-Maghreb, anti-Arab sentiments already prevalent in the Western world." Rachel Kushner accused *Charlie Hebdo* of "cultural intolerance" and the promotion of "a kind of forced secular view." But I've never heard satirists like P. J. O'Rourke being criticized for having a "forced Catholic view."

All this is too ridiculous. These pampered, self-cocooning writers need to get out into the world and see what's happening. The difference between attacking someone with a few strokes of the pen and attacking someone with guns and bombs should be abundantly clear.

[September/October 2015]

As is now common knowledge, the number of Republican candidates for president has now become so gargantuan that they could field both the offense and the defense of a professional football team. I use that analogy advisedly, because nearly all the candidates are offensive in one way or the other, and a fair number of them are having to play defense: former governor Rick Perry has already been indicted; Governor Chris Christie (the Ralph Kramden of American politics) is likely to be indicted; and Governor Scott Walker would have been indicted for fairly obvious campaign finance shenanigans were it not that a state appeals court—most of whose judges he conveniently appointed—quashed an investigation of the matter.

But of course all eyes have lately been focused on the exquisite buffoonery that is Donald J. Trump. Rarely has the political world seen such a melding of the showmanship of P. T. Barnum with the intellectual vacuity of the Kardashians. Of late, Mr. Trump has gotten himself into hot water on multiple fronts. First, he denied the status of war hero to Senator John McCain because, during the Vietnam War (where Trump himself was exempted from service by reason of some unspecified foot trouble—presumably the one that keeps finding its way into his mouth), he suffered the humiliation of being captured and tortured for five years. Then there were Trump's antics during and following the first Republican debate on August 6. Here, you will recall, he was confronted by that stellar exemplar of liberalism, Megyn Kelly of Fox News, for his unkind comments on women (he had referred to various women as "fat pigs, dogs, slobs, and disgusting animals"), to which he offered a flippant and unrepentant reply. Later he compounded his folly by referring to Kelly as a "bimbo"—a comment that led Erick Erickson, organizer of a Red-State conservative forum, to disinvite him.

Trump went on to say that there must have been something wrong with Kelly to make her question him so aggressively: "There was blood coming out of her eyes, blood coming out of her wherever." Many took that latter comment to refer to the supposition that Kelly was having her period—and everyone knows, of course, how irrational women in that condition can be. (The Old Testament certainly does, prohibiting people from approaching women who are menstruating, lest they be polluted.) Trump fought back, saying he really was alluding to blood coming out of Kelly's nose and ears and calling anyone who thought he was referring to menstruation a "degenerate." Well, I have not watched tapes of the debate (I could not bring myself to do so, lest I lose my lunch, dinner, and anything else in my internal organs)—but I very much doubt that blood could be detected emerging from any orifice on Ms. Kelly's person.

And yet, Mr. Trump continues to lead in the polls by a large margin, and there is no guarantee that he will wither on the vine the way Herman Cain (remember him?) or Rick Perry or any other once-prominent conservative has done in the past. And all this is happening not only after Trump's grotesqueries regarding McCain and Kelly, but after his notorious comments that Mexico is importing "rapists" and "murderers" in the form of undocumented immigrants. Trump, of course, does not allow himself to be confused by facts—such as that whites commit more rapes (in proportion to their numbers) than Hispanics, and that undocumented immigrants commit substantially fewer crimes overall than the general population.

What, then, is the appeal of Trump? The eminent Mr. Erickson may have put it best when he said that the candidate is connecting with "so much of the anger in the Republican base." There you have it, folks! It is a distressing fact that a substantial number of people in this country (mostly on the right side of the political spectrum) are unregenerate racists, sexists, and bigots. They are infuriated with certain trends in this country—whether it be legalization of same-sex marriage, the unexpected success of the Affordable Care Act after so many predictions of doom from the right, the outrageous attempts by the EPA to clean up our environment (you know, the "war on coal" and things like that), and, most galling of all, the fact that we have a half-black (or is he half-white?) person in the Oval Office and the sky hasn't fallen. Where can these enraged patriots turn except to a bombastic loudmouth who thinks "political correctness" is one of the great evils facing this nation? Well, all I can say is that the cartoonish capers of Trump and his followers are rapidly relegating Republicans to the status of a permanent minority party—a consummation that cannot happen too soon.

An individual with the fantastic name of Dylann Storm Roof—a baby-faced man-child of twenty-one—recently entered a predominantly black church in Charleston, South Carolina, and blew away nine parishioners with a shotgun. The fellow was promptly arrested and is likely to spend the rest of his life in prison, assuming he is not executed.

I for one hope that his life is a long one. His actions have already resulted in the removal of the Confederate battle flag from the South Carolina state capitol and elsewhere. And if the white supremacist gunman lives to the year 2040, he will be an eyewitness to a momentous event—for that is when it is expected that whites will become a minority in this country. I fully expect that at that time our Caucasian friends will suddenly discover an urgent need for affirmative action—for themselves.

We persons of color should be magnanimous and grant their wish. They need all the help they can get.

[*November/December 2015*]

My friends, we are witnessing the implosion and imminent demise of the Republican party.

This is the only viable conclusion from the unexpected resignation of John Boehner as Speaker of the House, itself the culmination of a years-long trend during which an alarming number of Republicans—both rank-and-file individuals and (especially) politicians—have demonstrated an impressive ability to be simultaneously stupid, crazy, and evil. It is now becoming apparent that Republicans are not only incapable of governing the nation, but also incapable of governing themselves.

If someone like Boehner is regarded as insufficiently conservative for the foaming-at-the-mouth reactionaries of the Tea Party, one wonders who on earth short of Attila the Hun could satisfy them. There have been all kinds of wild ideas as to a replacement. Current hopes rest on Representative Paul D. Ryan of Wisconsin, who has done a remarkable con job in convincing both his party and the media that he is a "thoughtful" Republican, even though his policy proposals on refashioning the tax code and cutting or privatizing Medicare and Social Security both fail to make any kind of economic sense and also would radically exacerbate the income inequality we are already suffering under. But other gents—ranging from Newt Gingrich to Senator Mike Lee of Utah—have been put forth. For you see, by a quirk of our constitution, the Speaker of the House does not have to be a congressman—indeed, does not have to be an elected official at all. You, I, or Kim Kardashian can be Speaker. I'm beginning to wonder whether that last option is the best we have.

Meanwhile, the Republican presidential campaign follies continue unabated. A certain weariness seems to be setting in as far as the odoriferous Donald J. Trump is concerned: his inimitable fusion of bombast, insults, and absence of viable policy prescriptions appears to be heralding his ultimate demise as a candidate. But who are filling the Trump void? None other than the equally unqualified Ben Carson and Carly Fiorina! All three of these candidates are vaunting the fact that they are perfect novices at governing as an actual point in their favor, even though they would be the first to heap abuse on the idea that someone without training or experience could be a real estate mogul, the head of a major corporation, or a neurosurgeon.

Let us pause on the exquisite Dr. Carson for a while. He first got into hot water by declaring bluntly, "I would not advocate that we put a Muslim in charge of this nation. I would absolutely disagree with that." When it was pointed out to him that the U.S. Constitution specifically forbids a "religious test" for public office, Carson attempted to walk back his comments, saying he really only meant that he was objecting to a Muslim who wished to practice "Sharia law." Then, after a horrible mass shooting at an Oregon community college, he came up with a novel way to deal with such situations: "I would not just stand there and let him shoot me. I would say: 'Hey, guys, everybody attack him! He may shoot me, but he can't get us all.'" Well, I for one would be happy to see Dr. Carson engage in unarmed kamikaze warfare with a gunman, but somehow I doubt whether that would be a very effective solution to this problem. Finally, he claimed that President Obama was "politicizing" the gun issue by merely going to Oregon to extend sympathy with the victims' relatives. If *he* were president, he simply couldn't be bothered! "I mean, I would probably have so many things on my agenda that I would go to the next one."

Of course, the establishment Republican candidates aren't having a good time of it either. Jeb Bush has landed in trouble on a number of fronts. He first declared that African Americans don't want a lot of "free stuff" (i.e., welfare) but want to earn their money (he failed to point out that the great majority of the "free stuff" the government hands out goes to the wealthy in the form of preferential tax policies). Then, in the wake of the Oregon shooting, he shrugged his shoulders and said cavalierly, "Stuff happens." At least he didn't say that these gun deaths—along with 30,000 others that occur each year—are just "collateral damage" in the face of the overriding necessity to preserve the Second Amendment.

What is happening to the Republican Party? It is a priceless instance of the old adage: "Be careful what you wish for: you might get it." For decades, liberals have lamented the rise of conservative talk radio and the systematic gerrymandering of voting districts in conservative states; but both these things have come back to bite the Republicans in the posterior. Talk radio keeps the Republican base in a white-hot pitch of rage, resentment, and sense of victimization; gerrymandering means that Republican politicians have only to fear primary opponents to their right, so that they themselves drift farther and farther to the right. The result is the Tea Party, a classic case of the tail wagging the dog.

Republicans are facing a further difficulty. Many of the pressing issues of the day—income inequality, climate change, ongoing problems with health care in an aging population—require strong government intervention, creating a kind of existential crisis for Republicans whose idea of "limited government" is becoming increasingly untenable. Conservatives are seeing their vision of a white-bread America where women know their place and gays, Muslims, and atheists don't exist collapsing all around them—and good riddance to it.

[January/February 2016]

What would the Republican party be without boogeymen to send a thrill of horror up the spines of the faithful? One will recall that in the 2004 presidential election, the party craftily held up the horrible specter of married gay people as part of their strategy for corralling votes—and it worked. One suspects that with the nationwide legalization of same-sex marriage (and, more significantly, the support for such marriage by a majority of Americans), gays will have to take second or third place among Republican-conjured demons.

We are, however, now witnessing the emergence of several new villains—one of which is the numerically tiny but increasingly vocal cadre of the transgendered.

A recent vote in Houston—which apparently passes for a bastion of liberalism in the benighted state of Texas—laid bare the new strategy. A proposition—the Houston Equal Rights Ordinance, which would have protected citizens from "discrimination based on sex, race, color, ethnicity, national origin, age, familial status, marital status, military status, religion, disability, sexual orientation, genetic information, gender identity or pregnancy"—was put to the vote on November 3. It would seem to have been uncontroversial, but an unholy alliance of political and religious conservatives devised a campaign that managed to bamboozle the naïve citizens of Houston—and it revolved around bathrooms.

Yes, my friends, the political and religious right created out of whole cloth the petrifying image of transgender women (i.e., women who had once been men—or perhaps men who simply "identified" as women) lurking in women's bathrooms to molest our wives, mothers, daughters, and perhaps even our mothers-in-law. Let it pass that not one single instance of any such thing happening anywhere was ever brought forth. Nevertheless, the proposition lost by a landslide.

Meanwhile, the comic opera that is the Republican presidential nomination continues with unabated hilarity. Lately Dr. Ben Carson, the political novice who had been on the verge of challenging Donald J. Trump for supremacy in the polls, has been fading fast because of his perceived inexperience in foreign affairs. (Apparently his inexperience in every other facet of political activity was not held against him.)

As for Trump himself, I have come up with what I believe is a novel theory: *He is a Democratic political operative in disguise!* What he is doing—by design—is embracing views so outlandish and absurd that he is holding the entire Republican Party up to ridicule. Consider some of his pronouncements of the past weeks and months:

- He declared that he recalled seeing news videos of "thousands and thousands" of Muslim Americans in Jersey City, New Jersey, celebrating after the 9/11 attacks (every news organ has declared such an assertion to be false);
- He advocated a return to torture (in the form of waterboarding) of suspected terrorists, and also recommended killing the families of terrorists (thereby pointing to conservatives' inveterate tendency to reduce themselves to the level of their enemies);

- Following the terrorist attacks in Paris and San Bernardino, he first declared that all Muslims in America should be entered into a registry and monitored, then said that some mosques should be shut down, and then, most outrageously of all, that no Muslims from overseas should be allowed into the country at all until we can "figure out what is going on" (a long and difficult proposition if someone as brainless as Mr. Trump is in charge). Trump subsequently defended his position by appealing to Franklin D. Roosevelt's internment of Japanese Americans—as if anything FDR did must in itself be acceptable.

All this has Republican bigwigs and donors in a tizzy, predicting disaster in 2016 if Trump is the actual nominee. "It would be an utter, complete, and total disaster," said Senator Lindsey Graham. "If you're a xenophobic, race-baiting, religious bigot, you're going to have a hard time being president of the United States, and you're going to do irreparable damage to the party." What Mr. Graham seems to have overlooked is the very real probability that a substantial majority of Republicans are themselves xenophobic, race-baiting, religious bigots.

At this point, my cat Henry (named after Henry VIII because of his regal bearing) could beat any Republican candidate that the party has the misfortune to nominate. In fact, Henry would make a rather good president, it seems to me. I see nothing in the U.S. Constitution prohibiting cats from becoming president. And he meets the age requirement of being thirty-five years or older: Henry is eleven in human years, making him fifty-five in cat years. He is a strong leader (decidedly an alpha cat), says exactly what's on his mind, and is beholden to no one! (Well, maybe to me for doling out servings of Fancy Feast at frequent intervals throughout the day.)

And if there were not enough reason to loathe and despise conservatives, we now have a new justification for doing so—their contemptible and insane reaction to recent terrorist attacks, not excluding the shooting up of a Planned Parenthood clinic in Colorado Springs by a self-proclaimed devout Christian. In response, twenty-six governors (all but one of them Republicans) have declared that their states will not be open to Syrian refugees (a stance that happens to be unconstitutional, since this is a federal matter). Of course, there is a furious denial that the terrorists in question all had easy access to an appalling array of firearms—a point emphasized by the Senate's refusal to deny those on the government's no-fly list the right to purchase weapons. What tender consideration for the due process rights of terrorists!

There is no need to worry about Syrian terrorists coming into the country disguised as refugees. The terrorists are already here—and they have guns.

[*March/April 2016*]

There is a long and noble tradition of civil disobedience in this country; there is also a long and despicable tradition of greed, selfishness, and self-aggrandizement masquerading as civil disobedience. A pungent example of the latter was on display recently in a remote corner of Oregon known as the Malheur National Wildlife Refuge. On January 2 a band of armed ranchers (most from out of state) took over the refuge, evicting the federal workers there, and settled in for the long haul. One of the leaders of this venture was Ammon Bundy, son of Ted—er, that is, Cliven—Bundy, who himself is undertaking a valiant escapade in civil disobedience (some, however, would call it thievery) by refusing to pay about $1 million in accumulated fees for grazing on federal land; he himself has a ragtag bunch of armed men to enforce his "freedom."

The Malheur protest was purportedly based on the claim that the federal government was illegally preventing these worthy souls from using the land for cattle grazing—but to my cynical eyes it looks like a simple land grab. For all that our conservative friends vaunt personal responsibility, it looks as if these ranchers simply want to get something for nothing—the ability to use this land for their own purposes without paying for it. And while Ammon Bundy claimed to be acting in order to "preserve freedom" and claiming that federal lands belong to everyone, it seems highly unlikely that he would countenance anyone but himself and his compatriots making use of the property. As in so many such instances, the Bundys seem to want freedom for themselves but not for anyone else. Mercifully, these miscreants have now been rounded up like their own cattle and evicted.

It should be noted that the Bundys embrace a bizarre mix of Mormonism, libertarianism, and right-wing paranoia that leads them to believe that God is on their side. They apparently believe that the U.S. Constitution is an inspired text, just like the Bible and their own *Book of Mormon*. Here is Cliven Bundy's reasoning: "Don't we believe that Jesus Christ is basically the author of the Bible? Well, if the Constitution is inspired, who is the author? Wouldn't that author be Jesus Christ again?" Q.E.D.! But it would seem to be a singular oversight on Mr. Christ's part that he failed to mention himself or God or anything that could be taken as endorsing biblical precepts in this sacred document.

Meanwhile, the presidential campaign follies continue unabated, especially on the Republican side. Donald J. Trump's surprising defeat in the Iowa caucuses had some people (including myself) hoping that the bad joke that is his campaign was on its way out the door, but his resounding win in the New

Hampshire primary made it dismally likely that this carnival barker would continue his antics for some time to come. But what was most amusing in the prelude to the Iowa vote was the degree to which so many Republican candidates pandered to the plethora of Christian evangelicals in the state.

Senator Ted Cruz was the most shameless, stating, "We have to awaken and energize the body of Christ" (which sounds to me as if Christ is a Frankenstein's monster that some mad scientist has to electrocute into some kind of galvanic activity). Cruz went on to say, "Any president who doesn't begin every day on his knees isn't fit to be commander in chief." Not to be outdone, Senator Marco Rubio took pride in the fact that he regularly attends both a Catholic service and one associated with the Southern Baptists. How ecumenical of him!

Even Donald Trump got into the toadying act, maintaining that "Christianity is under siege," but not offering any evidence as to why this should be the case—but then, that seems par for the course in his policy-free campaign. By some miracle, Trump won the endorsement of the esteemed Jerry Falwell, Jr.—and this in spite of his gaffe in referring to one of the books of the Bible as "Two Corinthians" and his noting how, at a Presbyterian service, he consumed "my little wine" and "my little cracker." This must be the first time Trump admitted to devouring anything "little"!

Some mainstream conservatives are becoming so distraught at the prospect of Trump being their standard-bearer that they are engaging in a kind of self-flagellation that is most amusing to watch. Ross Douthat has lamented that Trump may represent "an agent of divine retribution for a corrupt and stumbling party, a pillaging-and-torching Babylonian invasion of which it must be said: *The judgments of the Lord are true and righteous altogether.*" Amen to that, brother!

As for the Democratic side of the contest, the debate seems to be between the head (Hillary Clinton) and the heart (Bernie Sanders). A lot of starry-eyed young white liberals are swooning for Mr. Sanders, blithely unconcerned that his radical policies do not have the faintest chance of being passed by a conservative Congress. Moreover, Mr. Sanders's record of legislative accomplishment is embarrassingly thin. In twenty-four years in the House and Senate, he has sponsored exactly three bills; two of them related to renaming post offices in Vermont, and I forget what the third one was. And it doesn't help that Sanders, who is pretty clearly a secular Jew, doesn't have the courage to come out and say so. His mealy-mouthed assertion that "Everyone believes in God in their own ways" does not comport well with his reputation as a fearless truth-teller.

As a member of the rational wing of the Democratic Party, I am a firm Hillary supporter. Here's a campaign slogan she can use: "Hillary for President! She can't possibly do worse than a man."

[May/June 2016]

The late unlamented Antonin Scalia was not cold in his grave when Senate Majority Leader Mitch McConnell stated that no successor appointed by President Obama would be confirmed—or even receive public hearings—or, indeed, would even receive the courtesy of being greeted by any Republican senator. What could have led him to engage in such an unprecedented spasm of mulish obstructionism? Don't you see that "the people must have a voice" in the matter? (Let it pass that people already did have a voice in the matter when they re-elected Obama in 2012.) McConnell suggested that it would be all but unconstitutional for anyone nominated in the final year of a president's term to be confirmed.

It seems that we have all been reading the Reader's Digest Condensed Version of the U.S. Constitution. Once this fact dawned upon me, I did some investigation and found, in a remote corner of the Internet, what appears to be the full, unabridged text of this key document, which states: "The president shall not nominate, and the Senate shall not confirm, any Supreme Court candidate in the final year of his or her presidency." (Note how forward-looking the Founding Fathers were in using gender-neutral language here!) The awkward thing is that, under this rule, the confirmation of Justice Anthony Kennedy, which occurred in the final year of the presidency of Ronald Reagan, would appear to be unconstitutional.

Seriously, folks, is it not crystal-clear to everyone that Republican senators' wall of opposition on this issue has nothing to do with "strict constructionism" and everything to do with not allowing a Democratic president to shift the partisan center of the court? Mr. McConnell made this point openly and brazenly when he stated: "I can't imagine that a Republican-majority Senate, even if it were assumed to be a minority, would want to confirm a judge that would move the court dramatically to the left." Let it pass that Obama's nominee, Merrick Garland, is hardly a radical leftist; let it also pass that the Republicans are overwhelmingly likely to lose their Senate majority after the election. Would that Democrats had been so charmingly partisan when they contributed to Justice Scalia's confirmation by a 98-0 vote!

It must be a horrible thing to be a conservative. You are so full of fear—fear of terrorists lurking at every street corner, fear of undocumented aliens working hard to pick your vegetables and clean your hotel rooms, fear of men marrying men and women marrying women (which in some mysterious fashion degrades your own marriage to your opposite-sex spouse), and fear of liberals compelling you to worship at the altar of political correctness (otherwise called civilized behavior and common decency). And now conservatives are even afraid to use public bathrooms! I am led to these dour reflections by what has recently happened in the South (where else?), where a number of laws that permit open discrimination against gay and transgender people have been enacted so that God-fearing individuals can still pretend they are living in the 1950s.

The legislature of North Carolina, criminally disfigured by partisan gerrymandering, passed a law that, among many other horrible things, revoked a measure about to go into effect in the city of Charlotte that would have allowed people to use a bathroom that coincides with their gender identification. The specter of a man who has become a woman entering a women's bathroom and causing nameless havoc is apparently so terrifying that it requires discriminatory legislation to combat it. Bravo! But wait a minute. Aren't there also women who have become men? This is the point made by just such a person, who sent a message to Governor Pat McCrory: "It's now the law for me to share a restroom with your wife."

The governor, who has shed bitter tears about a "vicious, nationwide smear campaign" to portray him and his fellow Republicans as crazed bigots, is now making tentative moves to step back from the worst features of the law—but the bathroom provision apparently has wide support in his party. What a noble thing it is to protect women's honor and virtue while they are engaged in the serious business of relieving themselves!

Loose lips are said to sink ships, but they may also sink presidential campaigns. Recently the ineffable Donald J. Trump, questioned about his stance on abortion rights (which he once supported), declared not only that he was now opposed to abortion but that he believed that "some form of punishment" should be inflicted upon women who undergo them. Given that about one-third of American women have had abortions, that would seem to make criminals out of a substantial proportion of our wives, daughters, mothers, and sisters. Trump quickly backtracked, saying that only abortion doctors should be punished.

The most amusing thing about this contretemps is the alacrity with which not merely supporters but even opponents of abortion denounced Trump's initial statement. But, here as elsewhere, he was merely acting as the unregenerate Id of the conservative movement, saying out loud what it is unwilling to utter but clearly believes. The misogyny and fascism that have always been at the root of the anti-abortion movement have now been exposed for all to see. Our valiant "right-to-lifers" maintain that women are really "victims" in something called the abortion industry—driven to snuff out their "unborn children" through external influence, usually a husband, boyfriend, or some other (male) authority figure. The idea that women could actually make such a decision themselves, after due consideration of the economic, moral, psychological, and other issues involved, would mean that women are viable moral agents when it comes to taking control of their own bodies—and that is a conception our anti-abortion friends can never countenance.

[July/August 2016]

There are many good reasons why it is an exceptionally bad idea for sports figures to speak on any subjects outside of their very narrow areas of expertise—for the danger of sounding like a moron, a scoundrel, or a buffoon are alarmingly high. Case in point: Curt Schilling, who earned deserved praise for helping the Boston Red Sox win the World Series a decade ago and who was—until recently—a commentator on ESPN. For reasons known only to himself, Mr. Schilling has decided to weigh in on some sociopolitical topics of the day. First, he posted a comment on Twitter (that priceless venue that allows so many people to write before they think) comparing radical Muslims to Nazis. That only earned Schilling a reprimand, but then he shared a Facebook post showing an overweight man wearing a wig and women's clothing and with accompanying text that read: "LET HIM IN! to the restroom with your daughter or else you're a narrow-minded, judgmental, unloving racist bigot who needs to die." In his own words, Mr. Schilling added the following: "A man is a man no matter what they call themselves. I don't care who they are, who they sleep with, men's room was designed for penis, women't not so much. Now you need laws telling us differently? Pathetic." Evidently this passes for illuminating commentary among the generally conservative cadre of athletes. Not to become indelicate, but what would this modern-day Solomon do with those transgender women who no longer have the male organ of regeneration? And what about the transgender men who have gained this sought-after appendage? I am still befuddled what bathrooms these latter individuals are to use without endangering the lives and virtue of our wives, daughters, sisters, mothers, an other helpless females of our acquaintance. I doubt that I can expect any insight from the likes of Curt Schilling.

The decline and fall of Dennis Hastert has been quite a spectacle. It is one thing to learn that this seemingly benign and grandfatherly individual—once Speaker of the House, or third in line for the presidency—been revealed to be a serial child molester; it is quite another thing to discover that some of his allies were urging leniency in his sentencing (not for the molestation itself but for the bribes he handed out to cover up his derelictions) because Hastert was an avowed born-again Christian! The exquisite Tom DeLay, no stranger to controversy himself, wrote to the judge in the case: "He is a good man that loves the Lord. He gets his integrity and values from Him. He doesn't deserve what he is going through." Let me get this straight. Hastert is a Christian; and though he presumably defied Christian moral teaching in the most shameless way, he deserves milder treatment? One would think that Hastert's violation of Christian dogma would make him liable to greater punishment, not less. Or is DeLay saying that God himself is a child molester and that Hastert was only following His "integrity and values"?

The killing of forty-nine people at a gay bar in Orlando by an anti-gay Muslim has inevitably brought out the worst tendencies from a certain segment of the political spectrum. Our conservative friends were at first so reluctant to express the slightest sympathy with the L.G.B.T. community that they became amusingly phobic about even using the word "gay" in relation to the shooting. Representative Pete Sessions of Texas (where else?) described the gay bar where the shooting occurred as a "young person's club."

Republicans' demonization of gay people may have reached its apotheosis about a month before the shooting, when Representative Rick W. Allen of Georgia (where else?) had the effrontery to stand up in Congress and recite a passage from the Bible about gays ("they which commit such things are worthy of death" [Romans 1:32]). Let us overlook the small point that our laws are not based on this Bronze Age farrago of lunacy. If Mr. Allen finds this verse a suitable basis for legislation, then why not pass laws inflicting the death penalty for adulterers (Leviticus 20:10) and people who work on the Sabbath (Numbers 15:35)? Why not decree that wives are the property of their husbands (Exodus 20:17)? Indeed, since the Bible emphatically declares that the sun revolves around the earth (Joshua 10:12–13), why not punish every high school teacher in the country (except maybe those in Texas) who brainwash their hapless charges into the obvious heresy and falsehood of the heliocentric theory?

Then there is the ineffable Donald J. Frump (that is his name, isn't it?). After the Orlando shooting, he doubled down on his contention that all Muslim immigration into the United States should be banned. In the case of the Orlando gunman, we apparently should have prevented his parents from entering the U.S. because, thirty years after settling here and giving birth on U.S. soil to an American citizen, they wittingly or unwittingly engendered a terrorist.

But why stop there? I note that certain acts of terrorism committed over the past few decades involve such figures as Timothy McVeigh (the Oklahoma City bomber), Robert L. Dear, Jr. (the Planned Parenthood shooter), Dylann

S. Roof (the shooter in a black church in Charleston), among many others who could be mentioned. All these estimable people were right-wing white men. It would then seem highly prudent to monitor (or perhaps lock up) all white men who are not card-carrying leftists until—to echo Mr. Frump's words—we can figure out what the hell is going on here!

This policy would have the added advantage of confining Mr. Frump himself in a concentration camp for the remainder of his sorry existence.

[*September/October 2016*]

It is often said that England and America are two countries separated by a common language. The truth of this utterance has struck me with particular force recently, as certain curious events across the pond bear uncanny resemblances to what is going on in our own land. I refer, of course, to Brexit.

To those of you who may not be aware of this event, this was a referendum held on June 23 in which the citizens of Great Britain (England, Scotland, Wales, Northern Ireland) decided to remain within the European Union or leave it and go their own way. The referendum was demanded by a cadre of ferocious "Euroskeptics," mostly in the Conservative (Tory) party, who have apparently never gotten over the fact that England isn't an empire anymore and think they can get along just fine without those pesky Europeans who purchase a lot of their goods and services. To their own evident surprise, the Leave faction collared several million more votes than the Remain faction, and the result is Brexit.

I can't think of a better exemplification of the old adage, "Be careful what you wish for—you might get it." Britain's recovery from the recent recession is already shaky and is now likely to get shakier still, because it is unlikely that the various countries making up the European Union will be prepared to give Britain unfettered access to its markets without forcing the Brits to yield on the very point on which the referendum was based—that is, a restriction of immigration by citizens in the European Union.

The Brexit referendum was led by a loudmouth politician with bad hair named . . . no, not Donald J. Frump (that is his name, isn't it?), but Boris Johnson, whose previous occupation was as a commentator who perfected the technique of telling lies about Europe. And what is more, the campaign was also fueled by bare-faced immigrant-bashing, as any number of commercials and billboards sponsored by the United Kingdom Independence Party (UKIP), led by the odious Nigel Farage, made pungently obvious. These lies were rabidly lapped up by the poorly educated British populace, and that is how Brexit happened.

Let me be frank. The British working classes are openly, unabashedly, and proudly racist and xenophobic. In the two or three months that I have spent in England over the course of several visits, I have experienced more racist jibes than in the fifty-three years I have lived in the United States.

But the Brexiters may have bitten off more than they can chew. First, it is highly likely that Scotland (which overwhelmingly supported the Remain campaign) will secede from the United Kingdom—and, incredibly, Northern Ireland may follow suit. With only England and Wales, we'll have to start calling that nation Not-So-Great Britain—or maybe the Disunited Kingdom. On top of which, in a whirlwind turnabout that might have seemed like a Shakespearean tragedy were it not a ludicrous farce, Mr. Johnson's quest to become prime minister was upended by betrayals from his own side, leading to the appointment of one Theresa May (who actually supported the Remain side in a lukewarm manner) as head of state.

And then there is the fate (still hanging in the balance as of this writing) of Jeremy Corbyn, the Bernie Sanders of England. This fellow—the leader of the Labour Party, who has adopted political stances far outside the mainstream and shown an utter inability to get his radical measures actually enacted into law—is now in deep trouble for his less-than-enthusiastic support of the Remain campaign. If the Labour Party has any sense, it will discard this decrepit socialist for someone who actually has some chance of challenging the Tories for the prime ministership at the next election.

Speaking of elections, our own is nothing to write home about. Mr. Frump seems to be actuated by a mania of self-destruction, his loose cannon of a mouth getting him into all kinds of hot water of late. Here are some choice examples:

- After the email servers of the Democratic National Committee were hacked (apparently by Russian agents) and released by Julian Assange, an accused rapist (I believe he also heads some organization called Wikileaks), Mr. Frump pleaded with his pal Vladimir Putin to hack into Hillary Clinton's server and release her private emails.
- After a Muslim-American family, the Khans, whose son died in Afghanistan in 2004, chastised Mr. Frump for making no meaningful "sacrifices" of his own, Mr. Frump attacked them for days on end.
- At a rally, Mr. Frump all but suggested that "Second Amendment people" might do well to blast Hillary Clinton to smithereens in order to prevent her from taking their precious guns away.

These are only the highlights of Mr. Frump's recent buffoonery, but they will do.

The difficulty of writing a column like this one is that it goes to press weeks after it is written, so that it is not easy to be up-to-date on fast-moving events. Let me declare, then, that I am writing this column on August 15. I expect that, within weeks or even days, ***Mr. Frump will bow out of the presidential election.*** Even he knows he cannot win; and in order not to be branded as the biggest "loser" of his time, he will declare (as he has done already) that the election is "rigged" and that the Washington elite and the media will not "allow" him to win. This will allow Frump (in his own mind, at any rate) to save face.

Of course, we anti-Frumpers hope he will remain to the bitter end, for he and his party are facing a defeat of epic proportions. It couldn't happen to a nicer bunch of people.

[*November/December 2016*]

Well, the bad guys won.

That is the only way to characterize this presidential election, with its appalling result. When given the choice between a vile, despicable, ignorant, narcissistic racist/misogynist/xenophobe and the most intelligent, capable, and experienced candidate since Thomas Jefferson—and the only candidate who would allow us not to be ashamed of being Americans—the unacknowledged legions of brainless deplorables came out from the rocks under which they have been cowering and elevated the most unqualified candidate in American history to the highest office in the land. I no longer recognize—or wish to recognize—the country I am living in. In a single day, we have become an immense banana republic.

Much as many of us wish to banish the specter of Mr. Trump from our collective memories, it is worth reminding ourselves exactly what he is and what he stands for:

- He proposed a "complete and total" ban on all Muslims entering this country (which is probably unconstitutional);
- He advocated killing the families of suspected terrorists (which would be a war crime, subjecting him to indictment by the International Criminal Court);
- He advocated going to war in order to pillage the oil and other resources of conquered nations (which would also be a war crime);
- He stated that he would come to the assistance of NATO allies only if they paid their "fair share" (whatever that might be) for their own defense (which would be a violation of the central article in the NATO charter).

This does not even begin to broach his many other loathsome derelictions, both personal and financial: his failure to pay his fair share of taxes over decades; his brazen claim that he had the freedom to molest women because he was a "star"; his repeated insults hurled at anyone who dared to show him insufficient respect (at the same time that he showed little or no respect to anyone but himself); and so on.

I have high expectations that Trump will soon be impeached for one or the other of the above derelictions, or some others that he dreams up. Otherwise, he is likely to be nothing but a puppet of the Republican bosses who pull the strings while he basks in the glory of the presidency.

It is particularly galling to see that this election victory was fostered by underhanded tactics long used by conservatives: gerrymandering, voter suppression, and the relentless lies and duplicities disseminated by Fox News and its analogues. (Hillary Clinton is a multiple murderer, isn't she? She worships the Devil, doesn't she?) I have little doubt that the racists and xenophobes of the alt-right movement, the Ku Klux Klan (who explicitly endorsed Trump), and other such charming people are celebrating this brave last stand in defense of the Caucasian male. But their jubilation will be short-lived: by 2040 whites will be a minority in this country, and we will see how they enjoy being on the short end of the stick.

Throughout this election we have heard ad nauseam about the lamentable plight of the poor, ill-educated white males who formed Trump's core of support. Pardon me for being uncharitable, but they have largely brought their miseries upon themselves. They have failed to grasp that our economy has for decades been shifting from one based on brawn to one based on knowledge. This "education gap" has also become a clear indicator of political preference, the better-educated tending Democratic while the less-educated remain Republican. Is it any wonder that they cling to "guns and religion," as President Obama so presciently noted? If their support of Trump is some kind of shriek of rage at the political dysfunction in Washington, they seem blissfully unaware that the Republican Party is almost entirely responsible for that dysfunction by their unprecedented obstructionism and their relentless attempts to delegitimize Obama (a process in which Trump, with his advocacy of the "birther" canard, was a prime mover). And yet, these deluded people think that Trump can somehow "drain the swamp" of political gridlock!

One needs to direct particular opprobrium to the religious right, many of whom disgraced themselves by open support of a foul-mouthed, adulterous con man. Their reasons? Chiefly it was because they could not bear to contemplate the prospect of a liberal (or even centrist) Supreme Court. After all, a court that has already legalized same-sex marriage, upheld the Affordable Care Act, and pulled the plug on deceitful and fascistic restrictions on abortion rights might do something so appalling as endorse climate change legislation, or campaign finance reform, or—horror of horrors!—rational limits to gun ownership!

There is only one saving grace in this nightmare scenario, and that is the old adage: *Be careful what you wish for, you might get it.*

Assuming that Trump evades impeachment, the likelihood that he will be able to enact any of his major policy prescriptions—banning Muslims, building the "beautiful" wall at the Mexican border, repealing the Affordable Care Act, bringing manufacturing jobs back to the Rust Belt—is vanishingly small. Indeed, since Trump has no coherent policies, it is difficult to imagine how his administration could be anything but a floundering mess. And since the Republican Party has become nothing but a knee-jerk opposition party, and since it is itself severely riven by internal discord, there is an overwhelming probability that the poor ignorant sods who supported Trump will find their lives and fortunes much worse than they were before. They will remain poor, stupid, and despairing—and when they find that their patron saint can't be bothered to help them, they will turn on him with all the venom of rabid dogs.

And when that happens, I trust I will be pardoned for laughing my head off.

[January/February 2017]

There has been a considerable amount of whining among supporters of (Not My) President Donald J. Trump. They are shocked—shocked, I tell you—that they themselves are being branded as racists and misogynists just because their paragon has so frequently and pungently expressed these same charming attributes.

I think they are protesting too much.

There is surely no need to rehearse the sorry tale of Trump's own derelictions in these regards. For decades, he has made his racism abundantly clear. As far back as the 1970s, he was sued not once but twice by the Justice Department for denying African Americans the opportunity to occupy his rental units in New York (their applications were marked with a large C—standing for "colored"). His more recent remarks on Muslims and Hispanics during the presidential campaign leave little doubt that he will be the president of white people—and specifically white men—only.

"But," his supporters protest, "I didn't vote for him for those reasons!" This is like someone saying in 1968, "I voted for George Wallace because I happen to like his economic policies" (Wallace was an economic populist, as Trump—probably falsely—claims to be.) "His bare-faced racism doesn't matter." But it does matter. In choosing a president, one is not choosing a set of policy positions (and that is especially the case with Trump, who couldn't be troubled to present policies of any detail or coherence); one is choosing a person. And if that person is so morally flawed as Trump, then everyone who voted for him is complicit in his racism and misogyny.

Early indications on these matters are not reassuring. His selection of the odious Stephen K. Bannon (head of the far-right Breitbart.com "news" outlet) as chief strategist (a position that does not require approval by the Senate) is a transparent sop to the many racists, xenophobes, and anti-immigrant fanatics who elected him. In an interview with the *New York Times,* Trump ludicrously defended his longtime friend by saying that Bannon himself was pained by the tsunami of accusations hurled at him that he was a racist. My heart bleeds for the fellow! It was only two weeks after the election that he expressed concern that "two-thirds or three-quarters of the CEOs in Silicon Valley are from South Asia or from Asia, I think." Bannon doesn't think very well, it appears—the number of Asian CEOs in Silicon Valley is under 15%. But don't forget—Bannon is no racist!

And who has Trump chosen as attorney general—in other words, the person chiefly responsible for protecting Americans' civil rights? None other than the ineffable Senator Jeff Sessions, who was previously denied a federal judgeship because of his manifest prejudice against African Americans and others. In a recent response to some embarrassing comments he uttered some decades ago, Sessions said: "I'm often loose with my tongue. I may have said something about the N.A.A.C.P. being un-American or Communist, but I meant no harm by it." Okay, Jeff, I'll follow your lead: Donald J. Trump is a pro-Russian traitor, a moron, and a scumbag who likes to grab women's genitals—but I mean no harm by it!

In an exquisite bit of timing, a motley crew of white nationalists calling themselves the National Policy Institute met only blocks from the White House on November 19–20, thrilled at the election of their Manchurian candidate. They went so far as to cheer Trump on with a Nazi-style salute while crying, "Hail, Victory! Hail Trump!" Their euphoria, however, may be a trifle short-lived.

What is now only starting to penetrate the thick skulls of these pathetic losers is that their apparent supremacy has largely been a result of centuries of prejudice against other races and genders. Now that they have to compete on a (more or less) level playing field, their inferiority is becoming painfully evident. I've long held that we need affirmative action for white people, specifically white men.

Before the election, these white-supremacist dead-enders had planned to gather to console themselves on the defeat of their paragon and to retreat into their caves. Now they are in a celebratory mood. And yet, even with a racist in the Oval Office who has vowed to make America white again, their plight remains lamentable—wasting away in their trailer parks unable to get jobs, dying of suicide, meth and heroin addiction, and general incompetence, they seem not long for this world. Maybe—given their curious emphasis on their "European" heritage—they should migrate en masse to, say, Germany, where they can while away the time beating up migrants while they live comfortably on the generous German dole.

"Wait a minute!" the Trumpistas say. "These horrible people don't represent me!" A glum supporter wrote a plangent letter to the *New York Times* objecting to its coverage of the National Policy Institute gathering, saying, "Stories like this thrive on the narrative that the right has a propensity to support leaders who are bigoted, prejudiced, Islamophobic, racist, misogynistic and homophobic." You said, it, pal, not me! At this point we surely don't need to rehearse the decades of prejudicial statements *and actions* taken by the entire Republican Party to circumscribe the rights of minorities, to depress their vote, and to maintain white supremacy wherever they can. These measures may ultimately be futile (whites are inexorably headed toward minority status in this country), but Republicans are evidently determined to go down fighting with their old, fat, angry white sycophants and lickspittles.

So if (Not My) President Trump proceeds from demagogic tweets to actual measures that target non-whites, then every Trump supporter—*every single one*—will be as guilty of racism as he is. The picture will not be pretty.

[March/April *2017*]

The question of the day (and, really, the century) is: Why are Republicans such slime?

Case in point: the horrible state of North Carolina. Although this state boasts such distinguished centers of higher learning (and, not coincidentally, fiery liberalism) as Duke University and the University of North Carolina at Chapel Hill, it has recently been so mutilated by extreme Republican partisanship that it is a shadow of its former self. Consider what happened after the recent election, which saw the Democratic challenger Roy Cooper narrowly defeated the incumbent governor, Pat McCrory. Initially, McCrory began howling about tens of thousands of votes cast illegally for his opponent. Ah, yes—the familiar Republican bogeyman of "voter fraud"! When these baseless accusations were refuted, the state legislature—still controlled by Republicans—passed a succession of laws truncating the new governor's powers to appoint members of his own executive office. One state senator piously stated that such maneuvers merely restored "power that was grabbed during Democratic administrations in the 1990s, and some in the '70s." Even if this were true (which it isn't), one would suppose that our valiant Republicans—if they had really been interested in good governance and not just partisan advantage—have passed these measures when a Republican governor was in office. But no! That would have been beyond their comprehension—or their code of morals. Amusingly, several state judges have overturned or suspended these new measures.

The incompetence and corruption of the Republican Party are, of course, writ large in the grotesque blundering of the nascent administration of (Not My) President Trump. It should now be evident that Trump was only elected by (a) an avalanche of fake news that tarred his opponent, Hillary Clinton, with the most preposterous and scurrilous slanders, and (b) the unprecedented and probably illegal interference of FBI director James Comey, whose assertion, less than two weeks before the election, that he had "new" information regarding her emails turned out to be bogus. If a mere 70,000 votes in three states had gone the other way, we would be talking about *her* sane and experienced Cabinet choices, rather than the motley crew of deplorables whom Trump is appointing to undermine the very agencies they are heading.

Let us consider this whole notion of fake news. It did not, of course, begin with this election cycle; for decades the right-wing media (Fox News, talk radio, and the like) has been pouring out falsehood after falsehood to its pathetically brainwashed devotees, nurturing in them a deep-seated sense of rage, resentment, and victimization, based upon the (correct) assumption that they are being left behind by history. As a result, these poor fools actually believed that Hillary Clinton was a murderer or had run a child-sex ring out of a pizza parlor.

"But," our beleaguered conservative friends whine, "you liberals do it too!" Actually, we don't. Interviews with those who generated fake news—many of them working overseas—have made this abundantly plain. These people did their work chiefly for the money, earning big bucks based on the number of dupes who accessed their Internet sites. One fellow from the Russian province of Georgia, Beqa Latsabidze, actually tried to set up a pro-Clinton and anti-Trump site, but wasn't getting much traffic. Then he switched to pro-Trump and anti-Clinton—and hit the jackpot! "My audience likes Trump," he said. "I don't want to write bad things about Trump. If I write fake stories about Trump, I lose my audience."

What all this means is that a significant proportion of our populace—mostly on the right side of the political spectrum—is living in a delusionary world of "alternate facts" and outright lies. A poll taken a few weeks after the election reveal some frightening tendencies. Consider the following:

- 40% of Trump voters believe that Trump won the popular vote (in fact, he lost it by nearly 3 million votes).
- 60% of Trump voters believe that millions of people voted illegally for Clinton (in fact, there is no evidence of widespread voter fraud anywhere in the country).

- 67% of Trump voters believe that unemployment rose during President Obama's terms in office (in fact, it went down from 7.8% to 4.6%).

What to do in the face of such self-induced ignorance? This whole troubling tendency is now being compounded by the incoming administration, which is now resorting to the puerile and ineffective rhetorical ploy of branding as "fake news" any reports that contradict its twisted view of reality. But the Slimeball-in-Chief and his partisans will quickly discover that dispensing with the truth is not as easy as it seems.

Are some Trump voters feeling a bit of buyer's remorse? It would seem so: one of them used his own favorite vehicle, Twitter, to declare him a "nincompoop." Others are standing firm (so far), blaming the usual suspects—liberals. Clint Bellows, a conservative talk radio host in Omaha, opined: "There isn't going to be any harmony: they're out to bring this guy down." You got that right, pal!

There is something of a civil war going on in this country; and if you're not on the right side, you're on the wrong side. One side is the side of liberal democracy, tolerance, religious pluralism, and devotion to fact; the other side is the side of fascism, racism, misogyny, sulking resentment, religious dogmatism and theocracy, aversion to plain truths when they are inconvenient to one's ideology, and a vile toadyism to the wealthy and powerful (with a concomitant disdain of the middle and working classes). It has become increasingly clear to me that nearly all Republican politicians, and a substantial proportion of Republican voters, are traitors to American ideals and civilized values.

And we all know what the punishment for treason is.

[May/June 2017]

Are you embarrassed yet?

Only a few months into the regime of "President" Donald Trump, the level of incompetence and corruption that his administration has displayed has already made the United States the laughingstock of the world. But what can one expect from a narcissistic ninny who knows not the first thing about running a country—a serial liar who screeches incoherently on Twitter the moment he hears any facts that puncture his fragile ego—an insecure imbecile who surrounds himself either with pliant sycophants or with fiendishly evil ideologues determined to drag this nation into an orgy of xenophobic madness?

I will say, however, that "President" Trump has attained one lofty pinnacle. The shades of such past luminaries as Millard Fillmore, James Buchanan, Andrew Johnson, Rutherford B. Hayes, and Warren G. Harding must be dancing jigs in Gehenna, for they have all been shoved aside to make way for the Worst President Ever!

Case in point: the much-touted repeal of the Affordable Care Act. Trump and his fellow Republicans were so eager to take health care away from tens of millions of people that they cobbled together a Frankenstein's monster of a bill that would do irreparable harm to many of their own supporters while lining the pockets of their fat cat campaign donors with billions of dollars in tax cuts. For a time the House of Representatives wanted to force a vote even before the Congressional Budget Office prepared its estimate on the overall effects of the bill; when the CBO determined that as many as 24 million people might lose their insurance, our Republican friends were undeterred and said, "That's the way the cookie crumbles, folks! Ya gotta be free!" I am not entirely sure that freedom to die through lack of affordable health care is a freedom I particularly cherish.

And yet, this gruesome "death-to-the-poor" measure (remember, though, that Republicans are the "pro-life" party!) didn't even come to a vote. When it became evident that many of the far-right wingnuts of something called the Freedom Caucus were opposed to the bill—because, forsooth, *it was too generous* and did not constitute a root-and-branch repeal of Obamacare—the Trump administration sought to make it even more draconian, offering to eliminate subsidies for maternity care, among other proposals. But even this was not harsh enough for the Freedom Caucus, and the bill went down in flames.

Throughout this whole sorry process "President" Trump exhibited the same blithering cluelessness that he has displayed on every other major policy issue. In a priceless admission of his own nincompoopery, he blithely stated, "Nobody knew that health care could be so complicated." As the *New York Times* dryly noted, "Nobody except anyone who had spent any time in Washington policy making."

Many other initiatives that Trump championed during the campaign have similarly been either quietly put aside or blocked by the courts. Injunctions have put the kibosh on two separate executive orders to ban Muslim refugees and immigrants. A lawsuit demands that an environmental impact study be conducted before any work on the "beautiful" wall between the United States and Mexico begins. The "president" has suddenly decided that China *isn't* a currency manipulator and that NATO *isn't* quite as "obsolete" as he had fantasized.

Meanwhile, imagine the exquisite misery of Vladimir Putin! Here's a guy who spent so much effort putting his stooge into the White House, and what does the stooge do? He drops bombs on Syria, messing up relations with Putin's other dictator pal, Bashar al-Assad. That's gratitude for you!

But there's more to the one-off Syria bombing than it may appear. Let us recall that the Trump administration itself had previously made it quite clear that it had no stomach for ousting Assad. Nikki Haley, the US ambassador to the UN, stated bluntly, "Our priority is no longer to sit there and focus on getting Assad out." Days later, Assad drops chemical weapons on his own people. I'd call that a pretty clear instance of cause and effect: I can do anything, Assad must have thought, and Trump will just sit on his hands.

It is said that "President" Trump was deeply moved by images of Syrian children dying of sarin gas poisoning. This tender-hearted man has throughout his life shown solicitude for the poor and underprivileged, hasn't he? And the children! Let us never forget the children! To the astonishment and fury of his isolationist supporters, Trump's equally befuddled secretary of state, Rex Tillerson, recently stated that the US would punish those "who commit crimes against the innocents anywhere in the world." *Anywhere in the world?* Has the proponent of "America first" suddenly become the world's humanitarian policeman?

I'd be horribly cynical—wouldn't I?—for thinking that this single air attack, in the utter absence of a coherent policy on Syria, was intended as a distraction—a distraction, that is, from increasing evidence of collusion between members of the Trump campaign and Russian hackers to subvert the presidential election.

And it is unsurprising that "President" Trump has expressed solidarity with both Bill O'Reilly, the blowhard political commentator, and Roger Ailes, the former chairman of Fake—er, I mean Fox—News. Sexual predators have to stick together, after all! With everyone telling them it's not very nice to grab a woman's private parts or make her sexual submission a precondition for advancement in her job, it's just becoming harder and harder for molesters to function.

Say, what's *with* the quotation marks around "President," you ask? Well, I'm just borrowing a stylistic tic of Trump himself, as exhibited on Twitter. For you see, Donald Trump really isn't president of the United States; but he plays one on TV.

[July/*August 2017*]

Let's talk a moment about treason.

There is a well-known quotation on this subject: "Treason doth never prosper, what's the reason? / Why, if it prosper, none dare call it treason!" This was written by a rather obscure English poet, Sir John Harington, all the way back in 1615; but it is of singular relevance today in the age of Trump. For what is now happening before our eyes is the striking spectacle of an entire political party engaging in treason against American and world ideals. This treason is being exhibited in the words and acts of nearly every Republican politician and, more crucially, in their many millions of followers.

Let it not be thought that I am crudely exaggerating political differences by tarring my opponents with a deficiency of morality and patriotism—a tactic, indeed, of which the Republicans themselves have become past masters. To be sure, I and many others have political differences with Republicans; but what is occurring now goes well beyond that.

I am not referring to suspected collusion between Trump and/or his campaign staff with Russian officials, spies, or hackers. No clear-cut evidence of malfeasance has emerged, although the sheer number of contacts between the Trumpistas and the Russians has to be a concern to anyone with a stake in the viability of American democracy. It is vastly amusing that Trump undertook the rash and self-destructive act of firing FBI director James Comey and then, the very next day, openly admitted to the Russian ambassador and foreign minister that the firing relieved "great pressure" on him. How's that working for you, Donny boy?

But Russiagate is—for the moment—a sideshow. It ought to be much more troubling to American patriots to see Orange Julius sidling up to a grotesque array of dictators around the world, from Egypt's Abdel Fattah el-Sisi ("He's done a fantastic job in a very difficult situation"), Turkey's Recep Erdogan, and, most egregious of all, the blood-drenched Rodrigo Duterte of the Philippines. How typical that Trump lavished praise on Duterte's mad campaign of summary execution of hapless drug addicts ("he's done an unbelievable job on the drug problem"). No doubt our Fearful Leader was wishing he had the power to do the same against his multifarious enemies here at home. But Duterte has been so fixated on the drug war that he has failed to pay attention to the rise of Islamic terrorism in his island fiefdom, with the result that militants are now happily chopping off the heads of his own beleaguered soldiers.

And who can overlook the exquisitely comical spectacle of Trump summoning his entire cabinet for a session wherein each one of them in turn sang the praises of their fragile and flattery-yearning boss in ever more sycophantic terms? But that was only to be expected of a motley crew of bootlickers and lickspittles who are determined to carry out their Führer's campaign promises, no matter what the cost to the American people.

On that front, the entire Republican delegation to Congress is equally guilty. Contemplate the spectacle of a health "reform" bill that was rammed through the House in May—a bill that is estimated to deprive more than 20 million people of health insurance. Meanwhile, the Republican members of the Senate are working—in secret—on their own version of Obamacare repeal. Reports have surfaced that this bill will not be quite so horrible: perhaps only 15 million will lose their insurance? I suppose that counts as benevolence among Republicans these days.

But it is worth emphasizing that the treason exhibited in the above acts is not restricted to Trump or to Republican politicians, whether in Congress or in the many red states where their corrupt gerrymandering has put them in positions of nearly unassailable power. The treason extends to a wide array of Republican voters who continue to support Trump and his agenda in spite of the fact that they themselves may be its victims. There are some plausible reasons for this seemingly baffling phenomenon. First, few of us like to admit that we have been bamboozled; and while there is some evidence that a minority of Trumpistas—especially among the young and the college-educated—have emerged from their brainwashing, a substantial proportion will probably cling to him to the bitter end. Second, as Jim Dempsey's review in this issue demonstrates, many conservatives are fired by a deep-seated resentment against all those smart-aleck liberals who hold them in such contempt: they'll stick to their man—and their party—if only to enrage their wealthier, better-educated foes on the Left Coasts. That'll show 'em!

The contortions of evangelicals on the subject have been particularly amusing to watch. They supported Trump overwhelmingly in spite of his manifest unfitness for office and in spite of plain evidence that he was not exactly the pious gent they generally preferred for high office. A poll recently taken among evangelicals asked them if they felt that an elected official who commits an immoral his/her personal life can still fulfill the duties of his/her office; *72 percent agreed.* In 2011—when a certain other individual occupied the Oval Office—only 30 percent agreed. Evangelicals are so determined to secure temporary advantage on the public policy matters that concern them that they will happily look the other way if only their flawed and corrupt leaders will take them to the promised land.

So there you have it. We have reached the stage where an entire party—and a wide array of its supporters—have openly discarded all constraints of morality and civilization for political advantage. They have unashamedly put party above country. If that is not a textbook definition of treason, then I don't know what is.

[*September/October 2017*]

Limitation of the suffrage—an idea whose time has come.

My views on this issue have been percolating for some time, and have been influenced by a number of astute commentators over the past century or more who have perspicaciously questioned the very principle of democracy. Herr Friedrich Nietzsche declared: "I have . . . characterised modern democracy . . . as the *decaying form* of the state." H. P. Lovecraft, writing in the

1930s, was no less emphatic:

"Government 'by popular vote' means merely the nomination of doubt-fully qualified men by doubtfully authorised and seldom competent cliques of professional politicians representing hidden interests, followed by a sardonic farce of emotional persuasion in which the orators with the glibbest tongues and flashiest catch-words herd on their side a numerical majority of blindly impressionable dolts and gulls who have for the most part no idea of what the whole circus is about."

We now are faced with the impressive-sounding Presidential Advisory Commission on Election Integrity, organized by "President" Trump and headed by the redoubtable Kris Kobach, whose enthusiasm for eliminating people from the voter rolls is rabid and unremitting. But let us not be too hasty in condemning him and his commission: the focus of their voter-purging efforts may be askew, but their basic principle seems sound. Too many people in this country are manifestly unfit to vote.

The Founders were clear on the need for an *educated* electorate if democracy (or representative government) were to function properly. It is pretty difficult to deny that that educated electorate, by and large, simply doesn't exist today. So what to do? I say we need some fairly strong measures to wipe these people off the face of the earth—er, I mean, stop them from voting. Here are some suggestions.

Our first step would be to ban any people who watch Fake—er, that is, Fox—News or listen to conservative talk radio more than three times a week. (With "smart" televisions and other technology, it should be easy to identify such miscreants.) For is it not abundantly obvious that these hapless buffoons have been brainwashed into becoming unthinking zombies whose votes can be manipulated at will? Tobin Smith, a self-confessed "hit man" for Fox has recently admitted that this kind of indoctrination was exactly the purpose of his network:

"By careful design and staging, Fox News manipulated (and ultimately addicted) the most vulnerable people in America to the most powerful drug cocktail ever: visceral gut feelings of outrage relieved by the most powerful emotions of all . . . the thrill of your tribe's victory over its enemy and the ultimate triumph of good over evil."

Well, we can't have drug addicts voting, can we? They're almost as bad as ex-felons or the millions of illegal immigrants who committed treason by voting for Hillary and denying "President" Trump a victory in the popular vote.

Tobin goes on to say: "One part of the Fox News strategy is the tried and true conservative media narrative to insulate their audiences from opposing views—in part, by continually denouncing the mainstream media (i.e., other news sources) 24/7/365 as 'liberal, biased, and not to be trusted.'" Well, of course: why didn't I think of that?

The elimination of these deplorable people might be enough in itself to save American democracy; but I think we have to go further. We must, of course, stop the staggering number of sleazeballs and scumbags in our midst from voting. I am aware that these are somewhat imprecise designations for our fellow citizens, but we can all detect such creatures when we see them, can't we? Certain things are dead giveaways: living in single-wide (or even double-wide) trailers; driving pickup tricks or Harleys; hair on one's back (if one is a man) or a prominent mustache (if one is a woman); and so on and so forth.

We would probably have to extend the ban to such dubious specimens as male (and especially female) bodybuilders, professional athletes (who, with rare exceptions such as LeBron James, appear to be mindlessly conservative), anyone affiliated with Liberty University, Bryan College, the Creation Museum, and other such bogus institutions. Surely no "education" can be going on at these places, can it? It is to laugh!

At first I was simply going to advocate a blanket ban on white people, or maybe just white males. But that would be racist and sexist, wouldn't it? We can't have that. Anyway, some of my best friends are white males, and I can assure you that they are not all hopeless opioid addicts or trailer trash or bigots. *Please* take my word for it! In any case, the latest polls suggest that even this motley crew are falling away from their unthinking support of "President" Trump, so perhaps there is hope even for them.

Let it not be thought that the inability to vote will relegate all these lamentable people to second-class status in their own country. There is such a thing, after all, as benevolent aristocracy; and the luminous, well-educated people who can still vote will no doubt extend a kindly hand toward their intellectual inferiors. These serfs will no doubt occupy a humble but respected place in the body politic. Perhaps we can even train them to bow (if they are males) and curtsy (if they are females) as we walk by them.

Nevertheless, on the issue of voting—as on the broader issue of government as a whole—the problems facing us are difficult and perhaps insoluble. Given recent developments, it seems impossible to deny H. P. Lovecraft's lugubrious pronouncement: "There is no such thing—and there never will be such a thing—as good and permanent government among the crawling, miserable vermin called human beings."

Index

Stewart, Jon 140–41
Stoics 92, 93
Stoppard, Tom 53, 56
Strange Gods: A Secular History of Conversion (Jacoby) 97–101
Straughter, Taressa 111
stupidity 127, 131, 132, 134, 138
Sunquist, Scott W. 78
Supreme Court 50–52, 60, 69, 70, 83, 94, 107–8, 120, 136, 144, 145, 154, 159, 161–62, 164, 165, 166, 168–69, 170–71, 174, 177, 196
Swinburne, Richard 23
Syria 186, 203

Tacitus 76
Taking Liberties (Boston) 42–44
Tea Party 40, 145, 153, 159, 161, 167, 177, 183, 184
Tebow, Tim 138
Ten Commandments 82, 86, 96, 130, 174
Ten Commandments, The (film) 82
Tennessee 155, 156
Texas 112, 164, 165, 185, 192
Thales 91
Theodosius I (Emperor of Rome) 98
Theogony (Hesiod) 90
Thomas, Clarence 160
Thompson, Emma 110
Thucydides 91
Tillerson, Rex 203
Tillich, Paul 79
Timaeus (Plato) 92
Tolkien, J. R. R. 112
Torode, Sam 131–32
transgendered persons 108–9, 184–85, 189–90, 191
Trudeau, Garry 179
True Paradox: How Christianity Makes Sense of Our Complex World (Skeel) 62–65
Trump, Donald J. 8, 70, 106, 107–9, 120, 122, 181–82, 183, 185–86, 187–88, 190, 192–99, 200–205, 207, 208

Twitter 201, 202
Tylor, E. B. 62

Unbelievers, The (Joshi) 8, 29n1, 33n1
Unexpected Christian Century, The (Sunquist) 78–79
United Nations 146, 179
United States Conference of Roman Catholic Bishops 135
Utah 162, 171

vaccination 132–33, 175–76
Vargas, Juan 156
Varieties of Religious Experience (James) 97n1
Vietnam War 83, 181
Vincent, Lynn 45
Vines, Matthew 85–89
Violence Policy Center 173
Voltaire (François Marie Arouet) 64, 93

Waldman, Michael 49–52, 173
Walker, Scott 171, 180–81
Wall Street Journal 81, 127
Wallace, George 197
Walmart 175
Wasp Factory, The (Banks) 132
Watt, James 59
Way Forward, The (Ryan) 172
Wesleyans 45, 46
Whitmarsh, Tim 90–93
Wiccans 111
Wilcox, Ann 111–12
Wildstein, David 163
Williams, Nick 175
Williams, Roger 100
Wolf, Nancy J. 113
Women Beyond Belief (Garst) 110–13
Worley, Charles L. 141–42
Wright, Ceal 111
Wyoming 167–68

Xenophanes 91

Young, Dean 161

Zardari, Asif A. 146
Zimbabwe 111
Zuckerman, Phil 19–21

90628985R00121

Made in the USA
Middletown, DE
25 September 2018